g at one time. Illustration from *Frank Leslie's Illustrated Newspaper*, October 15, 1859.

The American Maritime Library: Volume VII

Oystering from New York to Boston

Oystering from New York to Boston

by JOHN M. KOCHISS

PUBLISHED FOR *Mystic Seaport, Inc.*

BY *Wesleyan University Press*
MIDDLETOWN, CONNECTICUT

Library of Congress Cataloging in Publication Data

Kochiss, John M.
   Oystering from New York to Boston.

   (The American maritime library, v. 7)
   Bibliography: p.
   1. Oyster fisheries — New England — History.
I. Title.   II. Series.
SH365.N35K62   639'.411'0974   74-5965
ISBN 0-8195-4074-9
ISBN 0-8195-4075-7 (lim. ed.)

Manufactured in the United States of America
FIRST EDITION

To my family and Edmund E. Lynch

Contents

Illustrations

Acknowledgements

I am deeply indebted to many people for their help, advice, criticism, photographs and encouragement, but most of all to Edmund E. Lynch, former curator of Mystic Seaport, for without him this book would not have been written, and to the classic *Oyster Industry* by Ernest Ingersoll, which was an inspiration and guide.

Especial thanks go to Carl Anderson, oysterman, bridge tender and artist, who was the first to tell me of those hard but happy days aboard the old oyster sloops; to the late Captain Fred Lovejoy, patriarch of the Connecticut oyster industry; to the men at the Aquaculture Division of the Connecticut Department of Agriculture (the old Shell-Fish Commission) at Milford, John Baker, Director; to the men of the state boat *Shell Fish*: Captain Joseph W. Lauchor, Edwin Zajkowski, and Bill Ciaurro, who has seen oystering from the decks of sloops, steamers, diesel boats and scows.

My gratitude goes also to Milton Bond, friend, fellow admirer of old boats, artist, and descendant of a long line of oystermen; Mr. and Mrs. George Chase, Jr., for their many kindnesses; August MacTaggart, former oyster-boat captain and production manager of the Bluepoints Company, Inc., for his expert criticism and wonderful photographs; J. Richards Nelson, Manager of the New Haven branch of the Long Island Oyster Farms, Inc., Emil Usinger, Executive Vice-President of the Bluepoints Company, Inc., who was always so kind and informative; Loring McMillen, Director of the Staten Island Historical Society; Hervey Garrett Smith and Roger P. Dunkerly of the Suffolk Marine Museum, West Sayville, Long Island, for their information, time, attention and photographs; J. Fletcher Lewis, Harbor Master of Stratford, Connecticut and local maritime historian, and Fred W. Goodsell, Stratford shellerman and all-around waterman.

I am no less indebted to Harold Palmer, John W. Brown, George Edwards, Stanley and Clarence Chard, Eric and Elisha Ball, Fred Brown, Mrs. William Veale, Betty Kuss, Jim Ryley, Helen Brown, Mr. and Mrs. David H. Wallace, Nelson Still, Frank Rice, Mr. and Mrs. Edward Rogers, Robert Prindle, Tonis Locker, and the late Mr. and Mrs. John Thomas. Appreciation is also extended to Robert C. Mallory, Wellfleet Shellfish Warden, and John H. Hickey, marine biologist of the Massachusetts Department of Natural Resources; to the men at the Bloom Brothers' oyster shop, especially Chester Ayers; to Clyde L. Mac-Kenzie, Jr., and to Dr. Anthony Calabrese and others at the National Marine Fisheries Services at Milford, Connecticut.

Foreword

A COMPLETE STUDY of any part of an American fishery has been rarely attempted. Sources have not been readily available since the days of the U.S. Fish Commission—part of the Smithsonian Institution, and of Captain Joseph Collins of the commission's staff. The historian attempting to invade this great field soon finds that he must deal with geographic considerations, fishery techniques, shore installations, and boats employed—all from the colonial period to the present—as well as problems of conservation, production, and marketing.

Technical areas are numerous and important. Fishing vessels, machinery, and gear are examples; each has an individual history and an extensive bibliography of its own. But much of this material may be out-of-date for some fisheries, and some of it requires revaluation to meet the standards of modern marine research. The fisheries have been influenced by the technologies and the technologies, in turn, have been influenced by the fisheries. Ship and boat building are good examples. Fishing gear machinery and marine engines are others.

Mr. Kochiss has made a complete study of an important part of the North American fisheries—the New England oyster fisheries between New York Bay and Massachusetts Bay—one of the great oyster-producing areas—from the colonial period to the present. The working of an oyster bed—tonging and dredging, seeding and planting—is described in great detail, as are the operation of the shore establishments for shucking, packing, icing, and shipping, and the manning of the oyster boats. The illustrations, particularly plans of boats and related matters, add greatly to its value.

This report is one of the most concise and complete studies of an important fishery that has yet appeared, and offers a model for research and reporting on other American fisheries.

Howard I. Chapelle

Introduction

I T IS DIFFICULT for New Englanders and even New Yorkers to imagine oysters as the chief fishery product of the United States and the most extensively eaten of all shellfish. Yet at the turn of the century and before, the oyster was indeed king. Everyone, especially those living along the shore, knew all about this wholesome, nutritious bivalve and the multimillion dollar industry it spawned.

The northern oyster industry, and by this I mean that conducted in New York and New England, maintained a huge fleet of fascinating watercraft and employed thousands of workers from deck hands to openers in oyster bars. Oystering was of major importance in many communities and its influence extended far beyond local bounds to the West Coast and to Europe as well.

Those were busy, prosperous days but they have vanished and been forgotten. Most people, even those who live on the coast adjacent to the oyster grounds, know little about them. Like a piece of clothing, oysters have gone out of fashion in New York and points north. Oystermen and oyster boats are so few here that we are led to believe an industry does not exist or ever existed. But it does.

In the past oystering was sufficiently publicized in the daily press but otherwise not adequately covered for easy future reference. Books or pamphlets on the subject are mostly out-of-print government publications not usually available in the average public library. My aim, therefore, has been to record the history of the forgotten northern oyster industry and to provide a reference and starting point for further research. This is not an exhaustive study. Much still can be done, especially with the rich store of anecdotal stories of the sailing days crammed into the memories of the older oystermen.

Why the scarcity of material and apparent disinterest in an important industry? Probably it suffered by comparison with land industries that commanded attractive wages and unlimited opportunities. Perhaps being so close to the largest city in the world with its vast shipping had its effects also, for who would look at a lowly oyster sloop, let alone write about it, when in the same view one had lofty square-riggers and magnificent ocean steamers?

Yet more than anything else, it was probably the Chesapeake oyster and the wide publicity it received that overshadowed the northern oyster. The Chesapeake oyster industry led the country and the world in oyster production and in area oystered, and still does. Relative to catch and amount of oyster ground worked, the northern industry was indeed small. But it was perhaps the differences between the northern and southern industries that pointed to the significances of each. The north, due to its marginally survivable position and quite limited oyster ground, was forced before any place else in the United States to cultivate or farm oysters. Farther south nature is more kind in this regard as well as in the relative lack of the predators, the starfish and drills. Oysters were so plentiful naturally that even in the face of a continuously declining output few oystermen found it necessary to cultivate them artificially.

Oyster cultivation in the North created sticky problems of underwater land ownership which eventually led to the various systems of franchises, leases, and grants. In Chesapeake Bay the supply of oysters was so great and the beds so extensive that jurisdiction was left to the state or towns. There was no pressing need to own or control your own grounds. In other words, southern oystering was conducted on public property whereas in the North most of the oysters came from privately operated and controlled land. Furthermore, the northern states allowed private oystermen the privilege of using any kind of boat or dredge, hence the rapid rise of the relatively efficient steamer and other powered craft. Chesapeake oystermen, working largely on public oyster grounds, were not generally permitted to use power and, therefore, were forced to stay with sail and the small tonging boats.

Though people tend to associate the oyster industry solely with the Chesapeake Bay area and more southern regions, the North outranked all other oyster localities in at least four respects: it grew the most valuable oyster, had the largest fleet of oyster steamers and power boats in the world, cultivated the most privately operated oyster ground in the world, and shipped more oysters overseas than any other place in the United States.

The northern oyster was and is still considered the prime oyster of the country. Prejudice may have fostered a little of this feeling but even today the

Long Island Sound market oyster sells for between $17 and $20 per bushel, whereas the Chesapeake oyster goes from $7 to $8 in the same market. Value, of course, depends upon supply but also upon that subjective thing called taste. Northerners consider their oysters very tasty and superior because they are cultivated and grow in robust waters where only the best survive. But it must be said in all fairness that prime oysters are not only found in the North, for quality here and elsewhere varies from bed to bed and season to season. There are countless areas in Delaware and Chesapeake Bays, the Gulf of Mexico and other places that produce premium oysters. However, to settle the question ask any oysterman which oysters are the best and invariably he will say that his are.

The northern oyster is a hardy creature and keeps well in shipment. For this reason, most if not all oysters sent overseas by ocean liner in the past came from the north.

During the 1880s and 1890s Connecticut, in particular, held the distinction of having the largest fleet of oyster steamers in the world. So-called Yankee ingenuity probably had something to do with it, but it was also due to the foresight of the state in allowing oystermen to form companies to cultivate their own oyster ground. Restricted by a limited amount of available ground, they nevertheless farmed it intensively and successfully kept alive an industry that otherwise would no doubt have completely disappeared.

In addition to being a source of information for those interested in the fisheries, this book may provide old boat buffs with a new and absorbing study—the northern oyster boats. This huge, bygone fleet of sail and powered vessels has been ignored, for the most part, by marine historians. Consequently they are comparatively unknown even to those who regularly sail out of the old oyster ports and over the watery oyster farms.

Oystering from New York to Boston

CHAPTER 1

The Oyster and Its Cultivation

MORE is known about the oyster than about any other marine animal. Down the ages man has devoured and cultured it, farmed it, studied and dissected it, abhorred it, admired it. Yet today we are only on the threshold of fully comprehending all aspects of this unique marine food product.

What we do know, however, helps us to understand the huge industry that grew and flourished around this delectable morsel. A bivalve or two-shelled mollusk closely related to the clam, scallop, and mussel, and distantly linked with the single-shelled snails and periwinkles, oysters grow and thrive naturally on select areas of most temperate and tropical coasts around the world—generally where fresh and salt water mix.

Over 100 living species are classified by scientists but only a few are edible or of any economic value. In tropical seas oysters are prized for their pearls; in the temperate zone their food value is more important. Those pearls that are found in temperate water oysters are invariably misshapen, small, and have a rough surface.

In the United States only three species are important. Two grow on the West Coast: the Japanese or Pacific oyster—*Crassostrea gigas* (introduced in the United States in 1905), and the native Olympia oyster—*Ostrea lurida*. On the East Coast *Crassostrea virginica*, popularly known as the American or

Anatomy of the Oyster
(Crassostrea Virginica)

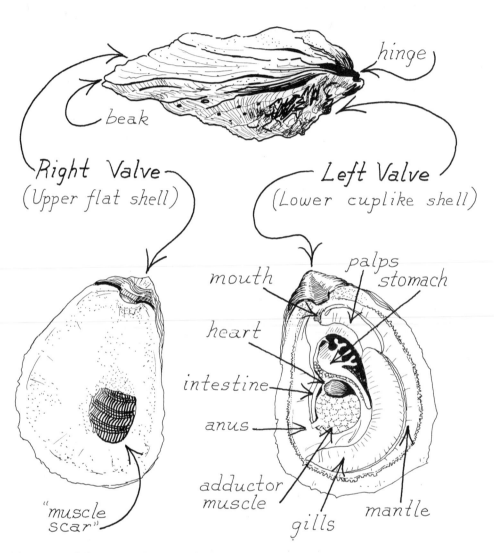

hinge

beak

Right Valve
(Upper flat shell)

Left Valve
(Lower cuplike shell)

mouth

palps
stomach

heart

intestine

anus

"muscle
scar"

adductor
muscle

gills

mantle

Anatomy of the oyster. Drawing by Joseph P. Kochiss

Eastern oyster, is found and cultivated from Prince Edward Island in the Gulf of St. Lawrence all the way down to Texas. Since this study is solely concerned with *Crassostrea virginica*, the word "oyster" will henceforth refer only to this species.

Although oysters from Prince Edward Island and those from Texas are of the same species, some of their characteristics show marked variations due solely to environmental forces. For instance, the warmer waters of the South increase the growth rate and lengthen the spawning periods, whereas in the colder northern waters the reverse is true. A Gulf of Mexico oyster reaches the marketable size of 3 1/2 inches in about two years, but it takes a Long Island Sound oyster four to five years to reach the same size. This, in turn, determines the activities of the oystermen: in different sections of the country they may have similar duties but their timing varies.

Oysters live best in certain shallow bays, sounds, creeks, and estuaries where the salinity, temperature, food supply, and bottom provide favorable combinations for reproduction or growth. Many areas in Narragansett Bay, Long Island Sound, and Great South Bay possess these ideal conditions. In Long Island Sound, for example, the salinity of 27 or 28 parts per thousand on the famous offshore beds from New Haven to Norwalk, Connecticut, is considered good. The minimum salinity for spawning runs from about 15 to 20 parts per thousand. This is found in estuaries and other inshore areas, though the salinity there fluctuates. In the open ocean, however, the salinity is so high, 35 parts per thousand, that oysters do not ordinarily reproduce.

Oysters can withstand a remarkably wide temperature range: they can be frozen solid, or heated in 90° F. waters, and yet somehow survive. Here, again, Long Island Sound and adjacent waters—with temperatures from a little below 32° F. to about 78° F.—are most favorable. When the temperature goes below about 43° F., the oyster slowly begins to hibernate.

Their growth depends not only upon the correct temperature and salinity but also upon the flow of the current and the amount and quality of food available. Oysters feed on a variety of microscopic sea life called phytoplankton, a portion of which comes from rivers and streams—by filtering it through their gills with as much as twenty to thirty quarts of water an hour.

Another important environmental influence is the location and nature of the bottom or bed upon which the oysters live. Their natural habitat lies anywhere between tidal marks—where they are exposed to the direct hot rays of the sun in summer and the freezing air in winter—out to perhaps a depth of twenty or thirty feet. In deeper water, temperatures seldom reach 68° F. (the

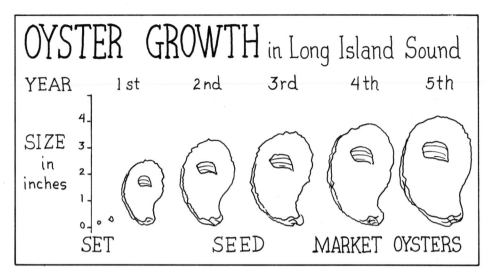

Oyster growth in Long Island Sound. Drawing by Joseph P. Kochiss

approximate temperature at which oysters begin to spawn) and thus spawning rarely occurs, though oysters can live and grow and are indeed cultivated in depths of sixty feet or more. In Long Island Sound the wild natural growth oysters inhabit these shallower regions, whereas the transplanted, farmed, or cultivated oysters can be grown in the deeper waters.

Young oysters prefer clean beds. Deep mud will smother them and they die when overgrown with other animals. After setting, they live a completely sedentary existence, resting on a bottom firm enough to allow them to open and close freely while filter-feeding the minute marine life in the water. All these delicate factors must balance in order to maintain life.

Some species of oysters exhibit a unique ability to switch their own sex: the Eastern oyster does not seem to be able to make up its mind whether to be male or female. But regardless of sex, ordinarily when the water temperature reaches 68° F. to 70° F. both male and female spawn, possibly several times during the season. In the Long Island Sound area this period extends from late June and early July to the end of August or the first week or so in September. In the colder regions farther north, the spawning period is later and shorter. Farther south it begins earlier and lasts longer.

Each sex emits its own generative products into the sea when spawning. Females release 23 to 85 million ova and the male an almost infinite number of sperm cells during the spawning season. When the sperm meets the ova purely by chance in the vastness of the water, fertilization occurs. Thanks to nature's self-regulating mechanism, not all cells are fertilized, for if the larvae set and the oyster developed and grew, within a brief span of time the bottom of Long Island Sound, for example, would literally rise clear out of the water. Probably one out of a few million eggs actually reaches the setting stage.

The fertilized eggs soon become free-swimming larvae called "spawn" by the oystermen. For a few days they have some locomotion, but are mostly carried by the tides and currents. The fragile, microscopic larvae have no adequate defenses and are thus drastically reduced in numbers by prolonged drops in temperature, lack of food, storms, and by predators such as jellyfish, sea anemones, and fish. At the end of the free-swimming stage, which may last up to two weeks, the larvae, now about 1/75 of an inch long, attach to firm, clean surfaces such as shells (which they seem to prefer), bottles, twigs, even boots or shoes, piles and floats. Here they cement themselves to the surface by their left valves and the young oysters, now metamorphosed, and called "spat" or "set," commence their sedentary life. If no such materials are available they eventually die.

In the warm summer and fall months the spat grow rapidly and within a year in Long Island Sound and vicinity they may reach a length of 3/4 of an inch to 1 inch. Now sexually mature, they may spawn every year, even if they live to the ripe old age of forty years!

The character of the bottom determines the oyster's shape to some degree: on soft mud, in sedgy or crowded places, the oyster seeking room grows long, slender, crooked, and ill-shaped. But on uncrowded, hard, sandy bottoms furnished with clean food-laden water, it becomes well-shaped and fat. The best looking oyster for the half-shell trade (the restaurant oyster) is one singly grown, with a width about one-half its length and a thickness of one-half the width.

Oysters of all ages are prone to attack from a host of enemies. Before metamorphosis, as noted, the eggs, embryos, and larvae are consumed relentlessly by jellyfish, crustaceans, fish. After they set some of the oysters' old enemies lose their force and others take over to feed on them or infest them with parasites or disease. Adult oysters with their tough armor of calcium carbonate face another formidable array of predators and animals that compete for space: drills, snails, winkles, drumfish, worms, starfish ("five-fingers"), and, the worst of the lot, "ten-fingers"—man!

Other than man, the starfish is by far the most destructive agent, particularly in Long Island Sound. An army of them can wipe out acres of oyster beds within days, one medium-sized starfish alone being capable of eating seven one-year-old oysters in a single day. It seems remarkable for such boneless, flabby creatures, yet the starfish accomplish it by wrapping themselves around their victim like a wrestler about his opponent, then pry the oyster's valves apart with their suckered tubed feet. After a prolonged tug-of-war in which the starfish is invariably the winner, the oyster relaxes its adductor muscle from sheer exhaustion and that is the end. The starfish turns its stomach inside out, inserts it between the shells, and devours the delicious meat at leisure.

Starfish have always plagued the oysterman and threatened his crops, but one severe gale or hurricane can finish it for both. The hurricane of 1938 and the subsequent series of hurricanes destroyed vessels, shore property, and oyster beds, and ended many an oysterman's career.

Despite these devastating natural agencies the oyster somehow manages to survive. Then comes man and all his foul industrial and domestic pollutants to upset the ecology. Overfishing, pollution, disregard for replacing spawning oysters to perpetuate the breed, poor farming methods, as well as other factors, virtually annihilated most of the naturally productive oyster beds of New England by the mid-twentieth century. The same thoughtless story repeats itself in England, Ireland, France and most other oyster growing countries.

As mentioned, oysters breed and thrive naturally in certain ideal, though limited, localities. These are known in the North as "natural oyster beds"; in the South the beds are called "bars" and "rocks"—which are not rocks at all but accumulations of oyster shells. In colonial times vast areas of these beds abounded in every state from Maine to Texas. In 1634 William Wood wrote in his *New England's Prospect*: "The Oysters be great ones in form of a Shoehorne; some to be a foot long; these breed on certain banks that are bare every spring tide. The fish without shell is so big, that it must admit of a division before you can well get it into your mouth."[1] Four years later Thomas Norton commented: "There are great store of Oysters in the entrances of all Rivers; they are not round as those of England, but excellent fat, and all good. I have seene an Oyster banke a mile at length."[2]

Oysters were then a staple, reliable food in many shore front communities. Even before the period of colonization, they were considered a limitless bounty and the Indians consumed them in prodigious quantities. Anyone could walk to the shallows and pick them as freely as he would pick wild berries in the fields. As time passed, however, a few fishermen and watermen began to specialize in oyster gathering, becoming, in effect, the first "natural growther" oystermen. for they worked on the naturally grown oyster beds for full-grown market oysters—those 3 1/2 inches and larger. Eventually these beds became completely depleted.

With most mother oysters, or brooders, or spawners removed from the natural beds, few remained to reseed them. Generally shells or "cultch" were not returned to act as receptacles of the larvae for future generations, and so by the early 1800s the dwindling natural supply could not be relied upon to meet the ever-increasing demand. The oyster was beating the buffalo to extinction.

Each state made some attempt to prevent the destruction. In Rhode Island, King Charles II's Charter of 1683 had given the right of free fishing to the inhabitants of the colony. In spite of these privileges the state, foreseeing the possibility of the oysters' extinction as early as 1766, made it unlawful to use "draggs" (dredges) since these instruments were assumed to damage oysters and to harvest more than the beds could afford. Only tongs were then permitted. And in 1834 a law was passed forbidding the burning of oyster shells for use in making lime for house builders.

The Connecticut legislature, in about 1750, recognizing that each shore town possessed its own individual problems, permitted each town to enact by-laws regulating the taking of shellfish belonging to or found in the adjoining waters. One of the earliest Connecticut laws, a carryover from England, prohibited fishing during the spawning months to allow the young oysters a chance to survive and, as voted at a town meeting in New Haven on February 22, 1762, read as follows:

> Whereas many persons has made a practice of Catching and Destroying the oysters in the Harbour of New Haven in the month of May June July and August which is to the Great Detriment of the Inhabitants of the Town of New Haven which to prevent Voted that no person shall be allowed to Rake up and Catch any oysters in the Harbour of New Haven or the Cove from the first day of May to the first day of September [the old saw that oysters should not be eaten in a month in the name of which there is no letter *r* probably had its origin in schemes to protect mollusk rather than man] upon a penalty of 20/ per Bushel and the Same proportion for a lesser Quantity (467) Provided nevertheless that nothing in this vote Shall hinder the Selectmen of the Town or any one of them to Give Liberty to any person to Catch a Small Quantity of oysters in the Case of Sickness or necessity. And Whereas Many persons make it their Practice to take the young oysters and shells and the Culch on which they grow on shore whereby the Growth of oysters is much obstructed and unless prevented will be a means of entirely Destroying the Growth of oysters which to prevent Voted that no person Shall carry of any oyster shells or Culch from of the oyster Banks below the New Wharf and East Haven Wharf and below a parrelel line from the oyster point

to the Lower Building yard at the west Parrish or shall be allowed to Carry any under the penalty of 20/ Bushel or in proportion for a Lesser Quantity.[3]

Paralleling the closed season restrictions, other prohibitive measures were placed on methods of gathering the oyster. Another New Haven Town Meeting voted sometime after 1766: "Whereas the catching of oysters in the Harbour in summer months, and with drags at any time of the year, is found prejudicial to the growth and increase of this useful article, therefore it is ordered that no person do catch any oyster . . . in the months of May, June, July, August, and September, save on the Monday and Tuesday before the Publick Commencement, nor with a Dragg at any time of the year."[4]

Besides the closed season law, two other common laws were observed: the two-bushel law, which limited a person's daily catch to two bushels; and the town-residents law, restricting oyster taking to town residents only.

In New York State as early as 1679 a local Brookhaven ordinance reflected the concern of unchecked pillage: "To prevent the destruction of oysters in South bay, by the unlimited number of vessels employed in the same, it is ordered that but ten vessels shall be allowed, and that each half-barrel tub shall be paid for at 2d., according to the town act of Brook Haven."[5]

And well before the War of 1812, by which time Staten Island's natural beds had gradually failed, the New York colonial legislature passed protective legislation aimed at keeping New England and New Jersey men from exhausting the natural beds by restricting them to local inhabitants only. The preamble to a law of 1737 states: "since it has been found by daily experience that the Oysterbeds lying at and near Richmond County, within this Colony, are wasted and Destroyed by Strangers; the preventing of which will tend to the great Benefit of the poor People and others inhabiting the aforesaid Colony." The act goes on to forbid any one "directly or indirectly, to rake, . . . any Oysters within this Colony, and put them on board any Canoe, Periauger, Flat, Scow, Boat or other vessel whatsoever, not wholly belonging to, and owned by, Persons who live within the aforesaid Colony."[6]

This and subsequent laws failed to prevent the virtual extinction of the oyster grounds of Staten Island, the mouth of the Raritan River, and the beds off Shrewsbury, New Jersey. Some of the natural beds off Keyport and Perth Amboy, however, continued to prosper right up to the immediate past.

In Massachusetts, extinction of the natural resources came sooner than it did farther south, perhaps because of the state's marginal location. In colonial days, oysters grew naturally in the Charles and Mystic rivers at Boston and in other points north to Portsmouth, New Hampshire, in quantities large enough to satisfy the local inhabitants. When Wellfleet's oysters suddenly gave out in 1775, it provoked commentaries that continued for generations. Henry Thoreau even wrote about it: "Various causes are assigned for this, such as a ground frost, the carcasses of black-fish kept to rot in the harbor, and the like, but the most common account of the matter is,—and I find that a similar superstition with regard to the disappearance of fishes exists almost everywhere, —that when Wellfleet began to quarrel with the neighboring towns about the right to gather them, yellow specks appeared in them, and Providence caused them to disappear."[7]

Oyster cultivation was not known in the United States prior to the 1820s, although the ancient Chinese, the Romans, and the French in the last century practiced some form of it. Shortages led New York and Connecticut oystermen, instead of relying upon natural set, to experiment with catching free-swimming larvae on artificially prepared beds, then rearing them to maturity.

By the 1860's oyster cultivation on a simple, practical level was mastered, although planting with natural set continued to be practiced. Enterprising oystermen experimented with planting and oyster culture in order to maintain the supply and stay in business, and thus began a new and prosperous phase of the northern fishery. When natural beds no longer provided market size oysters, the smaller "seed" oysters still found there were transplanted to the oystermen's own underwater lots to grow to maturity. It was a simple, relatively inexpensive way of maintaining an oyster reserve.

This, in essence, was oyster planting. However, the oysterman did nothing to perpetuate or propagate the stock. Throughout the nineteenth and twentieth centuries, planting and short-term variations of it called "bedding" and "laying down" continued to be the only type of oystering possible in certain areas.

Cultivation, on the other hand, consists basically of catching the larvae after the free-swimming stage on artificially prepared beds, then rearing them to maturity. First, however, the oysterman has to select the setting ground for his oyster farm. He seeks a clean, smooth, hard, silt bottom free of soft mud or shifting sand and possessing a good current of water laden with fresh food. The oysterman's property is staked and continually maintained much the same as any farmer's land, each lot being accurately mapped by the state or town with the aid of precise sextant readings. The corners of the watery farm are buoyed with twenty- to thirty-foot cedar or bamboo poles that float upright and are

Star mop or tangle made of long cotton strands entangles starfish when dragged over the sea bottom. Captain Thomas Thomas of New Haven, Connecticut, was the first to use the mop commercially in the 1880s. Courtesy of National Marine Fisheries Services.

Planting shells from a barge. Courtesy of August MacTaggart.

tied by rope lines to stone or concrete anchors weighing 100 to 250 pounds. Little flags fly from their tops with the owner's name, lot number and position painted on. New bottoms are cleaned of trash with dredges and swept clear of starfish periodically with starfish entangling mops and deposits of lime.

Spawning and setting beds are sometimes positioned next to each other, usually in shallow water near shore where the spawning temperature will be reached. The ground may be one of the oysterman's previously owned beds or he may acquire new land from the state or town. If the new area is near a bed of oysters capable of spawning, then all is for the good; if not, he may plant brood oysters nearby to supply the needed spawn. These brood oysters are saved from other crops or purchased from someone else. At any rate, he must clear the beds first, then "shell" the space with clean oyster, scallop, or jingle shells to catch the larvae at the end of the free-swimming stage. The cultivator either buys the shells from men who specialize in harvesting them— like the "shellermen" of the Housatonic River (see Chapter 11)—or he may save his shucked oyster shells, as most oystermen do.

Shelling, as the careful planting of the cultch is termed, lasts a few weeks beginning after the fourth of July in Long Island Sound, and corresponds hopefully with the larval free-swimming stage. If deposited a few days earlier, the shells acquire a thin layer of organic slime in which the larvae cannot survive. Shelling after the larvae have set is obviously too late, for to catch the maximum number of spat, it must be done at the time of spawning or slightly before. What makes it really difficult is that no one knows precisely when and if the larvae *will* set. The old-time oystermen would spot open some oysters to look for "spawn in the neck" which told them the oysters were ready to "let go." Science has helped a little here by notifying the oystermen when water conditions are at their optimum for spawning and setting.

The amount of shells required per acre depends upon the nature of the bottom. Ingersoll reports 250 bushels per acre as an average, but today they may plant 1000 to 2000 bushel per acre. Generally, oystermen try to cover as much ground as they can.[8] If there is no set the shells are dredged up and allowed to dry on land ready for the next year's shelling.

With a little cooperation from nature the brood oysters or others in the vicinity will spawn and set on the cultch. Since most of the setting areas are in shallow water subject to devastation by winter storms, the young (two- or three-month-old) set are dredged and transferred to safer growing beds offshore in deeper water. Here they are prone to become thin and tough, though

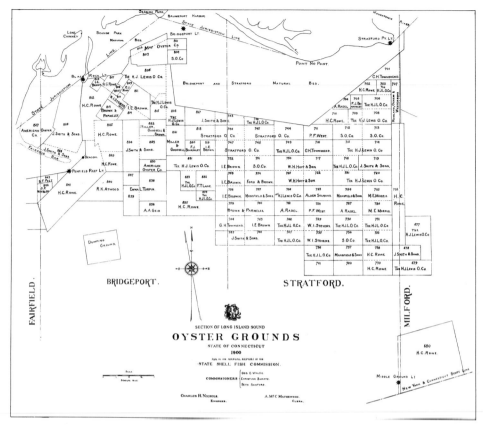

Connecticut state and town oyster beds have been accurately surveyed, mapped and kept updated since 1881. Map from *Annual Report of the Shell-Fish Commissioners, State of Connecticut*, 1900.

hardy, from the more saline and highly mineralized offshore water. After two or three years they are moved again to select growing or fattening beds such as those of Gardiners Bay and Peconic Bay where the pure, diatom-rich water promotes rapid growth. Possibly a final transplant will be made to the choicest "market" ground for further development in size, quality, plumpness, and flavor. Thus an oyster is ready for the table after four to five or even six years of constant care and attention.

CHAPTER 2

The History of Oystering in the North

Connecticut

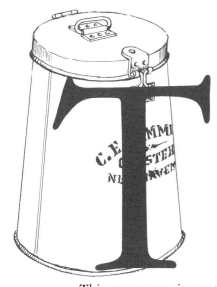

OWARD the end of the eighteenth century when overfishing continued unabated in southern Connecticut and laws failed, as usual, to prevent wholesale plunder, oystermen bought oysters from other places. At first imports for immediate use or short-term storage came from neighboring communities. When these could not furnish enough oysters, they were obtained from New York and Delaware Bay and, finally, by the first quarter of the nineteenth century, from the seemingly inexhaustible Chesapeake Bay.

This commerce in oysters from the Chesapeake, called the southern or Virginia trade, was confined in Connecticut almost exclusively to New Haven, where the largest oyster shops were located. Oysters were shipped by schooner from the South, and initially sold directly off the boats. Later they were laid down in the spring, fattened on the sandbars (known as "the beach") off City Point, taken up in the fall, and prepared for market. Captain Merritt Farron is reputed to have been the first man to carry Virginia oysters to New Haven around 1830,[1] although certain evidence points to 1823 or earlier. At any rate, by the 1850s New Haven had become a booming oyster community, chiefly due to the southern trade. Ingersoll reported that in 1858, 250 schooners imported 2 million bushels of oysters to Fair Haven (a section of New Haven). Business improved to such an extent that Fair Haven oyster firms opened houses inland as far as Chicago and St. Louis. One firm alone—Levi Rowe and

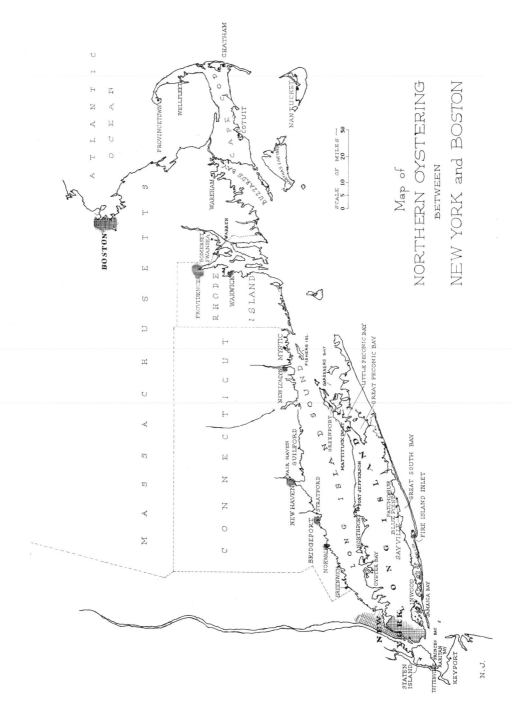

Map of
NORTHERN OYSTERING
between
NEW YORK and BOSTON
Drawing by John LaPresle.

SCALE OF MILES
0   5 10   20   30

Map of northern oystering from New York to Boston. Drawing by John LaPresle.

Co.—in 1856 was said to have employed twenty vessels and 100 openers, and to have sold 150,000 gallons of opened oysters. Other houses shipped 1,000 to 1,500 bushels daily.[2]

Southern imports, amounting to over one-quarter of the total New Haven trade at times, reached a peak between 1855 and 1858 and gradually fell to practically nothing by World War I. The rest of the trade involved taking market-sized oysters directly off the natural beds or from transplanting local natural bed oysters. This was before the era of oyster propagation that commenced about the 1860s. Despite prosperous times some New Haven firms, seeing a gold mine in the Chesapeake Bay area and sensing impending oyster failure at home, moved or opened branch houses in Baltimore. Such celebrated New Haven houses as H. M. Rowe & Co., D. D. Mallory & Co., C. S. Maltby, and H. F. Hemingway & Co. soon established themselves there, causing it to be said that "all the great Baltimore firms of old standing originated in Fair Haven."[3]

While oystering boomed in New Haven, circumstances transpired elsewhere that eventually altered the character of the entire business. It was common knowledge that oyster larvae set on almost any clean underwater object, especially oyster shells, in the summertime. Surprisingly, however, no one in the United States prior to the 1820s bothered or probably even thought of deliberately planting shells to catch set. Eventually, though, some people did, and Ingersoll in 1880 related the story of these first attempts at true oyster culture:

> The City Island oysterman, therefore, began to save his shells from the lime-kiln and the road-master, and to spread them on the bottom of the bay, hoping to save some of the oyster-spawn with which his imagination densely crowded the sea water. This happened, I am told, more than fifty years ago, and the first man to put the theory into practice, it is remembered, was the father of the Fordham Brothers, who still pursue the business at City Island. In 1855, Captain Henry Bell, of Bell's Island, planted shells among the islands off the mouth of Norwalk River, and a short time after, under the protection of the new law of 1855, recognizing private property in such beds, Mr. Oliver Cook, of Five-Mile River, Mr. Weed of South Norwalk, Mr. Hawley, of Bridgeport, and others, went into it on an extensive scale. Some of these gentlemen appear never to have heard of any previous operations of the sort. Discovering it for themselves, as it was easy and natural to do, they supposed they were the originators; but if any such credit attaches anywhere, I believe it belongs to the City Island men.[4]

Regardless of when it actually began, oyster culture thus prolonged the life of the state's oyster industry, and on the basis of these techniques and the nature of her oyster-growing areas, Connecticut developed into the leading oyster seed producer north of New Jersey.

State and local governments reacting to the changing industry enacted further protective legislation. More important, moreover, from early planting days the law had recognized and eventually granted underwater land to individuals. There were furious objections to this. Objectors claimed the state had no right to grant "public property" to individuals. They obviously believed that all underwater ground was common to all. Those in favor of titles argued "nobody's property, everybody's prey." In 1845 an ordinance permitted any state citizen to plant in Connecticut waters oysters brought in from another state. One year later the privilege extended to native oysters transplanted within the state. Both laws encouraged the southern trade and the new ideas of oyster cultivation.

In 1855 an important act was passed by the Connecticut Assembly. Known as the "two-acre law," it empowered coastal towns to grant two acres or less of underwater land to individuals for planting oysters. Land under water was gradually approaching the status of onshore property. Additional provisions stipulated that the natural beds were not to be touched, and that applications, designations, and transfers of oyster ground should be in writing. The chief outcome of the law was the encouragement of oyster cultivation, even though the two acres, while enough for one man to handle, proved insufficient for the large oyster companies. But the law was evaded by the oystermen, "who induced their neighbors and friends to aid them by each making application for 2 acres, at the same time signing a quitclaim in favor of the person for whom the action was really taken. Large areas were obtained in this manner by some individuals; indeed, there is on record a deed or quitclaim transferring to one man the ground rights of 224 men."[5]

In 1864 another statute directed that designations and transfers must be recorded and then, for the first time, denoted that oyster grounds were subject to assessment and taxation in the towns where the property was situated. The succeeding year only a duly appointed town committee had the right to stake out grounds. In an effort to define rights and privileges and establish standards for regulating grants, all existing Connecticut oyster laws were codified in 1866.

Oyster cultivation before 1865 was confined to the rivers and harbors of the state and to the shallow areas inside the Norwalk Islands. In that year, offshore cultivation in 20 to 25 feet of water began off Norwalk. By the early

APPLICATION.

To EDWARD B. THOMPSON, DANIEL H. BROWN, ALFRED HEMINGWAY, WILLIAM E. GOODYEAR and ALFRED HUGHES, Committee of the Town of East Haven, in New Haven County, State of Connecticut, to designate suitable places in the navigable waters of said State, within the limits of said Town, for the planting of Oysters:—

The Undersigned, being a citizen of Connecticut, and residing in the Town of *East Haven* in said State, is desirous of planting Oysters in the navigable waters of said State, within the limits of the Town of East Haven; and he therefore, respectfully requests that you will designate a suitable place to be used by him for that purpose, not exceeding two acres in extent, pursuant to the statute in such cases made and provided.

Dated at East Haven, upon this the *28th* day of *April* A. D. 186*6*

John J. Dayton

———— ◆ ————

DESIGNATION.

Upon the application of *John J. Dayton* of the Town of *East Haven* in the County of New Haven, and State of Connecticut, dated the *28th* day of *April* A. D. 186*6*, requesting that we, as a Committee of the Town of East Haven, duly and legally appointed for that purpose, will designate a suitable place, not exceeding two acres in extent, in the navigable waters of said State, and within the limits of said Town, for the planting of Oysters; we, the undersigned, believe, and are of the opinion that the public interest requires the granting of said Application; and we, therefore, as said Committee, have designated and allotted to the said *John J. Dayton* and for and in consideration of the sum of *Ten 50/100* dollars, received to our full satisfaction, do hereby designate, assign and allot to the said *John J. Dayton* and to his heirs and assigns forever, for the purpose of planting Oysters thereon, a certain piece or parcel of land, covered by the waters of New Haven harbor, situated within the limits of the Town of East Haven, and known and designated as Lot No. *105* on a certain Map now on file in the Town Clerk's Office, in the Town of East Haven, entitled "Map No. *1* of East Haven "Oyster Grounds, being a portion of Morris' Cove, surveyed by William Hartley, C. E. and County "Surveyor, April 1866, for and under the directions of the Committee appointed by the Town of "East Haven, to designate suitable places within the limits of said Town, for the planting of "Oysters;" said Lot is bounded North, by Lot No. *106* of said Map; East, by Lot No. *94* of said Map; West, by Lot No. of said Map; and South, by Lot No. *104* of said Map, and contains *One acre*

This designation, allotment and description, is made by us at East Haven, upon this the *28th* day of *April* A. D. 186*6*.

EDWARD B. THOMPSON,
DANIEL H. BROWN,
ALFRED HEMINGWAY,   } *Committee as aforesaid.*
WILLIAM E. GOODYEAR,
ALFRED HUGHES,

Application for a two-acre lot in 1866, when Connecticut law limited two acres to one person. Courtesy of John Baker.

Watchman in a shack on the "beach" in New Haven harbor guarding oyster beds from thieves. Illustration from *New Haven Register*, April 29, 1900.

1870s all the available inshore property was designated, and the spacious floor of Long Island Sound, always considered completely unfit for any kind of oystering, remained the only underwater land left in Connecticut.

Continuing under faulty assumptions, oystermen did not believe larvae or the oyster could survive the often turbulent sound and its deadly hordes of starfish. But it did not take long for an intrepid soul to wonder, then experiment. In 1874 "Mr. H. C. Rowe first showed the courage of his opinions

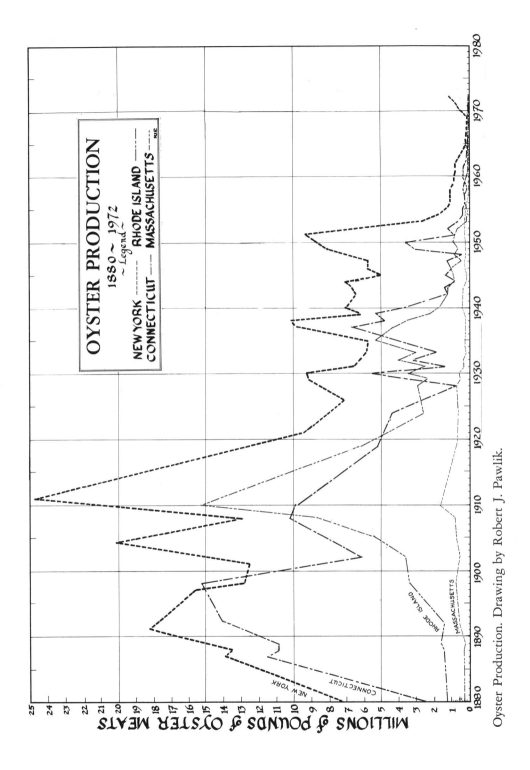

Oyster Production. Drawing by Robert J. Pawlik.

enough to take up some hundreds of acres outside [New Haven], in water from 25 to 40 feet in depth, and to begin there the cultivation of native oysters.[6]

Alterations and additions in the statutes followed, mostly aimed at establishing underwater land operations on a basis of law and order. Notwithstanding, conflicting claims among the owners of private ground and between them and the natural growthers continued, illustrating further the inadequacies and deficiencies of the laws and regulations. With cultivation extending into ever deeper water, the vast tract of ground offshore, now eagerly sought by the enterprising deep water cultivators, was not available because the state had granted no authority to designate it. Finally, under these and other pressures, the General Assembly in 1881 passed a significant act which, among other provisions, established a State Shell-Fish Commission with powers over all shell fisheries within state jurisdiction. It assigned to the commission the full authority to grant a perpetual franchise to designated oyster grounds and the right to receive the proceeds of their sale (at $1.10 per acre). The much evaded, two-acre limitation of 1855 was also removed by this legislation. At the same time, the Connecticut-New York boundary line in Long Island Sound was established.

The law of 1881, which became a model for oyster legislation in other states, read in part as follows:

> Section 1. The state shall exercise exclusive jurisdiction and control over all shell-fisheries which are located in that area of the state which is within that part of Long Island sound and its tributaries bounded westerly and southerly by the state of New York, easterly by the state of Rhode Island, and northerly by the line following the coasts of the state at high water, which shall cross all its bays, rivers, creeks, and inlets at such places nearest Long Island sound as are within and between points on opposite shores from one of which objects and what is done on the opposite shore can be reasonably discerned with the naked eye, or could be discerned but for intervening islands. And all shell-fisheries not within said area shall be and remain within the jurisdiction and control of the towns in which they are located under the same laws and regulations and through the same selectmen and oyster committees as heretofore.

> Sec. 2. The three fish commissioners of the state now in office and their successors, shall also be and constitute a board of commissioners of shell-fisheries, and be empowered to make or cause to be made a survey and map of all the grounds within the said area in Long Island sound which have been or may be designated for the planting or cultivation of shell-fish; shall ascertain the ownership thereof, and how much of the same is actually in use

WAITING FOR THEIR SUPPLY OF BLUE POINTS.
GREAT SOUTH BAY OYSTER FLEET IN NORTHPORT HARBOR

Oyster schooners in Northport Harbor. Courtesy of Richard Simpson, Northport, Long Island.

for said purposes; they shall also cause a survey of all the natural oyster beds in said area, and shall locate and delineate the same on said map, which survey and map when completed shall not cost a sum exceeding twenty-five hundred dollars, and shall report to the next session of the legislature a plan for an equitable taxation of the property in said fisheries, and make an annual report of the state and condition of said fisheries to the legislature.

Sec. 3. The said commissioners shall also be empowered, in the name and in behalf of the state, to grant by written instruments, for the purpose of planting and cultivating shell-fish, perpetual franchises in such undesignated grounds within said area as are not and for ten years have not been natural clam or oyster beds, whenever application in writing is made to them through their clerk by any person or persons who have resided in the state not less than one year next preceding the date of said application.[7]

The perpetual franchise system of private ownership then adopted was replaced in 1915 by a ten-year leasing plan with renewal privileges. Though ownership now rested with the state, there was nonetheless a measure of security of tenure. In 1973 four types of oyster ground existed in Connecticut: the natural beds; franchised ground—some of those old beds held since before 1915; the leased ground; and certain town-owned ground north of the state jurisdiction line, which ran roughly parallel to the coast line.

New York

New York State has consistently outproduced Connecticut, Rhode Island, and Massachusetts in marketable oysters. By the 1880s New York City had become the center of the northern oyster industry and led the country in overseas and transcontinental oyster shipments. Oysters flowed into the New York markets from New England, Chesapeake Bay, and Delaware Bay, but most significantly from its own waters—Staten Island, City Island, Raritan Bay, some select points up the Hudson River near Nyack and Ossining, and practically every inlet and bay on Long Island. At one time fine oysters were even grown and eaten from beds around Manhattan Island.

From colonial times New York has abounded with oysters, enough at least to supply local needs. But by the 1880s pollution—that sourge of mankind—nature and the expanded population had dwindled its resources to such an extent that to maintain an oyster industry and meet the demands placed upon it New York was forced to rely mainly on Connecticut's readily available oyster seed and, to a minor extent, on southern oysters. By 1909 less than 17 percent of the annual crop from the principal oyster-producing area, Great South Bay, originated there.[8] It was estimated again in 1947 that only 5 percent were indigenous and that the remaining 95 percent came from Connecticut transplants. New York's oyster industry, as Rhode Island's at the turn of the last century, would probably never have prospered without help from Connecticut.[9]

Perhaps no other New York oyster, or northern oyster for that matter, equaled the national and international fame of Great South Bay's Blue Point. Even today with the industry at rock bottom production, Blue Points are still remembered and asked for wherever oysters are eaten, though Great South Bay no longer harvests them. The bay was one of the leading oyster-producing areas of the North. In fact in 1881 it was called "the most populous oyster-ground north of the Chesapeake bay."[10] Since earliest times thousands of men and boys living on the bay had oystered, clammed, fished and, since the latter part of the nineteenth century, gone yachting in the summer. To them the land was to live on and farm, but the bay sustained them. And it was their own Blue Point that made some of them millionaires.

Blue Points originally came from the area off the town of Blue Point, near Patchogue. The small, roundish oysters found there were considered the half-shell oyster par excellence because of the shape, flavor, and whiteness of their meat. As time went on though, any small, well-formed oyster from any part of the bay took on the magic appellation Blue Point. Originally, Great South Bay oysters grew large, but by the 1830s (from some unknown cause) oysters ceased to propagate there and completely disappeared. In 1839 they spawned and increased again apparently as a result of transplanting Virginia oysters, so much so that the bay rapidly regained its former prosperity.[11] Many oystermen, however, do not believe that Chesapeake oysters can spawn in these waters.

To prevent other regions selling oysters under the Blue Point name, the New York Legislature in 1908 enacted a provision that unfortunately applied to sales in New York State only: "No person, firm or corporation shall sell or offer for sale any oysters, or label or brand any package containing oysters for shipment or sale, under the name of Blue Point oysters, other than oysters that have been planted and cultivated at least three months in the waters of the Great South Bay in Suffolk County."[12]

Not all Blue Points, however, were eaten locally. A lively European trade in northern oysters, mainly from New York to England, with Blue Points, East Rivers and Sounds leading the way, developed about 1870 when George H. Shaffer of New York sent twelve barrels to England by steamer. From then until its decline along with the rest of the industry, the trade flourished. In 1896 *The Fishing Gazette* reported that we were shipping 100,000 barrels annually to England alone.[13] The oysters were consumed raw, but a portion were planted for future consumption and further growth. One Whitstable, England, oysterman told me in 1968 that he never approved of that planting decades ago because it brought with it oyster predators previously unknown there.

Oysters for planting were also sent in large quantities by train from New York to the West Coast, beginning sometime prior to the 1870s. The oysters thrived and grew very rapidly there but never seemed to propagate successfully because of the cold water.

Although all eastern United States oysters are of the same species, the purity and thermal conditions of Great South Bay added something special to this famous bivalve. And even though no big cities or industries pollute its shores with sewage and industrial wastes—thanks to the vigilance of its concerned citizens and town and state laws—no oysters have been harvested from there for the past few years due to the parasite MSX (*Minchinia nelsoni*), which—though not harmful to man—is infecting and killing adult oysters to such an extent that they cannot be harvested economically. MSX was first reported in the late 1950s in Delaware Bay; now it is doing untold damage in Chesapeake Bay as well.

Great South Bay, located some 40 to 50 miles from Manhattan, is about 25 to 30 miles long, 2 to 5 miles wide, and averages about 6 feet in depth, but does not exceed 12 to 13 feet. Fire Island, a barrier island on the south side, protects it from the Atlantic Ocean. Nature and man have created a number of inlets through this barrier island, but today only Moriches Inlet and, most tellingly, Fire Island Inlet admit ocean water, giving a tidal rise in the bay of only about 1 foot. Salt water from the ocean and fresh water springs, brooks, and rivers feeding the bay create areas of different salinities, which sustain a variety of shellfish. Since salinity differences influence oysters, the bay is not uniformly productive. The eastern end, between Smith and Nicoll points, is less salty than the western end, due to its distance from the ocean inlet. The salinity there is favorable for oyster spawning and setting, but unfavorable for starfish and drills. All this coupled with a harmonious sandy and somewhat muddy bottom makes the eastern end a natural setting ground. The western end, closer to Fire Island Inlet and the ocean's more salty influence, is more suitable for the fattening and maturing process. Generally, since the advent of planting in the mid-nineteenth century, the tendency has been for the cultivators to concentrate on the western end, that is, west of Nicoll Point, for growing oysters to market size, and east of it for harvesting seed.

The history of oystering in the bay began, as elsewhere, with the Indians. But it was the white man who seemed to have a penchant for plundering what nature gives so freely, and a multitude of statutes, restrictions, taxes, leasing laws, and the like accrued, affecting all facets of the bay's oystering activities. Controversies arose not only amongst baymen but with all parties concerned—state, towns, cultivators—and laws were enacted to solve their many problems. In many cases they served only to aggravate and even create more strife. Cultivators sought, mostly in vain, for a clear title to the grounds cultivated which would encourage rather than hinder their business. Baymen, among other considerations, fought for the right to work the natural beds or their own few acres without fear of the cultivator's encroachments—much the same feeling as prevailed in other states.

In general New York State controlled all shellfish grounds within her boundaries with the notable exception of Great South Bay. Between 1767 and about 1910 the town of Brookhaven, on the eastern end of the bay, and the Smith Heirs considered that part of the bay—containing 13,440 acres (21 square miles)—solely under their jurisdiction. This unique situation arose through a colonial grant to the town of Brookhaven by patent from the king of England: "Recognizing this grant, there was made an agreement in 1767 between William Smith, who was at that time the holder and representative of the rights and interests of the fishing in Great South bay, whereby the town, in exchange for the right to control the bay, contracted to give to him and his heirs forever one half of all net income accruing to the town from the use of the bottom of the bay."[14] About 1910 the oyster lands fell under the sole control of the town trustees, but these same 13,440 acres are now owned with full legal title by the Bluepoints Company, Inc. of West Sayville.

The western end of the bay was generally owned and controlled by the towns of Islip and Babylon. Before 1931 any town resident, upon application for a license, could work on town-owned ground not under lease. Those with leases were for lots not exceeding four acres and at an annual rental of $1 per acre. As in Connecticut, a four-acre lot was not profitable; therefore, additional lots were acquired under relatives' or friends' names. After 1931 the situation improved somewhat. Islip, for instance, discontinued issuing leases but allowed additional lots to be continued into legal holdings.

Oyster planting and farming in the bay began in the 1840s. One of the first plantings was carried on in the western end of what is called the California bed. An account of its interesting origin reads: "About the year 1847, certain Sayville oystermen staked off some ground on what is known as California bed and planted a number of loads of young oysters thereon from the eastern part of the bay, and in 1849 they went there to see how they were doing and found that the oysters had all lived and were in such large quantities that one of the men seeing the shells had a bright yellow color from a moss or sponge that grows in the locality, exclaimed: 'It's a California.' And the California bed has been its name until the present time."[15] Around this time the Brookhaven Town Trustees first issued leases, emulating Connecticut's example to an extent. As time passed more planting ground was leased all over the bay and by the 1870s and 1880s, with the advent of oyster cultivation, much of the bay had been parcelled off and divided into town lands and public beds. The industry expanded and prospered through the years, and during its heyday *The Fishing Gazette* reported that "recent figures compiled show that from the

South Bay there are annually shipped 150,000 barrels of oysters at $5 a barrel and 101,000 gallons of opened oysters at $1 per gallon."[16] In 1916 the total area under cultivation in the bay was upward of 50,000 acres.

Oysters were always consumed locally but the largest percentage was sent to the New York City market by sail before the Long Island Railroad was opened through to the bay in the 1860s and 1870s. Transportation then shifted gradually from sail to rail; oysters were sent in barrels by horse-drawn wagons to the railroad stations and forwarded to the city by freight or express. This form of delivery lasted until the coming of the motor truck after World War I. Truck service was more direct and about as fast as the railroad: jobbers did not have to call at the railroad piers to pick up the oysters—they arrived directly at their doorstep.

The gasoline engine not only revolutionized land transportation but boats as well. Jacob Ockers of West Sayville, Long Island, recognized as the "Oyster King" of Great South Bay because of his vast business, had the first gasoline-powered oyster boat built on the Bay in 1896. He called her, appropriately, *Jacob Ockers*. By 1910 all the oyster companies on the bay owned a powered oyster boat. Today many of these original gas boats are still working it— clamming this time—but nevertheless serving their owners just as well as before. And quite a number of men living today still vividly recall the industry's heyday sixty years ago.

Oystermen here as in Connecticut were grouped into two distinct classes: the cultivators and the natural growthers. On the bay the natural growthers were and still are usually called "baymen." They were all-round watermen who inherited their trade from their fathers and grandfathers. Unlike his Connecticut counterpart who generally oystered only, the bayman did almost everything. In the winter season he worked at culling in the oyster houses or dredging on the oyster power boats. In the spring he tonged seed oysters on the natural beds in the eastern end of the bay. Summer time found him tonging clams in the middle and western part, or perhaps he took city folk out on sailing and fishing parties in his little sloop or cat boat. In the fall he was back at oystering.[17]

The cultivators or planters consisted of two classes:

> The first is represented by the poor bayman, who, without capital, cultivates a small piece of ground by his individual labor, with possibly the assistance of some member of his family or of a similarly situated "partner." There are many hundreds of these who, by arduous toil, while subject to constant hard-

West Sayville oyster shop of Jacob Ockers (seventh from left), the "oyster king" of Great South Bay. Courtesy of Suffolk Marine Museum.

ship and exposure, manage to wrest from the sand and mud of our bays and harbors a frugal livelihood for themselves and families. The numbers of this type are constantly increasing. Second, the planter with capital sufficient to enable him to use every device and appliance necessary or convenient to large operations, including the employment of well-manned steamers equipped with dredges, starfish mops, etc. together with extensive oyster houses where oysters are opened or otherwise prepared for shipment and from whence the product is sent throughout the country and indeed to all parts of the civilized world.[18]

At one time or another the entire periphery of Long Island was studded with oystering communities. Going west from Great South Bay toward New York City, the great marshy lagoon with its complex of tidal creeks running from Jamaica Bay to the Rockaways excelled in growing and maturing oysters though it probably never had any natural beds. Oystermen here got their seed from Great South Bay and Connecticut. Though these "Jamaicas" and "Rock-aways," as they were termed, never exceeded the Blue Points in volume, they nevertheless acquired a fine reputation in New York and in Europe well before 1900.

Each oysterman on Jamaica Bay owned a skiff, and the planters all had scow-type planting boats, floats for drinking the oysters, and probably a sloop for marketing their product. Oysters were tonged for the most part, although dredging was resorted to where oysters were scattered. The oystermen of Inwood were about as typical as any. An article in 1891 describes their activities:

> The best season for planting, it is thought, extends from the middle of March to the middle of April, although this industry is frequently continued until June. The oystermen begin shipping their produce to market on September 1, continuing until December, when they cease their weekly trips to New York until March. Some of them who sell to speculators do not go to market at all, but in these instances, which are rare, half the joy of the oysterman's life is lost. The pleasant sense of ownership which attaches to a smart sloop well laden with valuable produce, and skimming merrily over the smooth water to the markets of New York, is perhaps as great a compensation to the oystermen whose heart is in his work as the more substantial rewards with which he returns a few hours later.[19]

Staten Island ranked with Great South Bay, prior to 1900, as another leading New York oyster-producing region. Their oysters—"Sounds" and "Prince's Bays"—were highly regarded and due to their excellent keeping qualities were sent to Europe and overland to the West coast.

Like so many other common, oyster-producing areas, Staten Island's natural beds gradually failed by the War of 1812.

It then turned to the abundant Virginia oysters to satisfy the market. Around 1816 oysters were brought from Chesapeake Bay but were not initially laid down for further growth. "Firsts" are always contested and difficult to prove, but Captain David Van Name of Staten Island, who entered the oyster business as a dealer in 1817, is said to have been one of the first two men to plant oysters in America.[20] Captain Benjamin Decker of Keyport also claimed to have carried the first cargo of Virginia oysters to Prince's Bay in 1825— about the same time Connecticut men engaged in the same southern trade.[21]

Planting soon demanded solutions to underwater land ownership problems. At first the plots were staked out as claims and worked on a "first come,

Tonging for oysters in Princes Bay, Staten Island. Note bull rake in the stern of the Staten Island skiff and the oyster poles marking the boundary of the oyster plots. Illustration from *Ballou's Pictorial Drawing-Room Companion*, September 29, 1855.

first served basis. . . . Each oyster planter was a law unto himself and to his neighbors as to his claims, and so long as he kept his plot staked and a small or large quantity of oysters upon his land, the courts, by mutual consent, upheld his claims to the bed."[22] In this way oystermen controlled themselves to some extent and made every effort, with the knowledge at hand, to improve their produce and increase their yield. Through the years the simple claim system evolved into a granting system with laws to control and settle disputes. Though regulations of this nature have never been perfect, it was the only practical way to carry on the oyster business.

Reports a contemporary writer, "the prosperity and rapid increase of the population of that island [Staten] is owing, in a considerable degree, to the oyster-trade of this city. Before Prince's Bay was laid out in oyster-plantations there were very few persons living on it, and it was almost wholly uncultivated. . . . A few years after the first beds were planted an extent of coast of from five to ten miles was covered with oysters taken from the 'rocks' of Virginia."[23] Staten Island for the most part prospered from oystering and related industries like shipbuilding; communities grew and many oystermen waxed wealthy. The industry depended chiefly upon southern stock until the Civil War, when this supply was cut off. After that more reliance was placed on oysters from the North and East rivers, Long Island Sound, Great South Bay, Newark Bay, and the Raritan River.

Between the Civil War and World War I conditions at Staten Island remained fairly constant: planters acquired ground from the state, seed came from out of the area, the oyster planters toiled with skiff (the Staten Island skiff), sloop, or power boat and sent their product to the great New York City markets. An excellent description of the work of a typical Great Kills oyster planter appeared in *Outing* magazine, April, 1903.

Here is Captain Thomas Colon, of the sloop *Jessie*, who was the first man to plant an oyster in the Kills, thirty odd years ago. At present he owns "ground" down in Prince's Bay and also in the Kills. It is spring time, and he has either bought a cargo of "seed" or dredged it himself from a set discovered somewhere in Long Island Sound. The *Jessie* is anchored upon the captain's ground—forty or fifty acres of ocean, the limitations of which are marked by the inevitable long saplings driven into the bottom at low water. From the deck of the sloop the seed is transfered into skiffs, and as the skiffs are rowed to and fro over the ground the seed is sown right and left by the shovelful. It falls upon the bottom of soft ooze thirty feet below the surface, soon adapts itself to the new surroundings, and, as before, congregates in clusters which point their bills toward the zenith. Having planted his seed, Captain Tom returns from the scene, allowing nature a period of about three years to develop his colony into a marketable commodity.

Three years have elapsed, let us say, and again it is spring time. The trim little *Jessie* sails out of the Kills for Prince's Bay. Captain Colon is about to enter upon another stage of oyster culture. The sloop is anchored on the ground, and from dawn until late in the afternoon he and his men, working in skiffs, rake the oysters from the bottom. This is arduous toil, as the water is turbulent and the rakes very heavy. As the rakeful of oysters comes to the surface it is seen that they have grown to three and four inches in length, and proportionately broad and thick, during the three years since they were planted. They are loaded into the skiffs dripping with the salt sea, and often covered with the algae before mentioned.

Each afternoon, the *Jessie*, towing a string of laden skiffs sails back to her anchorage in the Great Kills. Here the oysters are culled, that is, knocked apart, as they cling together in cluster's. The skiffs are now rowed slowly over the captain's grounds in the Kills and the oysters are thrown out in the same manner as was the seed in Prince's Bay. Here they will be "tonged" up for the market.

The reason for transferring the three or four-year-old oysters to the Kills from the bay lies in the fact that the Kills have a hard bottom, and during the six months or so that the mollusks repose there they grow rapidly. There is considerable loss in the handling, it being impossible to rake up the full quantity that has been planted.

For six months, then, the mollusks, whose career we have traced from birth, lie upon the bed of the Kills. Here, in favorable seasons, they fatten and improve. There are, however, years when no change is observable in them, and these are gloomy years for the planter. It is then said that the oysters "don't open good," and the price is much affected thereby.

September is here, and if the weather remains cool enough to render the market "stiff," Captain Colon and his crew begin to tong up his oysters from the bed of the Kills. Tonging is less arduous work than raking. Still, a day's tonging tests a strong man's endurance severely, especially if the sea is high and the skiff rocks and dances on the lumpy waves. The skiffs loaded, culling is again gone through with, and the oysters are counted. The dexterity with which a skilful oysterman culls and counts a boatload is a revelation to laymen. Should there be oysters of extra size among those tonged, they are placed by themselves to be sold as "box" oysters.

The much-traveled mollusks are now placed upon the deck of the *Jessie*. But they are not ready for the market yet. The sloop, in company with the *Emma Joy* and other oyster boats, sails for the Rahway River, New Jersey. Here are anchored long lines of "floats" or oyster bathtubs, built of huge timber. Into one of these the cargo of the *Jessie* is thrown, and there it is allowed to remain for the tide, during which the oysters "bloat" themselves by taking copious draughts of semi-fresh water. At the same time they discard such small solids as sand and gravel from the interior of the shell. Thus drenched, bleached, and bloated with fresh water, they are again transferred to the sloop, which now sails for the oyster docks of the great city, where among a heterogeneous tangle of craft she ties up. Until recently this was at a quaint row of oyster scows which lined a portion of West Street, and here the cargo of the *Jessie*, in bushel baskets, was wont to be transferred to one of the scows, and Captain Colon's responsibility as a planter to cease.[24]

Since 1927, when New York finally condemned all the waters around Staten Island and in New York Bay, that once thriving oyster business has been dead—thanks to uncontrolled pollution.

The waters lying between Montauk and Orient points on Long Island's eastern end developed after the 1890s into another important oyster center. Today with Greenport as the hub it is the largest oyster-producing region in New York—if we don't include the small enterprises at Northport, Oyster Bay, and Fishers Island. In the clear, clean waters of Gardiners, Great Peconic, and Little Peconic bays, seed oysters mature with remarkable rapidity into excellent, highly prized stock. Yet it was not until the late 1880s that oystermen began to take advantage of this quality in their waters. Before then baymen scalloped and fished rather than oystered, since from earliest time oysters as a rule seldom set or survived to maturity there, perhaps because of the abundance of starfish and other predators.

In spite of the apparently unfavorable condition of these waters, an attempt at oyster growing was made by L.T. Terry in 1888 when he founded the Greenport Oyster Co. Terry bought a large quantity of seed and planted it, but soon stars and welks destroyed it all and he was forced out of business. Seven years later, with renewed confidence, he bought Bridgeport seed, which made a phenominal growth. It was claimed that one bushel of seed planted yielded seven bushels of mature oysters. Others soon organized companies and planted seed, many from their own ground in Connecticut. Some baymen were successful enough to retire while others not so lucky just struggled along.

By 1900 Greenport and vicinity rose to prominence as a maturing ground for Long Island Sound oysters. Connecticut men, many with investments in the Rhode Island industry, acquired acreage on Long Island which proved much to their advantage years later. Great South Bay oystermen, equally as sagacious as the Yankees, also leased here. They, incidentally, pushed for the construction of the Shinnecock Canal, which opened the shortest route between Peconic and Great South bays.

Greenport, like towns on Staten Island, prospered from the oyster. Tourism added its share then as now, but it was oystering and the related industries of shipbuilding and repairing that brought the money into town.

It may be difficult today to imagine oysters growing in the waters below the traffic pattern of LaGuardia Airport, but during the last century Flushing Bay and vicinity were the scenes of a thriving oyster industry. And oystering did not stop there. Up the Connecticut coast to Norwalk and beyond, and across the sound in Little Neck, Manhasset, and Hempstead bays all the way to Port Jefferson oysters were gathered by countless oystermen in skiffs, cat boats, and sloops. This triangular body of water from Hell Gate to Port Jefferson on one side and Norwalk on the other was known then collectively as the East River—though today we are more inclined to place most of it in Long Island Sound. The oysters from here, called "East Rivers," went primarily to the New York markets by the oyster planters' sloops or power boats or were bought on the grounds by the New York City dealers in their own boats.

Keyport, New Jersey, packing room of the J. & J. W. Elsworth Company at the time
of World War I. Courtesy of Captain William Wooley.

"Saddle-Rock Fry," a character sketch in a Fulton Market oyster saloon. Illustration from *Frank Leslie's Illustrated Newspaper*, February 17, 1877.

Stanley Lownds Oyster Dock. *Narcisus* and *Rev. John Fletcher* in background. Courtesy of Richard Simpson, Northport, Long Island.

Perhaps the most famous oyster brand from this area was the Saddle Rock. Both Norwalk and Great Neck on the opposite shore lay claim to its origin. Ingersoll reported that South Norwalkers said the original Saddle Rocks came from around a reef in Norwalk harbor. Whatever the truth, Saddle Rocks were very popular in New York City and Europe as well during the last century.[25]

The ultimate delight for the oyster-loving thousands was the fancy oyster preparations at the countless oyster bars, bays, saloons, houses, and cellars of New York, Boston, and Providence.

New York City in the nineteenth century was the great shipping center of the northern oyster business. Being so close to the best oysters in the country, so they said, New Yorkers also knew and loved them as much as they do hamburger or even possibly steak today. Oysters were available anywhere along the streets and in the markets, hotels, and eating places of lower Manhattan.

Businessmen and politicans found it difficult to bypass the elegance and

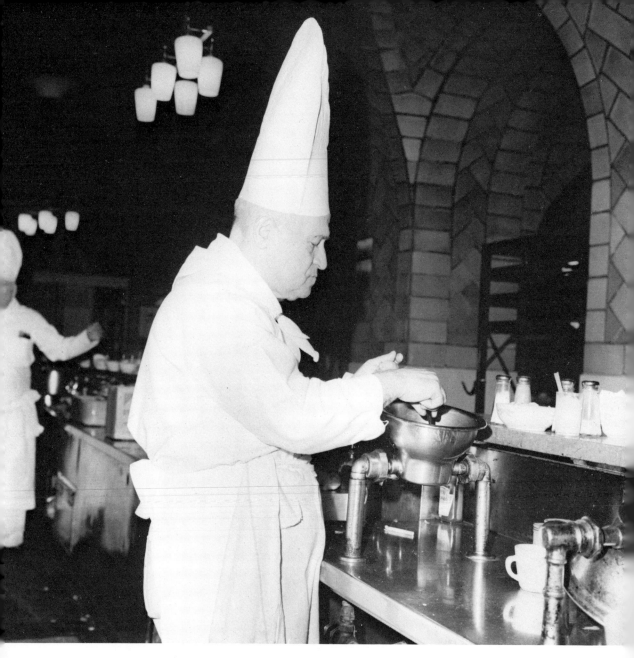

The well-known Grand Central Oyster Bar in New York City with Nick Petters making his famous oyster stew. Photograph by the author.

popularity of the oyster cellars of Canal Street and vicinity. Here oysters on the Canal Street Plan—or any other style—could be had at any time of the day. "The 'Plan' was to give the customer all the oysters he could eat for six pence, and the proprietors rarely lost money this way for if a customer became too greedy a bad oyster slipped onto the plate soon curbed his appetite."[26] Oyster cellars, as the name implies, were located below street level.

To attract attention an "oyster baloon" was hung over the entrance. A writer of the time described the balloons as "made of bright red muslin stretched over a globular frame of rattan or wire and illuminated at night by a candle placed within—the swinging crimson beacon serving to inform the hungry lover of the bivalve where he might procure the humble 'shilling stew' or the more expensive fry or roast."[27]

One of the popular New York oyster cellars of those days was Downings'. This and other cellars are "apt to surprise the visitor with luxurious fittings, not evident from the exterior: mirrored arcades, damask curtains, gold-carved work, splendid chandeliers, and magnificent carpeting down the broad center isle. Downings', at No. 5 Broad Street in the basement of two small buildings, was run by a Negro proprietor. This cellar was a popular gathering place because of its proximity to the Custom House (at Pine and Cedar Streets), the medium-sized stores, the Merchant's Exchange, and the banks."[28]

The oyster establishments, once so common in the larger cities 100 years ago, have succumbed to the times. But fortunately, a few old oyster houses and bars still operate to serve those who know or remember that "delectable morsel." The Union Oyster House of Boston, founded in 1826 is one, while in New York, Grand Central Station's famed Oyster Bar reminds us of the days when oyster was king.

Massachusetts

After 1880, when reliable data for all the states was first recorded, oystering in Massachusetts never surpassed the yield of either Connecticut, Rhode Island, or New York. And except for Maine and Portsmouth, New Hampshire, which had no significant volume, it was always the lowest producer.

In the early-eighteenth century Boston began transporting oysters by schooner from the famous beds at Wellfleet, Cape Cod and Buzzards Bay. When Wellfleet's oysters finally gave out in 1775, oysters were shipped from Buzzards and Narragansett bays directly to the city in winter. In the spring they were bedded at Wellfleet for summer and fall transshipment to Boston. Oysters were also planted on the flats at Boston.

In those spirited days Boston bustled with vendors hawking their wares at markets and from door to door like the friendly Good Humor man of today. One small group peddled fresh oysters from bags. Their lives are revived for us by the descriptive words of a writer in 1887:

Oyster men usually appeared in the evening, carrying their heavy burden, in the shell, on their shoulders in a kind of saddle-bag, crying, "Oys! Finey Oys! Buy any Oys?" They opened their bivalves at the purchasers' door, throwing the shells into another part of the bag. Hand-carts were afterward introduced, and were found a great convenience. Many people declare that they have never had such delicious oysters as those that were sold in this way. The first cooked oysters in Boston were sold by Peter B. Brigham under Concert Hall at the head of Hanover Street. The business proved so remunerative that its enterprising founder became a millionnaire.[29]

The oyster house in Boston originated soon after the Revolutionary War and quickly rose to prominence as a gathering place of the socially elite of the city. The house remained popular during the nineteenth century, but by 1900 or so had declined and nearly vanished. A writer in 1916 sketched their history when he said they

> became important institutions, taking the place of the coffee houses of London, such places as those in which Samuel Johnson and his confreres were wont to gather and dispute (though Johnson preferred to drink tea). . . . There one could go and devour . . . the bivalves fresh from the shell over the counter, or sit at a table and have them served in any of the various ways oysters are cooked, from a plain stew to a fancy roast. They were places of resort for the politicians and public men of their time as some of the hotels and pretentious refectories are today. There the bewigged, powdered gentlemen of the early days met to drink the ale or beer that was provided, smoke their long-stemmed "church-wardens" and discuss affairs of state. . . .

> Along the waterfront, where the fishing boats come in one could eat his fill of oysters for a few cents, but when more pretentious resorts were opened where one could sit at his ease and have the oysters cooked as well as raw, such places came into immediate popularity and displaced the coffee houses and the taverns as places of conviviality.

> From about 1810 to 1875 these institutions flourished and were a conspicuous feature of a part of Boston life. There were then no night restaurants, no quick lunch counters, no places for serving "hot dogs". . . . So the oyster houses, some of them serving only food, became a feature of Boston life, especially of night life.[30]

Boston in the 1880s boasted of some of the most famous oyster houses in the country. It was New England's largest city and its populace cherished the oyster as much as New Yorkers.

Oyster houses at the railroad bridge in Wellfleet, Cape Cod. Left to right: Wellfleet Oyster Company, a fish house, the R. R. Higgins Company (parallel to the tracks), the D. Atwood Company (next to the tracks) and outboard of them Williams & Kemp. Courtesy of Earle Rich.

By the mid-nineteenth century, in spite of her lack of natural beds, Boston became a leading oyster shipping center in New England, rivaled only by New Haven. Shipments from points as far as the Chesapeake poured into Boston's wholesalers. From here they were sent to all parts of Massachusetts, and to Maine, New Hampshire, Vermont, and Canada. In Boston alone there were about one thousand retail shops, fish markets, hotels, and restaurants where oysters formed a regular part of the sales.[31] Most of the seven to ten wholesalers operated in conjunction with their eating saloons, restaurants, lunch counters, and shops. From this it is easy to understand why practically a million dollars worth of business was transacted in the trade's heyday and why few other large cities consumed a greater percentage of oysters than Boston.

Full credit for Boston's position as market hub of the oyster industry down east goes to the renowned men of Wellfleet. Boston merely sold oysters, but Wellfleet grew and nurtured them, and endowed them with their superlative flavor. "No part of the world has better oysters than the harbour of Wellfleet. Time was when they were to be found in the greatest plenty, but in 1775 a mortality from an unknown cause carried off the most of them. Since that time Billingsgate oysters have been scarce, and the greater part that are carried to market are first imported and laid down in our harbor, where they obtain the proper relish of Billingsgate."[32]

The real cause of Wellfleet's depletion, as well as of most other Massachusetts beds, was ascribed by knowledgeable oystermen to overfishing and excessive taking of shells for lime. Out of plain ignorance or indifference the shells were not replaced to make cultch for succeeding oyster sets. Using typical Yankee ingenuity, however, Wellfleet oystermen survived the calamity with no real difficulty by purchasing oysters from Buzzards Bay and places all along the coast down to New York. These were bedded in the harbor just as the men of New Haven had been doing with Chesapeake stock. Schooners began unloading their cargoes over the shallow waters at high tide in February and continued until the trade terminated in April. The transplanted oysters were left to increase in size, quality, and flavor until the fall, when they were forked or raked off the exposed bars at low tide and sent by schooner to the Boston market. Frequently one hundred bushels laid down in April yielded three hundred bushels in the autumn, realizing a profit of 30 cents per bushel.[33]

Initially the bedded oysters came from all available nearby sources, but high oyster prices forced Wellfleet oyster dealers in the 1840s and possibly earlier to the plentiful and cheaper Chesapeake stocks. The adventurous ocean trade with the South reached its peak about 1850 when some 150,000 bushels were bedded in the harbor.

After the Civil War oyster dealers in and around Boston realized that bedding in their own waters was almost as effective as having it done at Wellfleet. Besides, it saved freighting expenses. Wellfleet suffered by the shift, though the same men and schooners engaged in the Boston bedding. Furthermore, Buzzards Bay and Narragansett Bay oysters for the Boston market were now beginning to be shipped directly by rail and steamer.

Though Wellfleet lost some of its prominence as an oyster center it did not abandon the business. Short-term bedding continued, but by World War I the trade in southern plants gradually gave out. Growing of native set and long-term maturing of seed oysters from New England replaced bedding. In 1881 E. P. Cook first planted seed from Somerset and kept it down for a few

Illustration from *A Report Upon the Mollusk Fisheries of Massachusetts*, 1909.

years. The oysters grew well and improved in flavor—so much so that other oystermen, such as Higgins, Atwood, Oliver, and Stubbs, followed Cook's successful experiment. By the early 1900s Wellfleet rose again as an important oyster producer. Even people from out of state—Thomas Thomas and the Lancraft Brothers of New Haven and the Sealshipt Oyster System of New York, Connecticut and Rhode Island—planted Long Island Sound oysters at Wellfleet.

The bedding and particularly the maturing of seed created legal questions similar to those in other states. For example, who was to plant where and under whose jurisdiction? Initially shellfish grounds were generally state controlled, but in 1880 the towns assumed this control, and the mayor, aldermen, or selectmen of each coast town were given absolute authority over the shellfish industries within their borders.[34] Unfortunately, lack of uniformity in the laws has resulted in a tendency toward loss of foresight and was responsible perhaps for destroying, or at least restraining, the growth potential of the industry.

Because of oyster farming and the bedding of southern oysters, an extensive grant system developed on Cape Cod and Buzzards Bay. Beginning in 1869, Swansee was the first to allow the selling of oyster privileges, and about this time Wellfleet was probably the first to obtain grants to bed Virginia plants. But these and other laws fanned long-standing hostility among oystermen, quahaughers, and shore-front property owners. Oyster farming is dependent upon some form of private ownership but the quahauger and shore owner saw in this privilege a monopoly and an evil.

Many oyster laws have evolved through the years in the various oyster communities throughout the state. Yet, not all have proven to be in the best interests of the industry. Though the grant system, for instance, was initially successful in keeping alive the declining industry, it had many faults. Besides its restrictive elements and the antagonisms it created, it did not give the oyster grower the legal protection and security he needed for his oyster ground.

This antiquated system with its many unwise features still exists today in Massachusetts. The state gives the towns the privilege of granting leases but not all towns have chosen to issue them. In those cases the oyster grounds are left open for public, recreational use only, and therefore there is no commercial oyster fishery. The towns that do issue grants restrict them solely to local residents. It is believed now that these old repressive laws, in preventing outside capital, for one thing, from entering are inhibiting the development of a potentially promising oyster industry. However, there are new laws before the state legislature due for passage in early 1974 that are expected to change this situation drastically.

Rhode Island

From the time Roger Williams settled Rhode Island in 1636 to the beginning of the nineteenth century, oysters grew abundantly in most rivers and inlets of Narragansett Bay. Prior to the 1800s the oyster fishery was primitive, unorganized, and supplemental. Local part-time oystermen tonged oysters from skiffs on the natural beds in the fall and stored them in their cellars for winter consumption. Those oystering for a living on the natural beds, called "free fishermen," also tonged from skiffs, but picked the load up on shore by horse and wagon and carried them to the small oyster houses for shucking. Though the fishery was small, indiscriminate and widescale plunder increased with the expanding population. And although laws appeared on the books to preserve this natural product, they were not enforced sufficiently and reckless fishing continued unabated.

Eventually all this reaping without proper attention to sowing resulted in near depletion of the natural stock, and Narragansett Bay could no longer meet the increasing demands for oysters. In the 1830s Rhode Island began to draw upon the unfailing oyster supply of Chesapeake Bay and its neighboring states. As usual at that time, the imported oysters were planted in the spring and taken up in the fall. Thus from the second quarter of the nineteenth century the majority of oysters grown in Rhode Island, even though termed "natives," originated in Virginia, Connecticut, New York, or Buzzards Bay. The local natural beds never recovered enough to supply seed except in a few scattered places such as the Warren and Seekonk rivers.

In 1822 an act of the General Assembly encouraged the infant industry for the first time by leasing to two men two acres apiece of bottom in Providence River for planting. In 1848 sixteen acres were leased to four men who planted Virginia and Fire Island oysters. Heartened by this, oystermen from all over Rhode Island eagerly acquired bottoms. Incidentally, Virginia oysters never seemed to spawn here: they were simply left down for a few months—before the ice of winter set in—in much the same manner as at Wellfleet and New Haven.

Then, in 1864 the Commissioners of Shell Fisheries was organized to cope with, aid, and administer the growing industry. Since the founding of the colony, all oyster ground had belonged to the state, a condition which eliminated many jurisdictional disputes. This fortunate arrangement was simple and much more effectual than that in Connecticut and New York, where authority in the early years was divided between state and town governments. Rhode Island oyster laws, however, long conflicting and obsolete, were codified in the 1860s. Unlike Connecticut, where a perpetual franchise was obtainable, Rhode Island leases ran for a period of only ten years but had a renewal option. The rent—ranging from $5 to $10 an acre per year—always stayed higher than in any other oyster-producing state.

But even with relatively encouraging new laws and a good market, oystermen did not take full advantage of these opportunities. Onshore ground was readily leased, however, and soon became scarce, leaving only deepwater property. But the men hesitated to invest in these comparatively untried grounds, and thus conditions continued fairly static for decades.

Most attempts at cultivation in Rhode Island prior to 1890 met with repeated failure due to carelessness, environmental hazards, and unknown factors. Furthermore, a devastating starfish attack decimated the existing stock in 1866, generated a slump in the entire industry, and caused additional discouragement to the oystermen. The industry, still relatively small and beset with continued obstacles, coasted along during the last quarter of the nineteenth century. Then, in 1890, an unexpectedly excellent set on the natural beds in the Warren River showed that with proper attention artificial propagation or oyster culture in Rhode Island waters might be feasible. However, nothing further

The oyster boats *William M. Merwin, Loretto, Governor* and *Stratford* at the East Providence, Rhode Island, oyster plants of Wm. M. Merwin & Sons Co. and the Stratford Oyster Co. about 1910. Courtesy of Hobart Beers.

Oyster shell pile. Courtesy of Hobart Beers.

developed from this experience, and the industry lingered on unchanged until about 1895.

Then, Connecticut oyster growers, spurred on by the scarcity of their own local maturing and growing ground and realizing that the Rhode Island oystermen were not using the deep waters of Narragansett Bay, literally took over the Rhode Island industry. Ground was leased in a resident's name, seed planted, and crops harvested and freighted back to Connecticut for shucking and processing.

Local oystermen at first feared and opposed the intrustion of the huge out-of-state companies but eventually realized the benefits of the unprecedented expansion in business. The quaint old shucking houses gradually disappeared in the shadow of revolutionary, immense new plants employing hundreds of workers. Large steam- and gasoline-powered oyster boats with their labor-saving machinery and the gigantic planting barges with capacities reaching thousands of bushels appeared brazenly alongside the venerable and smaller vessels and sailing craft. By 1908, over 100 powered oyster boats sailed Rhode Island waters, and those thousands of formerly barren offshore acres habitually shunned by Rhode Islanders were leased and worked successfully by Connecticut operators. Even some of the previously long unproductive natural and artificial beds "set" again. Within a decade, oystering exploded into a million dollar enterprise, with Connecticut ingenuity and capital for the most part rebuilding the dawdling industry. Under the stimulus of private ownership and intelligent state fishery laws, the tiny state forged far ahead of its previous indolence. The Rhode Island industry, with Providence as its center, flourished as never before.

The Oyster Ashore

THROUGHOUT the seventeenth and eighteenth centuries new towns and cities arose inland under the pressure of an expanding population, and oysters in sacks and casks of all sizes followed by horse, wagon, cart, coach, or other means. By 1800 a lively trade between New Haven, the oyster capital of Connecticut, and Albany, Montreal, and other cities and towns was well established. A similar situation existed in Boston. The widespread desire for oysters on the half shell at home or in public eating places kept the shell trade alive.

The early oystermen's shop did nothing but prepare and package the oyster for shipment in the shell. Oysters from the beds were usually "floated" or "drunk" near the shop prior to barreling in order to clean, freshen, and ostensibly improve the meat. Floating or drinking is the practice of placing oysters in the shell on floats, or on the bottom of a creek, harbor, or bay, usually over one tide, in water of less salinity than that in which they grew. There they purge themselves of their salty taste and dirt and also freshen, bloat, swell, and improve their appearance.

After this practice was outlawed in 1909, because of the possibility of infection due to pollution as well as adulteration, oysters reached the shop directly from the boats just as they came up in the dredge or tong, replete with all kinds of trash— shells, crabs, stones. Sometimes, however, the oysters were culled or separated from this unwanted material by the tonger or dredger right at the beds and the debris thrown overboard. As a conservation measure, most states legally require the natural growther to return all this trash, except starfish, to the natural beds.

In the shop the oysters were further culled and clusters were separated with a blunt, knife-like piece of metal called a "culling iron." The desired result was a clean, single oyster. They were then graded according to size, and finally barreled or bagged for shipment. The entire operation is sometimes referred to as culling, and the shop or building is called a culling house— although this is only part of the culling-packing operation.

Actually, a building is not absolutely necessary. The work can be done anywhere outside in good weather, on or near the docks of the oyster establishments—as it used to be along the Quinnipiac River in Fair Haven, Connecticut. Today the Bloom Brothers of South Norwalk cull and gunnysack their oysters as they sail in from the oyster beds and while at dockside. Only in severely cold weather are they lugged inside the shop for handling. Details of preparation and working with shell stock have always varied slightly with custom, location, and destination—whether for the consumer's market or for replanting—but the culling shop is probably much the same today as it was earlier.

Not everyone wanted shell stock. Many found opened oysters more convenient, and, since the oyster is somewhat difficult to open, requiring a skill gained only from practice, opening them for the market must have begun sometime in the eighteenth century, if not earlier. It is known that pickled oysters were sent in glass jars and earthenware from New York City to the West Indies in the mid-eighteenth century.[1] And after the Revolution, opened oysters were also in demand for oyster bars and houses of the larger coastal cities.

The inconvenience and cost of shipping heavy, bulky, barreled shell oysters by wagon farther and farther inland also spurred the development of the opening business. In the early nineteenth century Thomas Kensett introduced canning in glass jars into New York City when he preserved salmon, oysters, and lobsters, but it was not until 1839 that metal cans were common and thousands of oysters in small packages replaced an entire wagonload of shell oysters. The North, however, never did as much with packing cooked oysters as the South did.

Opening shops, far more elaborate than the old culling shops, soon sprang up all along the coasts to supply the oyster houses, bars, saloons, and housewives with shucked oysters ready for the stew, fry or whatever. These shops, located near the oyster beds on the shore front or partly over the water, served also as convenient unloading docks. The oyster business assumed new dimensions and functions, and by the nineteenth century the oyster opening house was a common sight along the coast.

By this time, too, oystering was a well organized business, if not an industry, complete with a hierarchy of positions from the gatherer to the oyster shop workers, from the dealer to the retailer and to the restaurant workers. The oyster shop now prepared shell or opened oysters, or both. Both operations were done in the same or in different buildings, depending upon the oysterman's specialty and circumstances. Generally these buildings were called oyster shops or houses. More specifically, those that opened oysters were referred to as shucking or opening shops, houses, or plants. And since packing of shell oysters was usually done in the same building as shucking, it was also called a packing house.

One of the earliest and certainly elementary types of opening establishments were the basement shops of many of the private dwellings built during the last century at Fair Haven. There, within yards of the Quinnipiac River, these ground level cellars had extra wide doors opening onto the street to permit easy entrance of laden wheelbarrows. Dugout canoes and sharpies filled with fresh oysters from the nearby waters unloaded in front of these houses. Housewives sat on stools and opened the oysters like New York oyster market bargemen. Later in the day the dealers or openers kegged the oysters and took them back to the packing house for shipment. Thus handy employment was available to many who were otherwise not able to work in the local oyster shops.

By the 1840s and 1850s the practice of opening and shipping oysters had become well established. Oystering developed to such an extent that companies multiplied, business flourished and branch houses opened in the Chesapeake Bay area. Many of the largest and longest established northern oyster companies were founded around this time: H.C. Rowe & Co. of New Haven, founded in the late 1850s; Robert Pettis of Providence, Rhode Island, around 1840; the F. Mansfield & Sons Co. of New Haven, in 1846; R.R. Higgins Co. of Boston, in 1828; and George Still of New York, in 1857.

One of the earliest detailed accounts of an oyster shop appeared in *The New York Tribune* of January 9, 1857. It describes the practices in a Fair Haven shop and may be considered typical of the day. Most interestingly, the methods correspond closely with those in use decades later.

The oysters, as they come from the vessel, are heaped upon the center of the room, the operators occupying the wall–sides. Each person has before him a small desk or platform, some 3 feet high, on which is placed, as occasion requires, about half a bushel of oysters, from which the opener takes his supply. On the stand is a small anvil, on which, with a small hammer, the edge of the shell is broken. The operative is provided with a knife and hammer, both of which are held in the right hand at the time the shell is broken, when the latter is dropped and the knife does its work. Two tubs or pails, of about three gallons capacity each, are placed within about 3 feet of the workman, into which he throws, with great dexterity and rapidity, the luscious morsel which is to tickle the palate and gratify the taste of some dweller in the far West. The object of placing these vessels of reception so far from the operator is to prevent, as much as possible, the deposit of the original liquor with the oyster. . . . From the opening-room the oysters are taken to the filling-room, and thence to the packing department. In the filling-room, on a platform, are placed a dozen or more kegs and cans, with the bungs out. The oysters are first poured into a large hopper pierced with holes, in which they are thoroughly washed and drained, when they are ready to be deposited in packages. This is done by placing a funnel in the aperture of the keg, by one person, while another "measures and pours." This operation is performed with great rapidity, two or three men being able to fill some 2,000 kegs in a day. After depositing the requisite number of "solid oysters," as they are termed, in each package, a pipe conveying fresh water is applied, and the vacant space filled with nature's beverage—the bungs placed and driven home—when it is ready to be shipped.

Sometime before the mid-nineteenth century, the industry's most unusual and picturesque, yet least known feature—the New York City oyster market— came into being. The oyster dealers, unable to purchase expensive waterfront property, built one- and two-story floating scows or barges and moored them to the city wharfs. Fresh oysters came in regularly from nearby Connecticut, Long Island, and Staten Island and to some extent Massachusetts, Rhode Island, Delaware, and Virginia, and here they were stored, barreled, opened, sold, and shipped for the local, West Coast, and European trade. From this floating market the great city was supplied with countless millions of oysters. The barges hummed with more intense energy, activity and business than even the famed Fulton Fish Market.

The oyster market survived a century in the city, all the while shifting from one point to another along the Hudson and East rivers to make room for the liners and ships of a more prestigious service. The last barge, that

Oystering at a glance. Illustration from Harper's Weekly, September 16, 1882.

of Geo. Still Inc., left the market—then located near the Brooklyn Bridge—during World War II. All that remains today are a couple of land-based shell-fish shops, memories, and remarkably few published descriptions.

An early account of the first scows appeared in *The New York Herald*, May 12, 1853.

> There are nine scows in the dock at Oliver slip, the value of which is estimated at four thousand dollars. They might not improperly be called oyster depots, for they are used almost exclusively for the storage of oysters as they arrive by the boats. Their length is about thirty feet, and breadth about twelve, and they are capable of holding from one thousand to fifteen hundred bushels. Some of these are owned by companies of two or three persons, the majority of whom plant their own oysters. The amount of oysters sold every year by these dealers is estimated at about five hundred thousand dollars. This is exclusive of the amount brought from the boats, and which is estimated by the dealers themselves at one million dollars. . . .
>
> The scows are all roofed over and contain an office at one end. The hold where the oysters are placed is divided into a number of compartments for the reception of the different varieties and sizes. They are all sold in the shell, while those sold by the retail dealers are opened.
>
> The oyster trade of Oliver slip is not so extensive as that of the dealers doing business in the dock opposite to Washington market. There are twelve scows in this dock the value of which is about fifteen thousand dollars. They are very handsomely fitted up and strongly built.

Another newspaper article of the early 1870s vividly depicts the scenes at the barges:

> When the wind changes, the fleet comes up the bay, and then there is a busy scene in the neighborhood off pier No. 54. The dock and its approaches are covered with cartmen, wagons and horses, stevedores, and oyster-dealers. The vessels are fastened to the wharf by means of strong hawsers, and the hatches are off fore and aft. In the hold are men filling baskets rapidly, and others stand on the deck, rail, and pierstring, ready to pass them to the cart being loaded. All is rush, bustle, and trade, flavored with copious dashes of profanity. In front of the scow-warehouses are men continually employed on these days, filling barrels with oysters and heading them up. Inside of the scows dozens of men are opening, while others can them ready for trans-mission by rail to Canada, country hotels, and restaurants. But the city trade creates the hurry visible on every side. All day long, until the cargoes, which are

J. & J. W. Elsworth Company oyster scow at the foot of Bloomfield Street, New York. This company, one of the biggest in New York, had a large fleet of vessels and extensive oyster grounds off Connecticut, Long Island, Staten Island and Keyport, New Jersey. Courtesy of Emil Usinger.

Oyster scows or barges on the Hudson River at the West Washington Market, New York City. Photograph from *The Oysterman and Fisherman.* September 1912.

always bespoken, are landed, the work goes on, and when they are discharged the vessels are sent away immediately for more.[2]

In the 1880s the barges had evolved into fancy two-story affairs

made with unusual strength and of the most durable materials, and which closely resemble the conventional "Noah's Ark" of the toy-shops, and the Sunday school picture-books, except that they have flat roofs. . . .

The deep hold, well-floored, serves as a cellar, cool in summer and warm in winter; oysters will never freeze there when the hatches are closed. Over the whole craft, flush with the outside, is built a house, two stories in height, as I have indicated. The floor of the first story is the deck of the scow. This is the general business apartment, and gives room for storage, and opening of oysters, and transaction of business. Above is a loft where are stored barrels, baskets, and machinery. In the rear, usually—sometimes in the front end—is fitted up an office. The daily capacity of such a barge is about 700 bushels.

These scows are securely moored, side by side, to the wharf, or rather to the water-wall of the city, and are reached by broad swinging platforms, which allow them to rise and fall with the tide. At the rear end, therefore, they can always be closely approached by the sloops and boats which bring to their owners their stock. Such a barge is worth from $1,500 to $4,000, and, with an annual overhauling and caulking, will last as long as a man is likely to need

F. F. Brown & Son oyster dock, Fair Haven, Connecticut. Courtesy of Fred Brown, Branford, Connecticut.

it. There are 30 of these barges, representing at present, a value of $75,000. To these barges at the foot of Broome street come the oysters from East river and Long Island beds; also somewhat from Staten Island and Virginia, but to a small extent compared with the westside business in these two classes.[3]

Before the 1870s the common land-based oyster house, whether culling or opening, was relatively small. Demands on the individual oysterman or concern may have been high but only a limited volume of oysters could be handled per day. Human nature, the law, and the ancient tongs, dredges, and sailboats combined to hold down output. One or two men in a skiff or sharpie, or two to six men in a sloop, were not able physically to work or cultivate more than about two to five acres effectively. In 1855 the State of Connecticut, fully aware of man's limitation in this regard, legally permitted the lease of only two acres per man for oyster cultivation. The average oysterman, therefore, restrained by law and nature, owned no more than one sloop or a couple of tonging craft.

The northern industry, long heavily dependent upon Chesapeake oysters because of dwindling natural stock, began to move forward on its own initiative after the Civil War. As new laws were passed allowing leasing of larger tracts

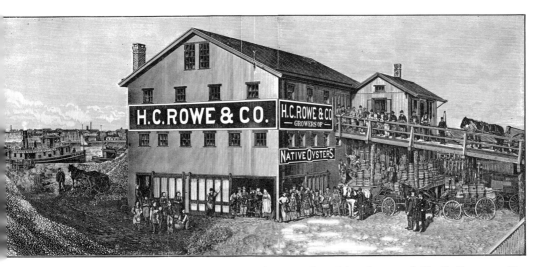

The principal storehouses, opening shops and packing house of H. C. Rowe & Co., of Fair Haven, Connecticut, built in 1885. From H. C. Rowe & Co. brochure.

of ground in deeper water offshore with legal protection and full property rights, men became more willing to sink money in an industry newly invested with tremendous growth potential.

A new and dominant factor affecting the size of the oyster shops and the character of the industry itself was the introduction in the 1870s of the steamboat to do the work of the sailboat. Power enabled the oysterman to harvest far more than previously; in fact, in 1881 it was estimated that the steamboat increased the harvest of oysters twelvefold.[4]

Now with thousands of acres available to work and harvest, the little old oyster house could not take care of the volume. Bigger and more efficient houses were built and more space, docks, and help acquired. Those businessmen with foresight and money gobbled up oyster ground and built steamers. Electricity, steam, gasoline—all the innovations of the times—were applied to oyster houses and vessels. Oysters sold, profits soared, and the northern industry reached its heyday between 1885 and 1910.

The steamboat and oyster cultivation based upon newly acquired knowledge of the oyster's biology boosted the industry and put Connecticut on the map. Connecticut could lay claim to being the "pioneer" of oyster cultivation and possessor of the largest oyster houses, boats, and cultivated beds in the entire industry. The leading oystermen of Connecticut for decades, H. J. Lewis, H. C. Rowe, and later Andrew Radel, owned the most cultivated ground anywhere, eventually about eleven thousand acres each. H. C. Rowe operated the largest steamers in the world, and his plant was considered one of the largest and best in the business. An advertising sheet printed in 1888 describes it:

H.C. Rowe & Co. have just added to their former facilities for opening oysters for shipment, by purchasing the best wharf in Fair Haven, and building a four-story shucking house. This building is arranged on an entirely new plan, contrived by Mr. Rowe, affording facilities for keeping the oysters in the best condition, and handling them with the least expense. Mr. Rowe claims that by means of these superior facilities he will be able to save $1,500 in expenses annually. For seven years the company's shops and wharves have been located near South Quinnipiac street, Fair Haven, Annex. This property, with 188 feet of wharfage and a capacity for forty shuckers, will still be used.

The new site is between the east end of Quinnipiac drawbridge and the Fair Haven marine railway. It has 340 feet of wharf front. There are two series of wharves; one wharf is intended for unloading steamers at low tide, the other at high tide. There is also a basin for the oyster floats. The oyster house is of four stories, 36 x 48 feet. The culling or sorting room is on the third floor. The floor is of two inch hard pine and two inch spruce, between which is a double coat of tar. This substantial floor is water-tight. As the oysters are sorted, they are thrown into different openings in the floor, communicating with the second floor. These openings are protected by trap doors. One of these hatchways is for seed oysters, and twelve other openings are for various sizes and grades of marketable oysters. To prevent the oysters from injury by falling to the floor beneath, an open frame, with a canvass bottom resting on a cushion of hay, is provided. As the oysters drop into this contrivance, they pass out between the open frame work without injury. The fourth floor is for the storage of packing barrels, and has capacity for 2,000 bushels of stock, and will also be for packing shell oyster.

The second floor is used for shucking; has accommodations for fifty shuckers, and will hold 3,000 bushels of stock. The arrangement here is unique. In most oyster shops a tub is located under each shucker's bench, for holding the shells. In the new shop all the space under the benches is ceiled, and under each bin is a trap door under which carts may be driven on the second floor. Each bin holds shells representing a day's work of one person, and by this arrangement the shells can easily be removed to the shell heaps. Connected with the lower floor are living rooms finished off for the family of the watchman. In the extension of the northeast corner of the main building is the general office, and in the rear is Mr. Rowe's private office. These rooms are finished in hard woods. The packing shop is conveniently arranged. The building is substantially put together, is triple sheathed with a coat of felting between, and has a heavily trussed roof. Each post rests upon a chestnut spile driven to the rock foundation. The big oyster house and wharf, with facilities

An oyster float for "drinking" oysters in Lemon Creek, Princes Bay, Staten Island, New York. Courtesy of The Staten Island Historical Society.

for handling 7,500 bushels of oysters per week, is the most convenient, and complete in the country, and cost $20,000.

These increased facilities are required by the rapid growth of the business since the firm has handled the native oysters only.

In may be observed that no mention was made here of the cleanliness of the Rowe plant or the hygienic and sanitary conditions of oyster handling. Responsible oystermen, like Rowe and most others, followed reasonable sanitary measures in keeping with the customs and knowledge of their day. Other than maintaining ostensibly at least a fresh, wholesome, clean oyster, little thought or worry was directed to the further possibility of infectious conditions in any plant, although diseases occasionally have been associated with oysters since Roman times. Despite the oystermen's belief that oysters had a better record in this matter than milk or drinking water, outbreaks of typhoid fever and gastro-intestinal disorders began to spot the country. One at Wesleyan University in 1894 and another at Atlantic City in 1902 aroused the nation and focused the blame on the oyster. The resulting newspaper and magazine stories were so maligning that people shunned oysters, and they rapidly went out of fashion as a food.

Health authorities, scientists, and medical men studied the problem intensely and found the oyster to blame in so few cases that it wasn't worth considering. But prejudice remained and the industry suffered. Oystermen trying to regain their floundering business responded to the accusations and fought to improve the oyster's lost image. In 1908 under the leadership of oyster packers and growers of New England and New York, they united to form the Oyster Growers and Dealers Association of North America (now with the operational name of the Shellfish Institute of North America, with offices in Towson, Maryland). The association's aim was to educate the public as well as to be the united, powerful spokesmen of the industry. Then, with assistance from state health departments, they requested the U.S. Department of Agriculture to help them produce a pure wholesome food. Stormy debates followed amongst scientists, government specialists, and oystermen on all conceivable health aspects of the industry from the spawning beds to the table. Eventually much needed rules, regulations, inspections, and recommendations resulted for the betterment of the industry and the public it serves.

One of the first important national rulings appeared in October, 1909, with the passage of the Department of Agriculture's Pure Food Decision No. 110. A provision of the law prohibited the floating of oysters, thereby reaching the heart of the problem—pollution. Oystermen nearly always floated oysters in the brackish waters at or near their oyster houses. But population centers, naturally grown oysters, and oyster houses were frequently concentrated in approximately the same place and by the turn of the century industrial and human pollutants from these centers reached the point where they were not only plainly destroying the old inshore oyster beds but infesting others. The decision proclaimed floating or drinking a potential hazard to health as well as an adulteration and the practice was prohibited. Another feature of that law banned the use of the common oyster shipping tub in which ice came into direct contact with shucked oysters. Furthermore, it was ruled that packages and shops must be kept absolutely clean. These and other features of Pure Food Decision No. 110 were directly responsible for radical changes in pack-

aging, shipping, and retailing. Never before had there been a keener awareness of proper hygienic conditions in all phases of the business.

In 1910, the Rhode Island Commissioners of Shell Fisheries quickly took
the lead in this matter and were among the first to adopt rules and regulations
for the sanitary operation of the oyster houses doing business within the state.
A look at some of those early measures shows the effect the new requirements
had on the oyster houses and their production methods.

Rule 1. Construction of Opening Houses: Opening houses must be well
lighted and well ventilated. All accumulations of shells and fragments of
oyster meats must be scrupulously avoided. Cleaning must be done at least
every day. The ceiling must be free from cobwebs and dust. (We recommend
that screens be placed at the windows and doors, as they will prevent flies from
bringing contamination to the opened oysters.)

Rule 2. Bins: If bins are used for holding oysters before they are opened,
they should be so constructed that all the oysters are delivered to the opener.
No beams or corners should be left where the oysters can collect. The bins
must be washed out thoroughly from accumulations of dirt and shells between
each filling.

Rule 3. Benches: The opening benches must be kept clean. Frequent flushings
and scrubbings will be necessary preferably with boiling water, at the places
where the openers stand. Openers should not be allowed to open oysters directly
on the benches but always into proper containers.

Rule 4. Utensils: All pans, measures, colanders, buckets, cans, etc., used for
holding opened oysters must be of such construction and such material that
they may be properly cleaned. They should be thoroughly washed with soap
and hot water, and then scalded out with hot water or steam at least once every
day. Knives used by the openers must be subjected to the same treatment.

Rule 5. Water Supply: An abundant supply of pure water must be available,
not only for washing the oysters, but also for flushing the bins, benches, and
floors, and for washing the utensils. If a tank is used for storing the water it
must be properly covered. Once every month it should be drained and scrubbed
out to free it from any sediment.

Rule 6. Hot Water: An abundant supply of hot water must be provided in
every oyster house; the hot water must be available both for washing the
utensils and benches, and also for washing the hands of the employees. This
will be insisted upon by the Commission.

Rule 7. Ice: Cooling of oysters must be effected as rapidly as possible. The ice box or refrigerating room in which oysters are held must be cleaned at frequent intervals, so that it will be clean and free from odors.[5]

The industry also launched a successful, vigorous advertising campaign to raise the oyster's sunken prestige, and the United States government helped by issuing an informative booklet, *How to Prepare Oysters 100 Ways*. But in spite of the revolutionary improvements and restored public confidence, with resulting higher sales, oyster demand actually dropped. Another factor had entered the scene—eating habits were changing in ever-changing America. The trend away from oysters to other foods gained momentum after World War I and continues right up to the present. Shrimp, tomato juice, fruit cocktail, herring, and clams have almost driven oysters off the appetizer side of the menu in New England and New York, and meats and countless other dishes have entirely replaced them as an entrée except in select restaurants.

More trouble came when further outbreaks of typhoid fever—traced to eating raw polluted shellfish in New York, Chicago, and Washington in 1924 and 1925— shook the public, the industry, and the government far more than previously. Another industry-sponsored publicity and advertising campaign followed, with a measure of success as before. More importantly, an invaluable scientific research program was inaugurated by the Oyster Growers and Dealers Association of North America. Under the leadership of Dr. Herbert D. Pease, the phenomenal dietary and nutritional value of the oyster was demonstrated and its chemical composition minutely analyzed. With renewed vigor, the state, the industry, and the Public Health Services cooperated in a joint study and issued significant, nationwide regulations affecting the entire industry. In 1925 they published the *Report of Committee on Sanitary Control of the Shellfish Industry in the United States*. On the basis of this guide and its subsequent revisions in 1937, 1946, 1957 to 1959 the program has been successful in regulating, controlling, and improving the sanitary conditions of all aspects of the shellfish industry. The rulings were now more rigid and vastly more enforceable than those of 1909. As a result we have the combined efforts of the states, the Public Health Service, (now the U.S. Food and Drug Administration) and the shellfish industry, each responsible for certain features of sanitary control. In summary the three agencies assume the following duties as stated in the report:

1. Each shellfish shipping state adopts laws and regulations for sanitary control of the industry, makes sanitary surveys of growing areas, delineates and insures the policing of restricted areas, inspects shellfish plants, and insures that

shellfish reaching the consumer have been grown, harvested and processed in a sanitary manner. The states issue numbered certificates to dealers who comply with agreed upon sanitary standards, and forward copies of interstate certificates to the Public Health Service.

2. The Public Health Service makes an annual review of each state's control program, and either endorses or witholds endorsement of the program. The Public Health Service publishes a semimonthly list of all valid interstate shellfish shipper certificates issued by states, for the information of health authorities and others.

3. The shellfish industry cooperates by obtaining shellfish from safe sources, by providing plants meeting sanitary standards, by placing the proper number on each package of shellfish and by keeping and making available to control authorities records which show the origin and disposition of all shellfish.

In 1926 a Cooperative Sanitary Shellfish Program was instituted. Federal health authorities under the U.S. Public Health Service, state regulatory officials in the then-nineteen oyster producing states, and the industry through their Oyster Growers and Dealers Association held a series of workshops in which the combined knowledge and viewpoint of each group was brought into play, resulting in the production of a manual for recommended sanitary practice. This exists today and has been expanded to three volumes covering all aspects of growing waters, quality, handling of shellfish (oysters, clams, mussels), harvesting, plant sanitation and handling in the plant, and all phases of shipping such as required containers, proper refrigeration and bacterial standards. Workshops have been held periodically since 1926. The system has also been expanded and now takes in Canada, Japan and South Korea in so far as shipment of shellfish into the United States is concerned. Today bacteriological standards of quality for shellfish growing water are as rigid as for drinking water.

The epidemics before and after World War I and the shift to other foods were not the only factors adversely effecting the northern oyster industry. Frequent set failures and labor costs forced many companies out of business. For survival, some concerns combined resources, over the cries of "monopoly" from smaller, independent oystermen.

Between the wars a few new, modernized shops were built and the industry struggled on. Connecticut continued to produce seed oysters for her neighbors although she opened and shipped large quantities of market oysters. Rhode Island and New York matured and opened them while Massachusetts dealt largely in barrel stock.

CHAPTER 4

Shucking, Measuring, and Shipping

HE first oyster openers in America were the Indians. When the colonists arrived, the Indian taught them how to open oysters quite easily by placing them near hot rocks next to an open campfire: the heat popped them open. Oysters were also wrapped in wet seaweed and laid on hot coals to steam open ready to eat. Anyone can steam open oysters but, to many, steaming kills their "fresh tang of the sea."

No other activity in the oyster business attracts so much interest as the dexterous movements of the oyster shucker. His skill, sharpened by thousands of openings, enables him to shuck one in a few seconds. This skill has always been considered most valuable and indeed indispensable in the oyster shop or bar.

The oyster shucker in the North had a choice of three ways of opening an oyster. His choice depended upon the city or state he worked in and how the oyster was to be used. New Haven, New York, and other places developed unique opening techniques in response to specific needs or traditions. In any one shop, especially during the last century of little job migration, local traditional methods prevailed. Later on in this century with a scarcity of shuckers, oyster shops enlisted them from out of state and more than one opening method was then seen.

The three common shucking methods are:

1. Side knife: This is a difficult but rapid method requiring considerable

skill, and is practiced in most of New England's oyster bars, hotels, and restaurants serving raw oysters on the half shell. When skillfully executed, it is
considered the fastest and cleanest because it leaves the oyster shell nearly
intact—a most desirable feature for the half-shell service. The oyster is held in
the palm of the left hand, lower or deep shell down, hinge end away from the
opener. With the right hand grasping the oyster knife, the shucker inserts the
blade between the shells somewhere on the right side. The trick here is to find
the right spot, for invariably the separation between the two shells is barely
visible. After insertion the adductor muscle, which holds the oyster to the shell,
is cut from the top shell and the shell is flicked off with a twist of the knife.
Another quick stroke cuts the bottom side of the muscle, thus separating the
oyster from the other shell. The complete operation is performed in one continuous, smooth motion. (In eating places the opener serves the severed oyster
on the hollow bottom shell, or baked in the shell as oysters casino, oysters
Rockefeller, etc.) The other two opening methods differ from this primarily in
the manner of making the first knife insertion. From then on the procedure
is about the same.

2. Stabber or sticker: This variation of the side-opening method probably
originated in Massachusetts where it was traditionally favored. Oyster shops in
New Jersey also used it. The oyster is held down on the bench with the left
hand, its hinge end wedged against a wooden cleat or stop. The knife, slimmer
than the side knife and also held in the right hand, is thrust into the bill end
of the oyster. The muscle on the deep side is cut first, then that on the top,
reversing the order of the side-knife and cracking methods. Sticking is much
easier than side-knifing because it relieves much of the strain on the opener—
but it does take slightly longer.

3. Cracking or breaking: This originated in Fair Haven, was used by all
their native professional openers, and spread to the Long Island and Chesapeake
Bay opening shops. It is the least tiring and easiest but probably the sloppiest
of the three methods. An excellent description of cracking as practiced at Fair
Haven in 1881 appears in Ingersoll:

> The shucker stands or sits before a stout bench (which may be a long table
> partitioned off into working spaces for each one, or may be an individual bench
> that can be moved about) and has her oysters in a pile before her. Immediately
> under her hand is a block of wood into which is firmly inserted an upright
> piece of iron about two inches long, one inch high, and a quarter of an inch
> thick, called the "cracking-iron." The shucker is also provided with a square-

SIDE KNIFE USED IN RESTAURANTS

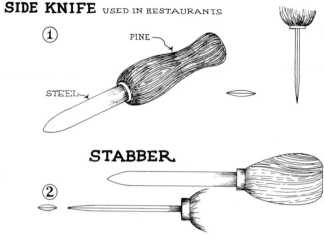

① PINE

STEEL

STABBER

②

NEW HAVEN CRACKING TOOLS

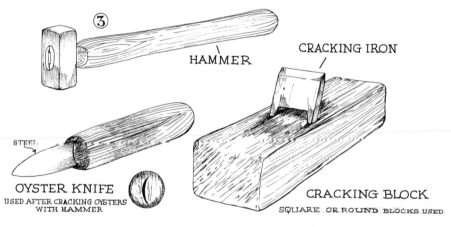

③

HAMMER

CRACKING IRON

STEEL

OYSTER KNIFE
USED AFTER CRACKING OYSTERS
WITH HAMMER

CRACKING BLOCK
SQUARE OR ROUND BLOCKS USED

NEW YORK OYSTER KNIFE USED IN THE N.Y. OYSTER SCOWS

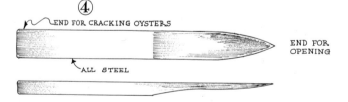

④
END FOR CRACKING OYSTERS

END FOR
OPENING

ALL STEEL

Oyster opening tools. Drawing by John LaPresle.

helved double-headed hammer, and a stiff sharp knife in a round wooden
handle. On her left hand she wears a rough woolen, rubber, or leathern half-
mitten, known as a "cot," to protect the skin. Seizing an oyster in her left
hand, with the hinge in her palm, she places it upon the cracking-iron, and
with one blow of the hammer breaks off the "bill" or growing edge of the
shell. In the fracture thus made the strong knife is inserted and pushed back

between the meat and the shell until it cuts off the attachment of the adductor muscle to the flat "upper" valve, after which, with a quick, dexterous twist, the other "eye" is severed, the meat tossed into the receptacle, which stands handy, and the shells are dropped through a hole in the bench into a barrel or tub placed underneath. Practice teaches extreme celerity in this operation. The knife and hammer are held in the same hand when the oyster is cracked, which does away with the expense of time and trouble in dropping one to pick up another; and the knife hilts very soon have a long spiral groove worn in them by the chafing of the hammer-handle.[1]

Man is a competitive creature and oyster opening frequently intensified this spirit. The long hours and admittedly dull work invited diversions, and contests for speed records were arranged. Unfortunately, I could not find any accurate, complete local or national records, but somehow a world record for opening 100 oysters against time was established in Rhode Island in the late 1870s. "Billy" Lowney, a crack culler and opener in the Robert Pettis shop in Providence, went down to Philadelphia with other openers from East Providence and New York and beat the champion of the South by opening 100 oysters in three minutes and three seconds.[2]

Every season contests were waged in the shops and in 1913 a national contest was held at Keyport, New Jersey. "The oyster opening championship of America was decided recently in an interesting contest here. Three oyster openers employed in local canning factories competed for cash prize of $100 in opening 500 bivalves. The contestants were Edward Brian, of Keyport, Neil Bradford, of Virginia, and Peter Lawson, of Connecticut. These men are said to be the fastest oyster openers in the world. Bradford recently made a new record by opening 41 gallons in one day's work. He and Brian open with hammer and knife, while Lawson, who practices 'side opening' uses a knife only."[3]

Shortly after the contests, a writer reported:

The recent oyster opening contest held in Keyport, New Jersey was watched with considerable interest by those who are paying high prices to shuckers. The result of the contest was remarkable. The record time was 20 minutes and 23 seconds, and the number of oysters opened in this length of time was 500. The first prize was $300. The wholesale dealers of New York city pay their shuckers $1.00 for every thousand oysters opened. If we assume that this shucker could keep this record up for a working day of 10 hours, he would earn about $14.00, and if he worked 6 days a week, he would earn $84.00

Women at their shucking stalls or benches opening oysters in a New Haven oyster plant. Courtesy of the Shellfish Institute of North America.

per week, and the enormous salary of $336.00 per month. We do not wonder therefore that the New York oyster dealer thinks the cost of shucking is too high.[4]

The last competitions attracting national attention were held before World War II at the sportman's shows at Boston and New York. The First (and last) National Oyster Shucking Championship, under the joint sponsorship of *The Fishing Gazette* and the Oyster Institute of North America, was held in New York City in 1937. Manuel Tavares, a side opener from the Warren Oyster Co., Warren, Rhode Island, won the contest after fighting his way up through the preliminaries, the New England championships, the semi-finals, and finals. Competing with men from as far away as Norfolk, Virginia, he opened 100 oysters (undamaged) in four minutes and fifty-two seconds. The speed certainly appears slower than Bill Lowney's old record back in the 1870s. Lowney may have been faster, but it seems more likely that the ground rules were different then.

However, men and women never worked in the shops at this terrific rate. Under steady, normal conditions and with fairly good stock (about 250 oysters to the bushel, with one bushel in the North equaling about one gallon opened), an average shucker opened two or three gallons an hour. The exceptionally fast opener working with single, big oysters can shuck a gallon in fifteen minutes or some thirty gallons a day.

Thousands of men and women, representing many nationalities and races shucked in harmony side by side in the opening houses of the North. In New Haven, during the greater part of the last century, American-born "Yankees," generally women, opened oysters in the oyster shops. With the influx of immigrants from Central Europe in the latter part of the century Polish women in particular dominated the shucking benches. Later still, after the two great wars, Negroes from the Chesapeake came north to work where few whites were left or were willing to work in the opening shops. In Rhode Island many of the workers were Portuguese and Cape Verdians. But their number has dwindled drastically along with the declining industry. Lack of shuckers and the high costs of paying the remaining few will, and has, influenced oyster production. Now that oystering seems to be reviving somewhat, renewed efforts are being made to develop a truly successful shucking machine to replace the almost nonexistant hand shucker. Many devices have been patented and tried, but none have been universally accepted by the industry. John L. Plock, of the Shelter Island Oyster Co., invented a mechanical shucker for home and institutional use, however, that has sold well. The Long Island Oyster Farms has developed an opener but it is not as efficient as the company would like.

High costs all along the line have thwarted the oyster companies' drive to survive and produce a worthwhile food product. It appears then, that a truly efficient mechanical oyster opener is one significant cost-saving factor which might eventually replace the traditional hand shucker. His job seems fairly secure, however, in the restaurants and oyster bars where customers like to watch raw oysters being opened.

Oystering has experienced many changes, but one element has remained untouched: the bushel and the bushel basket as the standard measuring unit. Practically all dealings aboard boats between natural growthers and the cultivators invariable dealt in terms of the bushel measure. The total yearly United States and foreign output universally employed the bushel as the basic unit of measure, although recently the pound appears to have displaced it in statistics. This bushel, an item of ancient lineage, varied slightly in size through the years and in different countries, but the standard American oyster bushel is a dry measure of volume of 2,150.42 cubic inches—a little over 1 cubic foot. The exact figure is theortical, for the baskets not only lost their shape in time but each man filled them differently; some packed them tightly, others loosely (cribbing), though they were always topped. The amount varied depending upon who loaded them, the buyer or the seller.

Oysters are handled at all ages and sizes. One bushel may hold as many as 15,000 of the young seed oysters or as few as 150 of the older and larger marketable oysters, but 250 to 300 was considered the average count per basket.

The common white oak (or ash) splint or lath-type bushel basket came from England with the colonists. Even before this it had been the universal oyster unit for centuries. Woven throughout with 3/4 x 1/4 of an inch wooden splints, and in some cases 3/4 of an inch x 1 1/4 inches, it stands about 1 1/2 feet high. The top is open and roughly equal in shape and area to the squarish bottom. Two handles on the rim are woven or made of the same wood and permit it to be lifted easily.

A few scattered basket makers in Connecticut supplied the industry there. During this century and slightly before, basket makers such as Scofield of New Canaan provisioned the Bridgeport and Norwalk area. On Staten Island oystermen and farmers made their own baskets as a rule. The demand was great, however, and some men like John Morgan and his son, Jim, of New Springfield, established their own business and catered to oystermen, farmers, or anyone, with baskets of all sizes and descriptions.

Everything has its day and so it was with the craft of basket making. It faded out before World War II and the popular and similarly shaped fisherman's "Daisy" wire basket made by The Massillon Wire Basket Company of Massillon, Ohio, took its place.

The barrel is another unit of measure of quantity. Domestic and foreign shellstock shipments were made and recorded in barrels although boxes and gunny sacks were used as well. Because the shape and size of the barrel is traditional and an effective and efficient container for bulk cargoes, it survived a long time. Today, boxes and sacks have replaced the barrel but it is still used occasionally in the North.

Oyster barrels looked much the same as the old flour or sugar barrels, and always contained from two to three bushels. By 1934 the United States government had standardized the barrel, making it equivalent to 3.03 United States standard bushels.

Most oystering communities boasted of at least one small cooperage, especially during the palmy days of the nineteenth century. As the industry prospered during the early and mid-nineteenth century, the demand for barrels increased. The small cooper worked unceasingly but could not keep up with orders, and large barrel companies applying primitive yet effective mass pro-

A variation of the cracking method. Note gloves, oyster hammer, block and gallon dipper on the right which held the oyster meats. Photograph by the author.

duction techniques based on the recently invented steam power sprang up to fill the demand. By the 1850s New Haven, the center of the New England packing trade, had two large "up-to-date" barrel companies supplying the oyster industry. Lieutenant P. deBroco of France, sent by Napoleon III to inspect the United States oyster business in 1862, commented about this type of manufacturing:

> The number of barrels and boxes or cases required annually, at Fair Haven, is so great that two large manufactories have been established for the manufacture of these articles, and they employ about one hundred and fifty persons. That for the making of kegs uses steam as a motive-power. Everything in the establishment is done by machinery. One machine cuts out the staves, a second the bottom; others pierce the holes, and form the plugs. The kegs at wholesale bring the following prices: Kegs containing a gallon, $1.08 a dozen; kegs containing a half-gallon, 94 cents a dozen. The kegs are made to contain two gallons, one, three-fourths, one-half, or one-fourth of a gallon, according to size. Tin cases are worth $5.50 a hundred.[5]

Filling cans with shucked oysters from the skimmer. Courtesy of Bluepoints Company, Inc.

By now the individual cooper, as a rule relying solely upon his own craftmanship and energy, found himself competing unprofitably with the barrel manufacturer, and eventually was forced out of business.

By 1900 the barrel–making business had improved substantially. One such establishment was the Bayport Barrel Company of Bayport, Long Island, supplier of the oystermen of Great South Bay. A newspaper article describing the company revealed changes since the 1860s:

> A spot of interest in Bayport is the plant of the Bayport Barrel Company, of which Mr. C.E. Hibbard is the proprietor. Mr. Hibbard has been manufactoring barrels on Long Island for the past eleven years [since 1904]. His barrel factory is an extensive structure, covering a half acre of ground, and for the immense output which is produced each season the Bayport Barrel Company has a railroad siding of its own.
>
> This company makes a specialty of barrels for the oyster trade, particularly for the Bluepoint oyster business. Such barrels must be particularly firm in construction, though numerous firms neglect the sanitary side of the question. Mr. Hibbard, however, has taken into consideration the worldwide fame of our oysters and realizing that sanitary packing is a most important detail, the Bayport Barrel Company is chiefly concerned in producing a barrel of the cleanest, most sanitary quality, so that the Bluepoint oysters may be shipped in a standard package of an absolutely sanitary nature.
>
> To accomplish this, all barrels manufactured by the Bayport Barrel Company are subjected to an intense heating process, thus sterilizing them and making safe, sanitary packing possible. The barrels are uniform in size and are sent to all parts of the Island from which the toothsome bivalve is shipped.
>
> This concern carries on an extensive trade with oyster men and their plant has a capacity of one hundred thousand barrels each season. There are fifteen men in the employ of the Bayport Barrel Company at the height of their busy season.
>
> The public at large will be interested to know that the sanitary packing of the oyster at its initial shipping is a very important factor, and in sterilizing his barrels, Mr. Hibbard has proved himself a champion of the "Pure Food" movement.[6]

Oysters in the shell were sent in barrels by either of two ways, depending upon their destination. For the European trade they were "double headed," that is, the top and bottom were identical, and made of wood. A "packer" carefully and closely packed them, hollow shell down, pressing them tightly with a heavy circular weight, and then "headed" or sealed the container with a wooden top the same as the bottom. Packing was so tight that not a single oyster rattled when the barrel was shaken. Dealers believed oysters kept better on the long ocean passage this way because the jamming prevented them from opening their shells and consequently they did not lose their precious liquor. The man who headed the barrel and whose work required more skill than the packer's was called the "cooper," although he did not make barrels.

Oysters destined for California or elsewhere in this country were shipped in the same barrels but topped instead with burlap. This necessitated a minimum of skill, was faster, and thus cheaper. Oysters were also transported in one- or two-bushel burlap sacks.

No exact figure can be given for the number of oysters per barrel. But an average amount recorded in 1891 for Connecticut oysters was:[7]

> 3 year olds—1500   per barrel
> 4 year olds—1200–1400 per barrel
> 5 year olds—1000–1200 per barrel
> 6 year olds— 800–1000 per barrel
> 7 year olds— 650– 825 per barrel

Oysters came in various sizes depending upon a number of factors and have become progressively more expensive, in fact, almost a luxury. To insure uniformly fair prices and an understanding of terms, local classifications and nomenclature evolved. The South spoke in different terms than the North and all measurments of size and weight have changed markedly since colonial days. Oystermen, fishermen, dealers, restaurant owners, and consumers frequently have had their own designations having similarities but no uniformity. For example, in 1891 Connecticut oystermen classified four grades of oysters in the shell relative to age.[8]

> cullentines   2–3 years old   }
> culls   3 years or more } for stews
> boxes   4–6 years old   }
> extras   5 years and over } in the shell

New Yorkers in the 1850s graded three kinds: culls, boxes, and extras. Shrewsbury oysters came in two sizes: boxes and cullings. The problem was so

Two ways of barreling oysters: left, "double headed" for long-distance shipment and better stacking; right, burlap-covered for shorter distances. Courtesy of Bluepoints Company, Inc.

perplexing and contradictory that the United States National Recovery Administration (NRA) in 1934 tried to help with a code of size standards for market oysters packed and sold in the shell for public consumption on the Atlantic and Gulf coasts:

Size A: LARGE—counting less than 185 oysters per U.S. standard bushel.
Size B: MEDIUM—counting 185 to 270 oysters per U.S. standard bushel.
Size C: HALF-SHELL—counting 271 to 350 per U.S. standard bushel.
Size D: SMALL—counting more than 350 oysters per U.S. standard bushel.

Nonetheless, many oystermen continued to use their own traditional terms when dealing among themselves. In 1972 one firm sized them: cocktail, half-shell, medium, and large. Another firm used half-shell and friers. There is still no uniformity but perhaps it is not necessary.

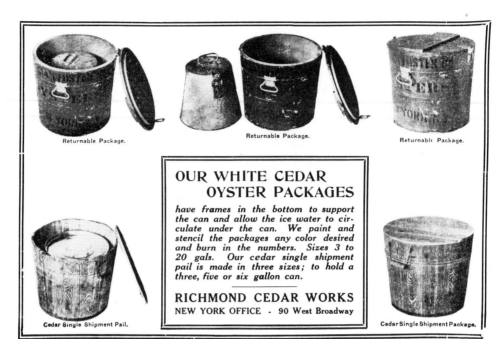

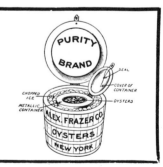
Common types of oyster carriers or packages that appeared around 1910. From
The Fishing Gazette, July 9, 1910, p. 1023; September 17, 1910, p. 1122.

Shucked oysters coming out of the washing tank into the skimmer. Courtesy of Bluepoints Company, Inc.

The history of oyster shipping containers is in a sense the account of the various solutions to the problem of keeping oysters fresh and clean in transport. Oysters in the shell, generally barrel-freighted in the cool months, presented no critical spoilage problem, though they had to be watched.

Preserving shucked oyster meats fresh, however, was always a problem, and was solved by sundry methods relating to the technology of the times. For a century and perhaps longer prior to 1880, fresh oyster meats were freighted out of New England and New York in wooden casks. One unit was the half barrel which contained eighteen gallons but only twelve gallons of solid meat. Another unit was the nine-gallon barrel, which contained only six gallons of solid meat. Fair Haven sent shucked oysters inland in common wooden kegs of varying sizes, the four-quart, nail keg size being the most common. In warm weather, kegs were encased in boxes packed with crushed ice.

A favorite oyster container for out-of-town orders up to the early 1900s was the returnable oyster tub. Made of wood and usually with a three-to twenty-gallon capacity, it was similar in shape to the butter tub—a truncated cone,

Kegging oysters. Illustration from Scribner's Monthly, December 1877, p. 225.

the bottom a little smaller than the top. A feature which later became the main objection was the cake of ice placed in the middle in direct contact with the oysters.

In 1909 the Department of Agriculture banned the use of the tub and ice combination not only for sanitary reasons but also because it was an adulteration, for oysters absorbed the ice water. Anticipating the ban, most oystermen had already shifted to the new returnable sanitary carriers that had appeared on the market a few years before the ruling.

The new wood containers were similar to the old tubs but some had nearly straight sides. They held a sealed metal receptacle, usually of galvanized iron, which in turn held the opened oysters. Enough space was provided between it and the carrier sides for crushed ice, thus keeping the oysters from unsanitary contact with the ice. Different patented locking devices held the cover down. The name and address of the oyster company was clearly marked and tagged on the containers—now termed "carriers" or simply packages.

By 1910 such carriers as the Bender, Vac-Jac, and the widely used Sealshipt were adopted by the oystermen. The last mentioned was a patented device used by the Sealshipt Oyster System, Inc. of Massachusetts, Rhode Island, Connecticut, and New York. By World War I, however, returnable carriers were being supplemented if not replaced by the more economical single shipment tin cans of various sizes.

Yet, tin cans were not new to the industry. After they were invented in the early-nineteenth century, the industry packed oysters at various times in 1/2 pint, pint, quart, 1/2 gallon, and 1, 2, 3, and 5 gallon sizes. These were also sent packed with ice in pine boxes as the Bloom Brothers of South Norwalk still do today.

World War I was roughly a pivotal point in the shipment of oysters. Before that time oysters arrived at the retailers in these bulk units, from which the retailer ladeled them out into cardboard holders for the customer. Health risks were always involved under these circumstances, leaving the customer and the oyster grower at the mercy of the retailer.

The newly aroused health awareness after the typhoid scare of 1924 and 1925—with the backing of federal, state and municipal agencies—forced oystermen to make radical improvements in all branches of their enterprise from the watery beds to the retailers' counters. As a result, the oyster became as sanitary as milk.

A related benefit was the increased use of the multishaped packages such as the highly successful "Nestrite" waxed paper container. Now small tin cans of improved tamper-proof design cooled with dry ice in fiberboard cartons were used by many companies. Frozen oysters also made their appearance on the scene at this time, though Captain Fred Ockers of West Sayville, New York, had experimented with them during World War I.

Up to about World War II, Railway Express handled the bulk of shucked oysters, re-icing as necessary. Today most of the oysters are moved by truck, but the difficulty of distribution to small towns and remote rural areas in particular has increased because no effective system has yet been developed to keep perishable products refrigerated with water ice.

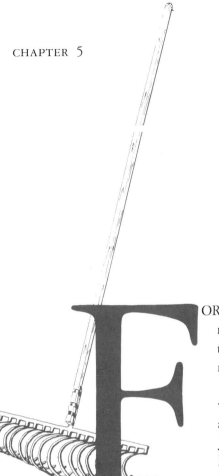

CHAPTER 5

Hand Implements

OR centuries man has fished oysters by hand, rake, tong, and dredge. All are still used today to some extent, as well as more complicated modern machinery such as the suction dredge.

Of the three hand implements, the rake was used by the American Indians before the arrival of the European settlers. In one of John White's famous drawings of 1585 an Indian is depicted with a long-tined rake made from a forked stick with which he is presumably oystering. The white man apparently copied it and followed the Indian custom of raking shallow bottoms for oysters.[1] The Indian invented the rake independently, to be sure, but it is known that the French had used this sort of tool in their fishery for centuries. It is uncertain when the oysterman's rake eventually developed into the more sophisticated blacksmith's (bull-type) rake with highly curved teeth. The prototype may have been the Indian rake, the French rake, or possibly both. At any rate one of the earliest recorded references to it was made by Baron Kalm in 1748. He observed rakes in operation in New York Bay and wrote: "We saw many boats, in which the fishmen were busy catching oysters; to this purpose they make use of a kind of rake with long iron teeth bent inward. These they used either single or two tied together in such a manner that the teeth were turned toward each other."[2]

The oyster bull rake is similar essentially to a garden rake and manipulated about the same way. The teeth end of the rake is formed of iron and is about three feet wide. The handle extends from five to thirty-five feet (in spliced sections), depending upon the depth of water worked. The teeth, seventeen to twenty-one inches long and spaced about one and one-half inches apart, are semi-eliptical in shape which permits them to hold the gathered oysters securely. Prior to World War I, they were custom-made by local blacksmiths on special order from oystermen. Now that blacksmiths have faded from the scene, companies devoted to fishing gear manufacture them in various sizes and forms.

Oysters can be raked while standing in the water or in a boat—the latter was the customary manner. Men working, for example, in Arthur Kill at Staten Island drifted in their skiffs square to the current and raked amidships with thirty-foot rakes. In southern Connecticut skiffs were anchored, and rakes half that length were operated from the stern or sides. In colonial days man undoubtedly used rakes extensively, but they have not been popular since the last quarter of the nineteenth century, except in these two places referred to and in Buzzards and Narragansett bays. Rakes were better suited to clamming than oystering and were employed more widely in the former occupation, being worked in the same fashion as the oyster rake or towed from a sailboat as did the clammers of Keyport, New Jersey.

Tongs, like rakes, were the tools of oystermen with small means and of part-time workers, who used them on the shallow natural beds or on their privately owned bit of ground. Tongs have been associated with the oyster fishery since the middle of the seventeenth century and may well be indigenous to the United States or Canada. Charlevoix, the French explorer, reported seeing them in the mid-seventeenth century on the "coasts of Acadia."[3] Lieutenant deBroca reported in 1862: "The tongs, which I have never seen except in America, is an instrument which ought to be introduced into France, as it would be of great service to our shell fisheries in general."[4]

Oyster tongs work much like the salad tongs at the dinner table of today. Take two ordinary long-handled garden rakes, fasten the handles together like shears, teeth facing each other, and you have a pair of tongs. They are worked in the water from a small boat such as a skiff, canoe, or sharpie by spreading the ends of the handles at arms length while the head or tongs on the bottom separate correspondingly. When the handles come together, the tongs do likewise and gather everything lying in between. Then the tongs are lifted to the boat, emptied of their catch, and the process is repeated until the boat is loaded.

The earliest tong heads were fashioned of wood or a combination of wood and metal. Their construction did not demand the services of a blacksmith,

Bayman of Great South Bay tonging for oysters. Courtesy of Suffolk Marine Museum.

Harold Palmer, oysterman of Riverside, Connecticut, with the three hand implements common to oystering—a bull rake, hand dredge and tongs. Photograph by the author.

so the oystermen made them to their own requirements and consequently many varieties existed. They were all rather light in weight and did not dig down as deeply as the later, all metal kind. An oak bar forming the width of the tong head received the metal or wood teeth. From the oak bar two to five wire or wood guard strips arced above concentrically to screen or basket the load.

After the wooden tongs were established during the nineteenth century, blacksmiths began to make the heads of metal to the oysterman's specification. Very few tongs were exactly alike in all respects. Local conditions, such as type of bottom and oyster size, fixed teeth dimensions and spacing. Individual opinion and custom tended to establish the configuration of the tong's basket or "bows" section. The basket above the bar of teeth varied widely in pattern. In one type it consisted of two to five parallel guard pieces of wood or wire as much as a foot high. For average size oysters the head piece might contain nine to sixteen teeth constituting a maximum width of 36 inches, with the 1 3/4 inch-long teeth set 1 3/4 inches apart, and run up to about 2 1/2 inch-long teeth set 2 1/8 inches apart. Tongs for set and seed oysters had shorter teeth spaced closer together. Stratford shell tongs had fourteen to sixteen teeth. In 1880 tongs appeared to be considerably smaller all around: 14 inches wide, teeth 1 1/2 inches apart and not over 1 to 1 1/2 inches long. Before World War II the stales or handles were made of longleaf yellow pine, white ash, or spruce from California. Their length ranged from 6 to 24 feet, depending upon the depth of water. The king pin or bolt was placed to give the oysterman the most comfortable reach for his tong. For the average man, this was 2 inches to the foot from the teeth. (On a 12–foot tong the pin came 24 inches from the teeth.)

The older type stales were cut straight for almost their entire length, then curved in near the head or basket to permit more room for holding the oysters. Before World War I, Captain Fred Lovejoy of East Norwalk, Connecticut, improved the stale by contriving a long curve at the head which eliminated the quick, short curve. Three straight handles could now be made out of a piece of stock that formerly yielded only two. Chas. D. Briddell Inc. of Cristfield, Maryland, one of the largest oyster equipment manufacturers on the East Coast, bought Captain Lovejoy's idea and sold it for years as the Connecticut model tong. Lovejoy, Hans Lingdell of Bridgeport and others "hung tongs," that is, they fitted the head, set the pin, and sold them to local tongers. Tongs sold for $3.50 to $5.00 in the 1880s, $7.50 during the 1940s, and in 1972 they were either purchased from the Chesapeake or a blacksmith on Long Island for about four times the 1940s price.

When oysters are found deeper than tong or rake depth or in open, unprotected water where they are scattered, dredges become necessary and desirable for harvesting. Dredging is faster, and covers a wider terrain than tonging or raking.

The dredge is essentially a kind of rake with a bag attached and a long rope, cable, or chain replacing the wooden handle. The small hand dredges consisted of a triangular metal framework with the straight base curved down and in toward the apex to form a scraping edge. Behind this edge was fastened a heavy twine bag (on top) and metal link or ring bag (on the bottom) to catch and hold the oysters. A sailboat pulled the dredge along the bottom with a "21 thread," 1/2 inch 8 to 12 fathom manila line extending from the boat's rail down to the apex of the triangular bar frame. When full, the dredge was hauled aboard by hand, dumped, and then thrown overboard again.

A hand winder aboard an open-deck sloop. Courtesy of the Coulter McKenzie Machine Company.

In the United States the dredge, also called drag and drudge, was popular in the North from earliest times and spread later to the Chesapeake in the early 1800s.[5] It apparently came to the United States from England where it had been used since the Middle Ages and perhaps earlier. Its exact origin or prototype is unknown, but it may have been invented by the ancient Romans for their famous Whitstable and Colchester oystery fishery.[6] An any rate, an evolution from the rake to the dredge seems plausible, although as far as we know, the English did not use the rake.

There are three types of New England dredges: those operated by hand, by hand-winder, and by power. All three are alike in funtion and general appearance; the differences occur in size, weight, structural details, and how they are hoisted. The hand dredge, the lightest and oldest of all, remained the common choice of oystermen using sail. In Connecticut its weight and size for use on the natural beds were restricted by law to no more than 30 pounds exclusive of the bag. One man could lift a dredge which held roughly three-fourths of a bushel and weighed about 80 to 100 pounds when full. Though the blade or width of dredge can vary, the average was about 26 inches long on the one-man dredge and about 32 inches for one handled by two men.

A heavy old-style dredge with dredge post at right. Courtesy of the Bluepoints Company, Inc.

The boom rig with bottom dumping dredge aboard the Bloom Brother's *Catharine M. Wedmore*. Photograph by the author.

A hydraulic boom with bottom dumping dredge on the Long Island Oyster Farms' *Captain*. Note side boards to hold in the piled up oysters. Photograph by the author.

Blacksmiths traditionally made the wrought iron framework and the oystermen wove the net and links which made up the bag, although a few companies manufactured them. With proper care a dredge lasted years—sometimes generations. Many of the hand dredges used aboard the Connecticut natural growth sloops in the 1950s were made a half century before.

Three types of blades were used on the hand dredges:

1. Scraper. A blade 2″ wide (in cross section), the scraping end hammered to a sharp edge. Good on sand and cobble bottoms like those off Bridgeport and Stratford. This was the most common style.
2. Oval. Also applied to sandy bottoms or those with jingles like the New Haven and Savin Rock beds.

3. Toothed. For big oysters on hard bottoms (not used very often).

A "cutting board" was occasionally attached to the dredge when the oysters were buried or when oystermen were working on a rough bottom such as a section of the Bridgeport bed. It was simply a sheet of metal a few inches wide fastened above and across the full width of the blade. When the dredge was towed the pressure of the rushing water on the board deflected the dredge downward, thus preventing it from skipping over the bottom.

The hand-winder, a hand-operated winch dredge, was the universal favorite of the natural growthers of the Chesapeake and Delaware bays, although it never gained widespread acceptance in the North, where oystermen were satisfied with the traditional hand dredge method and therefore reluctant to try the labor-saving winder. They claimed that the hand method was equally effective and did not break the oysters or damage the bottom as the hand-winder dredges reportedly did. In addition, six or eight or more hand dredges could be used simultaneously, whereas the hand-winder boat was limited traditionally to two. Some oystermen also claimed that the beds in Long Island Sound were not big enough for the hand-winders. Yet men like Edward Robillard of Milford oystered successfully with his hand-winder Delaware schooner *Ann Marie*, and Earle "Bezak" Svertesky repeatedly proved its worth on his *Priscilla, Ann Gertrude*, and the skipjack *Eagle*.

A boat with hand-winders (two winders, one per dredge) does not drift but sails, with a dredge off each side—power boat fashion. These dredges could not weigh more than 30 pounds in Connecticut, though they were wider than hand dredges—about 36 inches, holding two-and-one-half bushels. Their construction was therefore relatively lighter but stronger and more rigidly reinforced than that of hand dredges. The blade was also thicker—from 2 1/2 to 3 inches. Instead of a manila rope dredge-line, a 7/16 of an inch flexible cable led from the dredge to a horizontal protective roller on the rail and finally to the hand-operated winch positioned on the center line of the boat immediately abaft the mast. A vertical roller at the after end of the horizontal roller held the cable in place. At least two men were needed to handle each winch and dredge.

Power boat dredges operated on the same principle as the hand-winders except that all equipment was heavier and, of course, hauled by power. One dredge alone could hold twenty-one bushels and weighed about a ton loaded, and some of the bigger dredges held twenty-four to thirty bushels. Many dredges held about twelve bushels but an eight- or nine-bushel dredge is considered the best size by many oystermen. It is not so big that the chain bag "bills" or kills the oysters. At least three men were needed for the dredging operation, better six or seven: one to work the hoister (usually the captain in the pilot house) and two to six men on deck to trip or "break" and unload the dredge as it reaches the rollers at the rail.

Since the 1870s when power was utilized for the first time, dredges and dredge boats have progressively altered in size and design. The small blacksmiths could no longer produce these massive dredges easily, though some continued to make them. As a result concerns like the Coulter & McKenzie Machine Co. and the Automatic Machine Company, both of Bridgeport, supplied not only the dredges but the winders, hoisters, and the engines to operate them. It was not unusual for the Coulter & McKenzie Co., for instance, to design and manufacture all the dredging gear for a specific vessel.

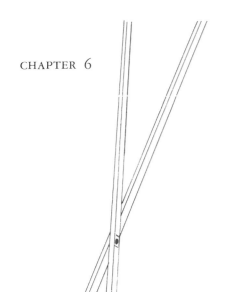

CHAPTER 6

Oyster Tonging Boats

YSTERING in New England produced a wide variety of watercraft. The pressures of an evolving industry, geographical factors, local maritime traditions, the needs and financial capabilities of individual oystermen, all influenced design. Therefore, there was no such thing as the typical New England oyster boat, although there were typical specific types.

At different times the oyster boat meant different things to different people. We can no more say, for example, that the Model A Ford is a typical car than we can claim the Fair Haven sharpie is the typical northern oyster boat. Both statements must be carefully qualified. The Model A may be described as the typical car of the average American in the late 1920s. The Fair Haven sharpie is likewise more accurately labeled the typical tonging oyster boat of the New Haven, Connecticut, area during the period of 1850 to 1910. Therefore, statements of this nature must include consideration of time, place, and use, if a proper perspective is desired.

"Oyster boat" may refer to anything from a skiff to a steamer. Essentially, it means any boat associated in some way with oystering. More specifically, it functions, solely or jointly, as a platform from which oysters are harvested (raked, tonged, or dredged), as a vehicle for freighting and shifting them, or for maintaining the beds. This chapter deals only with the sailing tonging boats.

The sailing oyster harvesting boat ranged from a diminutive 16 feet to about 65 feet. In the beginning, when oystering was a modest fishery and carried on close to shore, only small tonging craft were needed.

Generally, the tonger was the poorest of all oystermen. He earned his living oystering or fishing on the water near his home. His boat had to be inexpensive to buy or build and maintain, strong and long-lasting. In addition it had to be easy to work and big enough to carry at least a day's catch—something like 30 to 100 bushels. Many small, purely local boats evolved from these elementary needs and some were successfully borrowed from other fisheries. Like living creatures, all types evolved, flourished, and eventually disappeared in the course of events. Of all the tonging boats from Cape Cod to Staten Island, the oyster dugout canoe and the sharpie—both from Fair Haven—exemplify the evolution and demise of the one- or two-man northern oyster tonging craft. One was the product of the highly pragmatic aboriginal mind, and the other the refinement of civilized man's somewhat equivalent needs. The dugout represents not only the most primitive American watercraft but also one of the most functional craft known to mankind. It was a simple, rugged, durable, capacious, one-man tonging boat.

From the beginning the early settlers realized the value of oysters and wisely copied Indian ways of catching, opening, and preparing them. The dugout came directly from the Indian, who freighted, oystered, and performed similar rough work with it while using skin and bark canoes for lighter tasks. At first, log canoes were bartered or purchased from the Indians. Later, when the pioneering atmosphere stabilized, the settler hewed them himself out of the trunks, copying the model closely. With less patience than the Indian perhaps, he chose to work with the soft white pine log rather than the hard oak and chestnut the Indians so often favored. Pine, however, had advantages other trees did not, such as straight, long trunks of light weight. Through his newly acquired experience, the settler gradually modified and improved the original model. With superior iron tools he rounded the ends, flattened the bottom and, when needed, added a leeboard and sails. Thus, the primitive dugout passed gracefully from one culture to another.

Originally, New Haven dugouts came from the extensive local stands of pine, but soon these were depleted. Builders and oystermen, forced to look farther afield, discovered suitable timber in New Hampshire at the headwaters of the Connecticut River. One Zabina Allen constructed canoes there in the winter and rafted them down river to New Haven in the spring. Maine fishermen did the same in the slack winter season and towed them to New Haven by sail in warm weather.

Oyster dugouts and a two-masted sharpie on the Quinnipiac River in Fair Haven, Connecticut, probably taken in the 1890s. Courtesy of Eric Ball.

A fifty-bushel canoe or dugout on the Quinnipiac River. From *Annual Report of the Shell-Fish Commissioners*, State of Connecticut, 1901.

Due to widespread use of lumber in house and shipbuilding, the large virgin white pine tree became woefully scarce throughout New England after the American Revolution. Oystermen then searched westward and found good large trees still standing at Lake Cayuga in New York. From here came the last of the Fair Haven dugouts, although some may have been built from the few remaining local pines.

The Fair Haven dugout looked like a long trough with spoon-shaped ends. In frozen water the unturned bow enabled the craft to ride up and break down this barrier more effectively than a skiff or sharpie.

Canoes reached 30 feet in length, but the average size was 28 feet long by 36 or 39 inches wide, 18 inches inside depth, 3 inches thick on the bottom, and 2 1/2 inches on the sides. They floated light in 3 inches of water, but loaded with a ton of oysters, drew about 9 inches. They carried a maximum of fifty bushels but thirty bushels was about the average.

Sculling oar or sail propelled the dugout, choice depending upon the location of oysters, tide, and wind. In Fair Haven, oystermen kept their canoes along the banks of the Quinnipiac River deep in the harbor, for in the early days tonging was conveniently limited to the river right at their doorsteps: sculling was all that was necessary. Depletion pushed their territory farther out to Morris Cove near the breakwater, a distance of three to four miles from home. Then a sail came in handy. The men worked the tide, drifted and sculled with the outgoing tide, tonged a few hours, and returned with the flood. With a fair wind the leg-of-mutton sharpie-type sail helped the tonger coming and going.

Dugouts, though fairly stable loaded, were not considered very seaworthy. One observer in the 1890s claimed that they seldom or never ventured beyond the breakwater. Yet some men like Elijah S. Ball, a noted Fair Haven oysterman, felt differently. Once, when there was no local outlet for his load of oysters, he sailed his dugout to market at Mattituck Inlet, a distance of some twenty-one miles across Long Island Sound.

Dugout oystermen as a rule took pride in their craft, kept them painted and in shipshape condition. The men themselves often dressed unusually well for their rough occupation. A Mr. Rowland, for example, always tonged in New Haven Harbor in a white dress shirt and cuff links, topped off with a derby.

The exact number of canoes built for New Haven is unknown but Ingersoll reported a "few dozen" near the end of the era in 1879.[1] By 1900 there was only "a handful" left.[2]

Sculling a Fair Haven sharpie on the Quinnipiac River in light airs, Oystermen hand-drove two long wooden poles into the river bottom to act as anchors while tonging. Courtesy of August MacTaggart.

An acticle in an unidentified 1904 New Haven newspaper describes the canoes further and tells the interesting story of how they were purchased:

John Smith of Fair Haven, a veteran of the war of 1812, skilled in the art of canoe building, made periodical trips to the pine forests of Cayuga Lake, where the required number of canoes needed, were hewed and hollowed out. These were about 28 feet long, very narrow and with sides three inches thick. The price paid for the white pine trees was around one dollar a piece, standing. When the requisite number of canoes were made, they were tied together like a raft and towed to Albany through the Erie Canal by a sloop. The journey to New York was made by the Hudson River, the native power being a sailing craft bound for that port. From New York to New Haven the journey was made by the craft being towed by a craft bound for this port. As soon as the fleet of canoes reached their journey's end, they were drawn upon the beach, each one marked with a number, the duplicate of the numbers thrown in a receptacle . . . and the numbers drawn by those who had ordered the canoes. . . . The cost of the canoe delivered here was about $35.

The speed (under sail) at which the different dugouts would travel was oftentimes the topic of conversation over the cracker barrels in the village grocery, and many a night the merits and faults of various "private" yachts were discussed before an interested group of owners and admirers. A race was the only way out of it and this afforded plenty of excitement. Each canoe carried a lee board which consisted of a thin piece of plank some four feet long by two feet wide and half an inch thick. This was placed over the side of the craft and on a change of tack, the lee-board had to be lifted out of the water and transferred to the other side of the boat. This was the only thing that changed sides in a race, as the owners of the canoes seldom placed money on their boats.[3]

Around 1900 the Quinnipiac Canoe Club raced a couple of borrowed oyster dugouts in the Quinnipiac River at their annual regatta. A dozen men kneeling on the bottom paddled their canoes on a 100- or 200-foot course. The winner was awarded the grand prize of a ripe watermelon!

In time more sophisticated craft completely superceded the dugouts all along the coast, except in New Haven. As long as tonging lasted there— roughly until World War I—the dugout survived. The well-known sharpie replaced it but never entirely succeeded in ousting it, and when the last dugout finally rotted on the banks of the Quinnipiac, the sharpie—the darling of the Connecticut oystermen—soon followed its fate.

While the dugout remained the patriarch of the oyster fishery, other boat types, perhaps as old as the New England colonies, worked side by side with it. In New Haven there were "square-enders," (scow type boats) also called bat-teaux locally, and the ubiquitous rowboat or skiff. All did yeoman service for the watermen without gaining the fame and glory of the dugout or sharpie. Of all these, one type alone still survives in vast numbers as a work and pleasure boat—and is just as unsung as before. It is the skiff, the mother of the sharpie. In 1892 Henry Hall gave a good description of the skiff and its natural evolution to the sharpie:

The flat-bottomed skiff followed the canoe. The clumsy shape of the original skiffs is suggested by the name of "New Haven flat-iron boats." They were

The South Norwalk, Connecticut, cat-ketch-sharpie *Sword Fish*, a modified Fair Haven sharpie. Either the summer cabin aft was removed for working, or it represents a conversion to yachting. Courtesy of Fred Lovejoy.

pointed at the bow, were as broad aft as amidships, and were flat on the floor, with upright sides, having a little outward flare, two or three rowing thwarts, and rowlocks and rudder. They were easily constructed, were cheap and serviceable, and any boy who had learned to handle a hammer, brad-awl, and saw and to drive a nail straight could make one, no other tools being needed. . . . When canoes became expensive the skiff came into favor, and as soon as the gowth of the oystering business made it necessary to have boats of large size and broad beam an improved skiff became the popular model in Connecticut. The "flat-iron boat" was cheap and safe and drew very little water, which is all that can be said in its favor, as the broad, square stern neutralized the effect of the pointed bow and made rowing a difficult and tiresome occupation. The boat was short and had little capacity; but the remedy for these defects was found in increasing the length and in giving the bottom a gradual round upward at the stern, so as to permit the displaced water to flow in behind the boat easily, as it does behind a keel vessel with a good run, without retarding the forward motion in the slightest degree, and sometimes the floor forward was given a rise of 3 inches to help the speed. The sharper bow and the round upward of the floor at the stern have given this peculiarly American boat its good qualities and its name. It is now universally called the "sharpie," and is so good a fishing boat and so fast a yacht that it has been adopted in a great many other localities throughout the United States where the waters are tolerably smooth and a safe, comfortable and capacious boat is required. The sharpie is at present the oyster boat of Connecticut, and is also a favorite for all general pleasure rowing on the rivers and lakes of that state.[4]

George Graves before 1880, and Lester Rowe, and E. H. Thatcher after him were leading Fair Haven sharpie builders. The Hills of Guilford, Connecticut, designed and built sharpies that were reputedly faster than the renowned Rowe models. Differences were slight but enough to win admirers. Guilford sharpies were smaller and had greater flare to the sides, allowing the tongs to clear the chine more easily.

New Haven sharpies made ideal tongers but seldom succeeded as dredge boats. They were not powerful enough to pull dredges and never worked well in the relatively heavy seas frequently encountered in Long Island Sound. However, a modification of the Fair Haven sharpies developed south of New Haven and dredged successfully on the natural beds. These larger boats had more freeboard, a cabin up forward, often a square stern, and all were gaff cat-ketch rigged. Good examples of this type at the turn of the century were the *Martha*, owned by Hans Gaeger of Rowayton; the *Clarence*, belonging to William Redfern of South Norwalk; and the *Sword Fish*, owned by Captain Albert Geib of South Norwalk.

Like sports shirts and sweaters, sharpies came in three sizes: small, medium, and large. To the oysterman the choice depended upon his pocketbook and where he worked. Henry Hall reported the prices being asked for sharpies at the end of the last century.[5]

SMALL	About $25	Under 25′ Below 75 bushel capacity	Skiff-like, undecked or half decked, one mast sprit sail, or oars
MEDIUM	$200	26′–35′ 75 to 175 bushels	1 or 2 masts, spirt sail, half decked

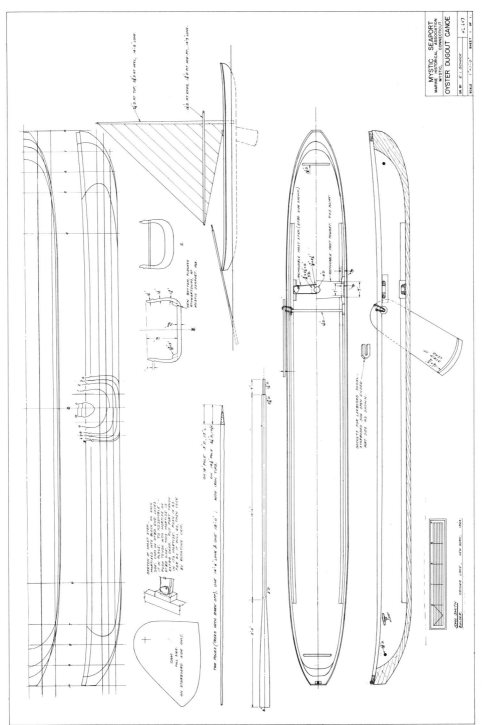

An oyster dugout canoe used in New Haven and now at Mystic Seaport.

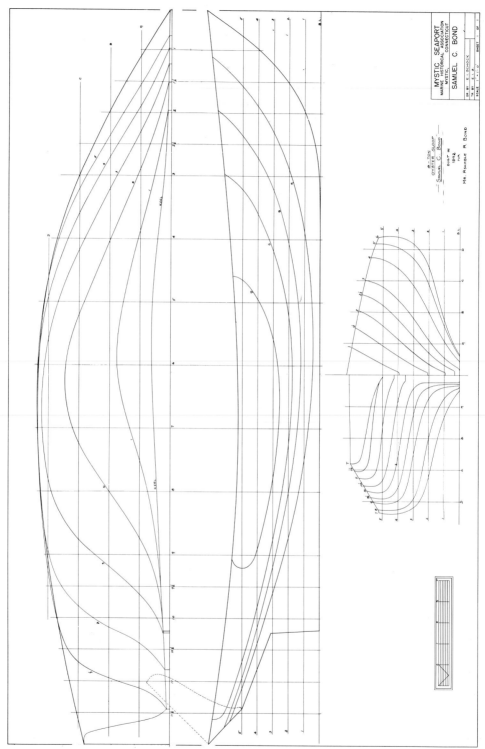

Lines from the half model of the *Samuel C. Bond*, a Connecticut-built oyster sloop.

| LARGE | $300 to $500 | From 35′ to about 45′ | Cabin forward, gaff cat-ketch, tong and dredge boat |

Because the sharpie was inexpensive, simple to build, and efficient, the model spread throughout the Atlantic and Gulf Coasts developing into all shapes and sizes.

A variation of the Connecticut skiff or rowboat appeared in the Staten Island oyster fleet and was called a bateau. It was not as handsome as the Connecticut prototype but it satisfied many of the area tongers.

The boatmen of northern New Jersey and Staten Island developed another very successful local type tonging boat known as the Staten Island skiff. It served the oystermen well for decades, though never attaining the widespread popularity of the sharpie. Commenting on this boat, Hall writes:

> At Amboy a great many oyster skiffs are employed by the fishermen of that busy locality, and probably 125 of them can be seen every day at nightfall gathering about the landing places on both sides of the Kill at that point. Two or three boat-shops are steadily engaged in their production. Unlike the Connecticut skiffs, these boats are regularly framed, and have a strip of flat bottom, tapering to a point at each end, with clinker-built sides nailed to frame timbers inside, placed about 20 inches apart, the sides being full and round and the stern perpendicular but V-shaped, as in a yawl. There are three sizes of these oyster skiffs, 18, 19, and 20 feet respectively. This is the length of the bottom. The boats over all are 4 and 4 1/2 feet longer. The beam is about 6 feet, and the depth from 20 to 22 inches. The planking is pine or cedar, strongly fastened with copper rivets through each lap; the frames are roots of white oak tree, selected as having the proper curvature naturally, squared and fitted to their places; and the bottom is floored over and the thwarts made removable, so that a large pile of oysters in the shell can be heaped up in the boat amidships. Most of the skiffs have a pole with small fore-and-aft sail, the mast being planted a little forward of amidships, but not in the bow. When there is a sail, there is generally a center-board also. About 250 feet of cedar are cut up for the planking and flooring. The boats cost $90 and $100 each, and one man with an assistant can make twenty of them in a year. The building of new boats and the repair of old ones is a pleasant and profitable local industry.[6]

On Great South Bay in Long Island the common tonging boat during the last half of the nineteenth century was the cat or sloop-rigged centerboarder.

Tonging from a Great South Bay catboat. A typical feature of these working boats was the convenient position of the tiller. Courtesy of the Suffolk Marine Museum.

The shoal draft gaff-rigged catboat ranged upwards of thirty feet, had a plum stem, with or without a bowsprit, graceful counter stern, and exceptionally low freeboard aft. A portable summer cabin for pleasure sailing, draped with canvas curtains, provided shelter from sun, rain, and wind. When tonging, the cabin was removed and the oysters stowed below in the hold. The larger boats with trunk cabins aft also had portable cabins placed over the hold. The baymen's catboat often had a short bowsprit and another mast step for summer conversion to sloop rig. Many of these boats, especially the sloops, dredged as well as tonged.

CHAPTER 7

The Sailing Oyster Dredgers

P to the twentieth century, during the age of sail, oyster boats were seen in large numbers from New York to Massachusetts. Taking a look at the dredger type alone, one is struck by the impression that almost any boat would do! Indeed, in lean times oystermen bought anything they could as long as it was able to pull a dredge and carry a load. Beyond this, however, no northern dredger type appears at the forefront with the same stamp of uniqueness as the Chesapeake's skipjack or bugeye. Unfortunately, marine writers and the popular press have furthered this illusion by almost completely ignoring the oyster dredging boats north of New Jersey; yet upon closer examination a family resemblance is discernible. They were nearly all round bottom, gaff-rigged, centerboard sloops. This broad description applies equally well to the common working sloop of the area, which originated as a general workboat for the shallow New York and Long Island waters and served its purpose so well that oystermen simply borrowed the model. The common northern oyster dredger then, with all its unique local variations, is an adaptation of this common workboat which the marine historian Chapelle calls the "New York sloop." He describes its general features:

> The New York boats were developed sometime in the 1830's, when the centerboard had been accepted. The boats were built all about New York Bay, particularly on the Jersey shore. The model spread rapidly, and, by the end

Tonging from a Great South Bay sloop. These boats either pulled dredges or were used for tonging. In Connecticut, where they only dredged, they were known as South-siders. Courtesy of Suffolk Marine Museum.

A Great South Bay working catboat under sail in light airs. Courtesy of Suffolk Marine Museum.

of the Civil War, the shoal centerboard sloop of the New York style had appeared all along the shores of western Long Island Sound, in northern New Jersey, and from thence southward into Delaware and Chesapeake waters. . . .

The New York sloop was a distinctive boat—a wide, shoal centerboarder with a rather wide, square stern and a good deal of dead rise, the midsection being a wide, shallow V with a high bilge. The working sloops usually had a rather hard bilge; but in some it was very slack, and a strongly flaring side was used. Originally, the ends were plumb, and the stem often showed a slight tumble home at the cutwater. V-sterns and short overhanging counters were gradually introduced in the 1850's, particularly in the boats over 25 feet in length on deck. Round sterns were rather popular in large sloops, after 1858. . . .

The rig was a simple jib and mainsail with a moderately long gaff and a very long boom to which the foot of the sail was laced. A very large jib was set on a long, hogged-down, plank bowsprit. The mast was rather well forward in the early boats, but as time passed it was moved aft somewhat. The early sloops usually had a marked rake in the mast, but this was decreased, and after the Civil War the mast became nearly plumb and the gaffs longer. . . .

Work-boats of the New York model were usually between 18 and 36 feet on deck. They were built very extensively on Long Island, in northern New Jersey, and along the lower reaches of the Hudson. When a particularly fast work-boat came out, it was usual for the boat to be purchased by a sportsman and converted to racing. Normally, however, the work-boats were much more burdensome and seaworthy than the "improved" type represented by the fast sandbagger.[1]

Chapelle's outline covers a wide array of boats. We can observe and arbitrarily classify three main styles of the New York working sloop that oystered in the New York-Connecticut area without, however, attempting to associate them in an evolutionary relationship. Within each group we may pinpoint some types equally as fascinating as the skipjack and bugeye. All three styles were sloop- or cat-rigged, sometimes with two mast steps for either rig.

1. The open deck boat. This has no cabin and so little deck space forward, along the sides and aft, that oysters must be carried down below at the open hold amidships. Usually up to 25 to 30 feet overall, this type was well represented by the famed sandbaggers which were frequently converted to oysterboats.

2. Open boat with cabin forward. This is similar to the open deck boat except for the cabin placed at or immediately aft of the mast. These boats were considered excellent for "running" oysters because they did not shift when the

boat heeled as they tended to do on the deck-loading boats. The cabin afforded protection from the sea as well as overnight accommodations. Their size was about the same or a little bigger than the open deck boat.

3. Deck boat with cabin aft and hold forward. This was the common Great South Bay and New York Bay style oyster boat for perhaps 150 years or more. And since the arrangement best suited the larger boats from 30 feet upward, most oyster boats this size adopted it. The boat was entirely decked except for the hold amidships. A trunk cabin stood forward of the steering gear and on the largest boats, those above 45 or 50 feet, a forecastle with crew accommodations was provided. The oysters were carried on deck and on top of the hatches, and stowed below only in cold weather, for ballast, or on long runs to the market or the buyers. Many natural growthers who sold to buyers favored the deck boat because the load was more easily busheled off than on the open boat. It was also a more watertight, and therefore a more seaworthy hull in this respect at least. The fair-sized cabin supplied adequate living accommodations for at least two men.

This classification is based solely upon deck configuration. Actually all hulls, whether flat, chine, round, keel or centerboard can be adapted to any of the three deck plans. But the dredgers were invariably round bottom, gaff-rigged centerboarders—a classification within itself. And no matter how general this deck classification, it was used commonly by many oystermen to describe their boats.

Buying ability, tradition, and practicability influenced the choice of overall length. Oystermen, always a rather independent lot, owned their boats or were in family partnerships and thus their individual or even group capability of buying a large boat was limited. The tradition of using only hand dredges also kept down the boat's length because the bigger the boat, the more dredges one was likely to use. And too many of these eighty-pound (plus) loaded dredges on any one boat were a nuisance. The 50-foot sloop *Nena A. Rowland* (built in 1883), one of the largest sailing dredge boats on the Connecticut natural beds since the 1880s, could pull eighteen dredges, but the dredges acted as so many anchors to slow her down, particularly in light airs, and shares for the huge crew also cut into overall profits. Furthermore, some claimed a large vessel on the comparatively small natural beds was clumsy among the smaller more responsive craft. So large vessels around 50 feet L.O.A. were never too popular in Connecticut, at least, since *Nena A. Rowland's* time.

The boat had to be large enough to carry a substantial load though, and a proper combination of length and beam resulted in a deck or hold which would

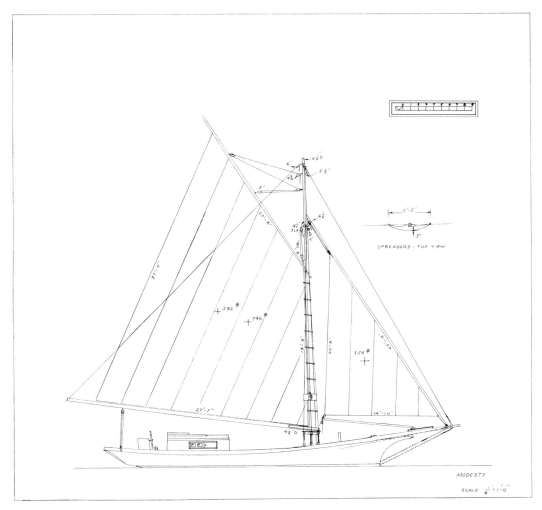

Sail plan of the *Modesty*

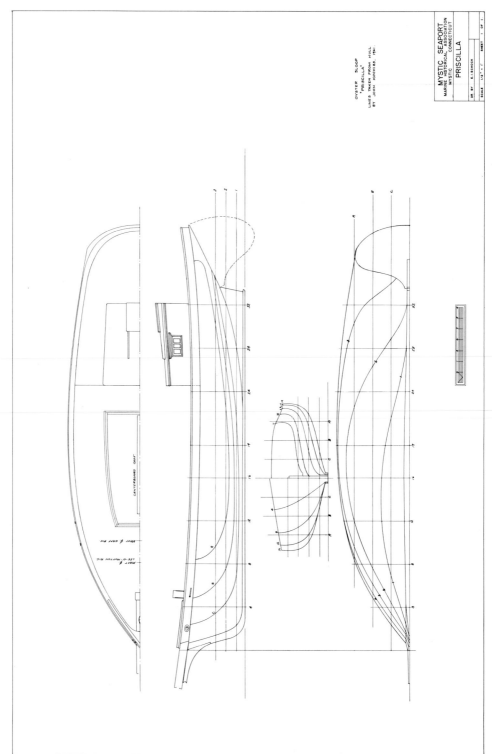

The South-sider-type oyster sloop *Priscilla*, built in Patchogue in 1888.

The 200-bushel oyster sloop *Amateur*—a cabin forward, hold aft type boat in Bridgeport around 1895. The topsail was used only in light airs and to get to the oyster beds and back. Courtesy of J. Fletcher Lewis.

carry 100 to 600 bushels of oysters—the common load range. Ample beam extending throughout the full length assured stability as well as cargo space. One characteristic of the mid-nineteenth century oyster boats, such as the *Ann Gertrude* and the New York City market boats, was their "cod's head and mackerel tail" deck outline: that is, full bows with greatest beam forward of amidships. Many oystermen, especially on the Connecticut natural beds, also

The *Nena A. Rowland*, one of the biggest oyster sloops in northern waters during the last fifty years of oystering, under sail in Narragansett Bay around 1900. Courtesy of Henry Treat.

preferred to own boats under five tons gross because the custom house license fee began at that figure.

Traditionally northern oyster boats were centerboarders that "drifted" while dredging. Good design, correct alignment of the centers of sail area, and lateral resistance with proper adjustment of the centerboard combined to produce a boat that would drift well. Most oystermen believed that only a centerboard boat could hold a drift. Actually keel boats like the Friendship sloop possessed advantages for oystering not found in centerboarders: they drift if properly handled and have no centerboard trunk to leak. When very close to shore or over shelving bottom the keel boat has maneuverability at all times even after bumping bottom. The centerboard boat skipper tends to raise the centerboard gradually while inshore to the point where he loses maneuverability. Light draft boats were, nevertheless, a necessity in the shallow Great South Bay and inshore Connecticut. A centerboarder was also appreciated because its long, straight keel and shoal draft permitted easy and inexpensive beaching for painting and repairs which most oystermen did themselves.

The lower the freeboard—from about amidships aft—the better. Dredges were lifted by hand and since the weight of anything increases when it is lifted out of the water, every inch saved in lifting above water eased the work. Dredges were not worked forward of the mast, so freeboard here was usually ample to insure a dry boat. Local sea conditions and the builder's notions determined the amount of freeboard forward.

The sloop with gaff main and jib was established early as standard rig for oyster boats. Main gaff topsails and jib topsails were used for running to market but were generally considered too much of a nuisance while dredging except in light airs. As a rule the oyster boats were too small for anything but the simple sloop or cat rig, yet the sail area had to be sufficiently large to sail the boat in light airs, powerful enough to pull from one to about eight hand dredges, but not too unwieldly for one to four men to handle. Since the burdensome hulls also demanded a sufficiently powerful sail plan to move them, sail area was usually large, but three rows of reef points were standard on the sloops to take care of heavy winds. Long, high peaked gaffs were common after about 1890. This meant that the boat would tend to point into the wind—a most desirable feature when dredging.

The shape of the hull, stern, and bow depended upon local traditions evolved by generations of dreaming, thinking, working men. The same held true for countless other details of rig and construction, unfortunately most of it lost to us forever through lack of documentation. It was usual to see full length (no butts) native oak or longleaf yellow pine planking and frames of sawed oak and/or chestnut on the older boats. The transom and keel were oak and the spars pine or fir.

Except for one or two sailing clammers working out of Keyport, New Jersey, as late as 1967, the age of commercial sail north of New York came to a melancholy end at Bridgeport, Connecticut, in the 1950s. Here the last fleet of sailing oystermen dredged for seed on the nearly exhausted Bridgeport-Stratford natural oyster bed. For over a century preceding, oyster boats of the New York model (all three types), as well as craft indigenous to other sections of the eastern coast from the Chesapeake to Maine worked on these and other

Connecticut natural beds. A study, therefore, of these Connecticut boats will cover most of the significant northern types.

The most common and probably oldest type oyster dredge boat of the last century and a half was the decked sloop with cabin aft and hold forward—type number three. And the model recognized as superior by Connecticut oystermen (and others) was one they called the "south-sider"—the Long Island bayman's sloop built for shellfishing on the south side of Long Island in Great South Bay. The larger sizes resembled in many respects the "carry away sloops" of Long Island, the scallop dredgers, and the menhaden fishing sloops of Greenport, the Keyport clammers, and common market boats of New York Bay. Differences appeared mainly in some proportions and details: in reality they were all close sisters. South-siders were built in various sizes with a variety of options. The larger models were over 35 feet, all either gaff cats or regular jib and mainsail sloops, usually with the old style clipper bow and counter stern. They were beamy, shallow boats having little freeboard aft but ample amount forward. Usually the tiller was long enough for someone sitting in the companionway to reach it, but a wheel was sometimes used instead.

A fine example of a big, old successful south-sider was the *Ann Gertrude*, long known and admired by Connecticut oystermen. Built in Patchogue in 1851 by either Oliver Perry Smith or Charles Baker, she was in Connecticut by 1894 where for many years she remained under the capable ownership of Benjamin F. Palmer of Greenwich. Her principal custom house dimensions were: 44-foot length, 16-foot beam, and 4 feet 4 inches depth, 14 tons gross and 13 tons net. Not only was she one of the oldest craft on the beds, but she had the distinction of having oystered longer than any other Connecticut sailing vessel. Her last owner, Earle Svertesky, worked her right to the very end of the fishery (sailing) in the mid-1950s.

Another large, old south-sider was the *J.F. Penny*, built in Moriches, Long Island, in 1884. She was owned by the Ventuletts of Bridgeport from 1935 until she was destroyed in a gasoline explosion in the 1940s. Her principal custom house measurements were: 45 feet 2 inches length, 16 feet 5 inches beam, 5-foot depth, 17 tons gross, 16 net tons, carrying capacity up to 1,000 bushels of oysters.

Two examples of medium sized south-siders on the Bridgeport-Stratford natural beds were the *Priscilla* and the *Ally Ray*, both built side by side in the same, but unknown, Patchogue yard in the winter of 1887 to 1888. *Priscilla* has had at least nine Connecticut owners oystering her since 1896, and oystermen have always regarded her as a moneymaker and an able, fast and "smart" boat. Her principal measurements are: 39-feet 7 inches length, 14-feet beam, 4-foot 2 inches depth, 10 tons gross, 9 tons net, and oyster capacity of 250 bushels. Incidentally, her present owner, John Woodside of Wappingers Falls, New York, sailed her with a skipjack rig to Maine and to the Bahamas without incident. Not bad for an old girl in her eighties!

The *Ally Ray* came to Connecticut in 1894 and had only three owners, a good testimony of her ability: Charles Ford, Harry Anderson and John Wagner. Her measurements were: 36-foot length, 12-foot 8 inch beam, 3-foot 2 inch depth, 6.85 gross tons, 6.51 net tons.

The smaller vessels from the Great South Bay, those used as clam boats and oyster tongers by the baymen, were generally unsuitable for Long Island Sound dredging because of their size. They were usually below 25 feet L.O.A. undecked or one-half decked with plumb stems and counter sterns, short bowsprits, and perhaps small cabins forward or sometimes aft. Oystermen tonged from these craft while anchored on beds located near their homes and overnight accommodations, therefore, were not generally needed. Baymen with more distant markets and summer tourists in mind constructed larger cats and sloops quite similar in most respects but 26 to about 30 feet or more in length.

Long Island boat builders on the south side were of English and Dutch heritage, whose ancestors had produced boats for generations. Their designs were satisfactorily tested by time and highly respected by all baymen. They turned out these New York models in untold numbers for over a century, and the Great South Bay, in particular, demanded the services of the small boat builders decades longer than did any surrounding locality, not only because of its unique marine environment but also possibly due to its isolation from the influence of industrial surroundings. The fame of south-side builders was such that when Connecticut oystermen wanted a suitable, well-constructed, handsome vessel, they headed directly for Patchogue—the workboat building center of Great South Bay.

Among the numerous builders here Oliver Perry Smith and his son Martenus stand out in particular. Oliver Perry built nineteen oyster sloops from twenty to forty tons burden between 1850 and 1872. These rather large craft probably freighted oysters or ran them to the New York market. He is known also for his speedy coasters and fruit schooners such as the *R. H. Vermilyea*, which made a fast trip from Cuba to New York in only six days. Another schooner, *Phebe (11)*, made the fastest passage from the San Blas Islands, near Panama, to New York—in twelve days![2] The illustrious schooner *Australia*, now exhibited at Mystic Seaport, is credited, though not yet fully authenticated, as being one of his vessels. His son, Martenus, preferred small workboats and turned out a couple a year for the baymen. Although oyster sloops were his specialty, a number of coasting schooners also left his yard, notably the *Grace Bailey*, built in 1882 and recently sailing with the Camden, Maine, dude fleet as the *Mattie*.

Another Patchogue firm well known for its yachts as well as work boats was Samuel C. Wicks and Son. Other builders from this locality included George Miller; Forrest, Charles and Filmore Baker; George Bishop; DeWitt Conklin. Other boat builders on the bay were Ottis Palmer of East Moriches, the Post brothers of Bellport, Sam Newey of Brookhaven, and Young of Great River. It would be difficult to record all the oyster boat builders on Long Island, for they all worked hard without fanfare and almost to a man left few if any records. Even the countless half models they cut have become the victims of time and the bonfire.

Connecticut oystermen, however, drew from two other localities on Long Island for their boats—Greenport and the North Shore (the communities from New York City to Port Jefferson). The same traditional configuration of cabin aft, hatch forward, was retained, but a huskier vessel with more freeboard and draft evolved. On the North Shore four names come to mind: the Harts (Pryor, Erastus, and Oliver) of Northport; Chas G. Sammis of Huntington; William Bedell of Glenwood (later of Stratford, Connecticut); and the Bayles' of Port Jefferson. They built not only oyster boats but also steamers, yachts, oyster schooners, and sloops. On the eastern end of the island, the Percy Tuttle Shipyard of Greenport built powered vessels, among them the oyster steamers *Magician* and *Wizard*. A fabulous story still being circulated concerning this shipyard tells of the rebuilding of the sloop *Nena A. Rowland* "around one piece of stem you can hold in your hand." Tuthill & Higbee and others as well built, converted, and repaired oyster boats in Greenport.

When scalloping petered out in Peconic Bay after World War I, a few scallop dredges like the *Modesty* found their way into Connecticut. *Modesty* was built by Wood and Chute of Greenport, New York, in 1923 and modeled after an old sloop built in the Great South Bay and called the *Honest*. She is a south-sider type designed to oyster and scallop, and was one of the last two sailing workboats built on Long Island. She is now owned and sailed by Leo Fagan of Stratford, Connecticut.

The Elsworth family of New York City were oystermen and yachtsmen, and one, Captain Philip Eleworth, was a designer. He modeled, among others, the famous schooner yachts *Montauk* and *Grayling*, and the oyster sloops *Ad-*

miral, Lieutenant, and *Commodore* which were later converted to power dredgers. At Tottenville, Staten Island, A. C. Brown & Sons and J. S. Ellis & Son were considered among the finest shipbuilders in the East. A. C. Brown built an oyster boat for a Connecticut oyster company in 1907 that does not appear on the roster in the back of this book. The day before the *Limit* was to be launched she and the yard burned. Brown continued to build, however, until 1932 when the demand for wooden ships fell, forcing him out of business. Although the yard built oyster boats, it was better known for its tugs, barges, and scows. Among these were the wrecking steamers *Relief, Rescue,* and the two *I. E. Merritts* for the Merritt, Chapman & Scott Corporation of New York.

Another prominent boatbuilding center in New York was City Island, long noted for serving yachtsmen and oystermen alike. There Benjamin Barstow built small tonging skiffs—a variation of the Staten Island skiff—for the local oystermen. However, many oyster sloops were also built there, particularly before the turn of the century, although the names of the builders have not been remembered nor apparently recorded.

A look at the north side of Long Island Sound reveals Connecticut boatyards producing models similar to those of Long Island's North Shore. The Chards of Greenwich designed and built workboats including the 34-foot oyster sloop *Susie C*, built on Brush Island (Greenwich) in 1894 by Samuel Chard. Later, incidentally, she was cut in half and lengthened 6 feet making her about 40 feet L.O.A.—a common practice in those days. William Chard, who learned his trade at the Palmer and Duff shipyard in Cos Cob, built the *Guiding Star* and the Southport, Connecticut, "onion schooner" *Mary Elizabeth,* the Stony Creek, Connecticut, schooner *James H. Holdane,* and the Hudson River packet *Locomotive.* The last boat built by the Chards and indeed the last sailing oyster boat built in Connecticut and in fact anywhere north of New York is the *Hope,* designed and built by Stanley Chard in 1948. She was built of oak from trees fallen in a severe northwest storm in 1945. Her design is rather unusual, in that she has regular round sides carvel planked above the waterline, but below she has a v-bottom.

Dexter Cole of Rowayton, Connecticut, later of Northport, New York, was one of the early oyster boat builders. His *Harp,* built in 1873, was considered by many to be one of the best oyster sloops on the sound. He also designed the *Supervisor* in Northport, one of the largest steamers specifically designed to oyster.

John Richards of South Norwalk, a contemporary of Cole, gained a fine reputation in Connecticut for building excellent workboats of all types and sizes. His best known oyster sloop, the previously mentioned *Nena A. Rowland*, built in 1883, was dubbed by oystermen the "queen of the sound." Three even larger vessels from Richard's yard were the oyster steamers *Falcon, Henry J*, and *Medea*—the last two are still afloat, both nearly ninety years old.

Richards also built a series of small boats—either for pleasure or work—that resembled the popular sandbaggers of his day. They were of the open deck type, 22, 24, and 26 feet long, although some oystermen later erected shelter cabins just abaft the mast. Though small they were quite seaworthy and more preferred in Connecticut than the similar sized tonging craft of Great South Bay. *Beatrice* (nicknamed *Dishpan*), *Mayflower*, and *Tiger* (early) were typical of this type.

Closely associated with this sandbagger or "rudder-out-doors" style in Connecticut was Commodore Francis Burritt of South Norwalk. He commissioned the building of quite a few of them, some of which he designed himself, and invariably raced them in the local and New York regattas. After a season or two he sold the newest one to oystermen—usually those who crewed for him. Then an improved model was built and the procedure repeated. John Richards retained Burritt as a steady client and supplied him with such boats as the *Champion, Broadbill*, and *Teal*. Incidentally, the *Teal*, since then, has been lengthened and even widened by being split in two down her length, a rather unusual feat. She has subsequently been converted to a regular power boat, with a big pilot house aft, and is still dredging oysters in Connecticut.

A small yacht yard in Bridgeport run by Henry B. Robbins and his son William seems also to have catered to Burritt's passion for sandbaggers. This is the same yard that in 1902 hauled the most famous oyster boat of them all—Joshua Slocum's world-circling *Spray*.

Frank Burritt's quest for speed also led him to the well-known yard of Tom Webber of New Rochelle, who built for him the *Amateur*, whose half model Burritt cut. She is believed to have been one of the few sandbaggers with a counter stern. After a couple of seasons of yachting and racing Burritt sold her to Captain Bill Lewis, oysterman and Connecticut Shell-Fish Commissioner. Under meticulous care and unusual skill the *Amateur* earned the title of one of the fastest oyster boats in Connecticut.

One of the best, yet scarcely recognized and remembered, boat designers of the sandbagger era was Christopher "Crit" Smith of Bridgeport. Though he was by occupation a natural growth oysterman, he designed many sailing craft of the sandbagger type. One of his designs was the aforementioned *Tiger* that once raced the *Bella* of Brooklyn. It was reported to be the first and last time

The *Tiger* in Southport, Connecticut: an open-type sloop with a cuddy cabin forward. She was probably the best-known converted sandbagger in Long Island Sound. Courtesy of Pequot Library.

A typical John Richards sandbagger in South Norwalk. These boats were frequently used for oystering when their racing days were over. Courtesy of Fred Lovejoy.

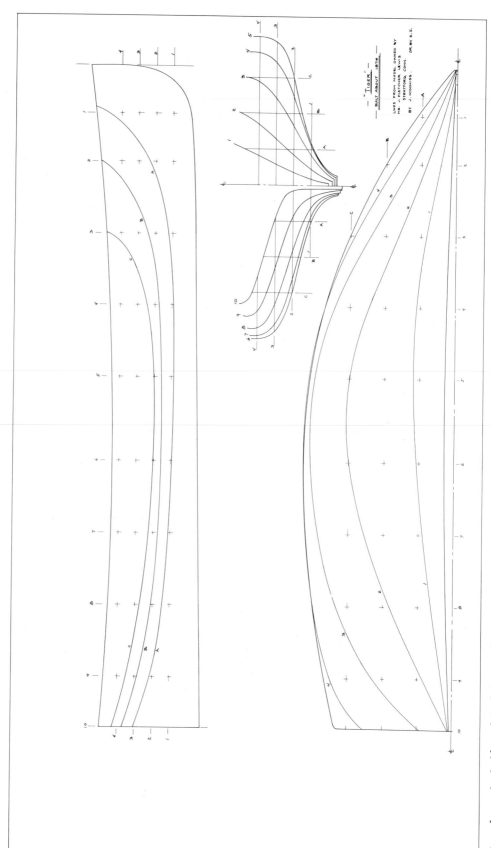

"TIGER"
BUILT ABOUT 1874

LINES FROM MODEL OWNED BY
MR. J. FLETCHER, LEWIS
STRATFORD, CONN.
BY J. KOCHISS.   DR. BY E.S.

Lines from the half model of the sandbagger-type oyster sloop *Tiger*.

Smith's boats lost a race. He also designed, all by half model, the sandbaggers *Pearl, Americus, Quickstep, Rival, Rippel, Whisper, Remona, Shadow* (built by Robbins and still active in 1972), and *E.Z. Sloat* (later converted to a shell-kicker). His designs also included some yachts such as the *Maggie B*, once owned by Tom Thumb and, as to be expected, a number of oyster sloops: the *C.D. Smith* (named after him), *Arrow, Broadbill, Pearl* (the second), *Rescue,* and the *Eaglet.*

Remarkably enough, after the 1870s or 1880s the bustling city of Bridgeport, in the very heart of the oyster industry, did not have any small sailing oyster-boat builders—unless a few backyard projects are considered. However, the Greene Brothers made up for it with power dredgers. Three brothers from Maine, Reuben, Ben and Fred Greene, settled in Bridgeport and soon concentrated on building powered oyster boats such as the *Climax* and *X-Ray*—two of the first gas boats built in Connecticut. They also built three large schooners, the *P.T. Barnum, Sylvia C. Hall* and *Greenleaf Johnson*, and the four-masted *Perry Setzer*, built in 1902. At the launching of the *Perry Setzer* the ways gave out under her, and the financial problems resulting therefrom apparently forced the brothers back home to Maine. Their well-equipped yard was eventually acquired by Simon Lake and his Lake Torpedo Boat Co. In addition to the submarines which made the yard famous, a few wooden work boats were built. One of these was the oyster steamer *Smith Bros.* (the second). Like the *Perry Setzer*, the largest sailing vessel built in Bridgeport, the *Smith Bros.* went a peg higher: she was the largest oyster steamer built in Connecticut.

After the 1880s, New Haven marked the eastern end of Connecticut dredge-boat building. A few were built farther up the sound, but as a rule only sharpies were produced there. E. M. Thatcher built some working sloops including the *Eaglet* in 1900. Crit Smith designed her from the half model of the *Eagle*, a square-sterned sandbagger from Bridgeport. These boats were quite similar except the *Eaglet* was built with a counter stern.

Besides Thatcher, John H. Mar & Son of West Haven and the Wyman shipyard of Fair Haven built and repaired oyster boats. George M. Graves, also of Fair Haven, who bought his yard from George Baldwin, a schooner builder, was one of the oldest and best builders in Connecticut. The *Luzerne Luddington, Gordon Rowe,* and *Emily Mansfield* are good examples of his excellent work.

Frank Anderson of Maryland, West Haven, and West Mystic, Connecticut, designed some boats, notably the *Clara C. Raye* in West Haven in 1931. John Alden, the noted Boston naval architect, used her as a guide when he designed the sisterships *General* and *Harvester.*

Three stages of the *Henry Ruppell*: as built in 1892 as a typical South-sider with trunk cabin aft and hold forward and carrying about 250 to 280 bushels. Courtesy of Mystic Seaport.

The *Henry Ruppell* in 1938 with the hold opened up, the trunk cabin removed and a small cabin built forward. Then she carried 300 bushels. Courtesy of George Chase, Jr.

The *Henry Ruppell* in 1970—with more changes and a diesel engine, she carried 500 bushels. Photograph by the author.

One of the most popular oyster boat builders in Connecticut and New York for more than a half century was William Bedell's shipyard in Stratford. Bedell's life and work, as written up in a local newspaper article, was typical of the shipbuilders of western Long Island Sound:

William Edward Bedell was born at Port Jefferson, Long Island, May 15, 1847. . . . While spending his youthful days under the parental roof, [he] attended the public schools at Glenwood, Long Island, for ten years. Later he went to work in his father's shipyard at Glenwood, thus acquainting himself with the business in principle and detail. . . . [Bedell] purchased the Peter White shipyard at the foot of Broad Street, Stratford, and carried on the business under the Bedell name until his death in December, 1924, at the age of 77 years. It is said that he built enough ships to reach from Stratford to New York if placed end to end. . . . During his career Mr. Bedell built about 90 vessels of various kinds propelled by steam, gas, and sail. Among the largest of these was the *Comanche* (a quarantine boat of New York City), the *Governor*, and the *Seba*, which were large oyster boats, and the yachts of Rose A. and Sarah Vreeland. He also built the *Rhoda Crane*, the *Sea Gull*, and the *Guess,* which were in the coastwide trade up and down Long Island Sound.[3]

Every boat, like every man, had special characteristics and almost a personality. Some were handsome, some were smart, dumb, fast, or average; others were so slow they couldn't, as the saying goes, get out of their own way. Some could hold a drift and others could not. Some were heavy air boats like the *Jewel*, that kept full sail when most others had to reef. A few, like the *Henry Ruppel*, were excellent light air boats that kept on working while the rest remained anchored to their dredges.

Of all the boats in the Connecticut fleet at the turn of the century, the *Samuel C. Bond* shared honors with the *Amateur* as perhaps the best sail boat in all-around qualities—looks, speed, and ability to work. Her owner, incidentally, Ashabel Bond, one of Connecticut's oyster pioneers, launched the *Samuel C. Bond* at Bond's Dock in Stratford. Initially she served a short time as a yacht, then was converted to a workboat. She may be considered one of the finest examples of a Connecticut working sloop at the end of the age of commercial sail.

The Long Island and Connecticut versions of the "New York sloop" predominated in the Long Island Sound oyster fleets. Other types filled in the ranks at various times, but few oystermen adopted them: these included the Noank and Friendship sloops, Delaware Bay oyster schooners, Chesapeake skipjacks, home-builts and mongrels. The most significant aspect of the use of these boats was that the skippers of some proved, at least to themselves, that other types could be employed successfully on Long Island Sound.

Almost every boat building area on Long Island had its own sailmakers. Sometimes they were closely associated with the builders, Samuel C. Wicks & Son of Patchogue and Charles Miller, for instance, whose sail loft was located directly above their shop. But much of the time they were independent, such as Frank C. Brown, also of Patchogue, and Frank Mills of Greenport.

The most prominent and virtually the only sailmaker of Connecticut for the last half century of oystering was Frank F. Upson of New Haven. He learned his trade in the 1880s at the Van Name & King loft on Long Wharf in that city, and in the 1890s opened his own business, continuing to make sails for the last of the schooners and almost all of the Connecticut natural growthers until about 1951. The only other sailmakers were James Cahill of Cos Cob (originally from East Street in New York) in the 1890s and Harrington and Whitney of Bridgeport, at least for oyster boats.

CHAPTER 8

The Sailing Freighters

N oyster boat generally functioned either as a harvester or freighter of oysters, and almost from the beginning of the oyster industry men tended to specialize in one or the other. It was rare, for example, to find a captain engaging in the southern trade in the spring and dredging oysters in another season. For one thing, the big freighters were not suitable for catching oysters; for another, the two activities attracted men of different temperaments. Freighter captains were men of the sea. Since trips lasted days or weeks, much of their life was was spent away from home. The harvester never went beyond bay, estuary, or sound: he lived at home most of the time and was seldom more than a few days away.

When oysters were still plentiful in New England during colonial days, freighting them locally was not a major problem. Small keel sloops performed the duty quite well. In Boston, however, the lively trade in oysters from Wellfleet required larger sloops and two-masted schooners. All were keel vessels of about forty-tons burden recruited from the local Wellfleet and Provincetown fishing fleets. They fished for mackerel in the summer and freighted oysters in the winter. For this a burdensome, but not necessarily swift, vessel was needed since the loading and unloading ports were not far apart.

After the oyster beds gave out at Cape Cod in 1775, oysters were shipped from Buzzards Bay, Narragansett Bay, and Long Island Sound, bedded at Wellfleet for a few months and then transshipped to Boston as before. Around 1830 or 1840, however, when the high–priced southern New England oysters forced Wellfleet dealers to the Chesapeake for their supply, faster and larger vessels were demanded. Oysters faced increased difficulties in surviving the long distances, and a short passage time became imperative. A fast or clipper-type model developed with emphasis on a long, sharp, beamy, shallow hull with a large sail area. In 1849 Samuel Hall of East Boston designed the *Express* and the *Telegraph*, each 100 tons, for the Wellfleet oyster-mackerel fishery.[1] They are reputed to be the first clipper fishing schooners built.

Lines of identifiable Wellfleet schooners are rare to come by, but those of the *Etta G. Fogg* may be representative of these early two-masted clipper schooners. She was built by Charles O. Story of Essex, Massachusetts in 1857. Her principle dimensions were: 94 feet 9 inches moulded length at rail, 24 feet extreme beam, 8 feet 8 inches depth in hold, 10 feet 4 inches draft at stern and 107.25 tons burden, oyster capacity around three thousand bushels.[2]

The evolving Wellfleet type eventually approached unsafe proportions, and by 1890 new and more seaworthy schooners appeared in the fishing fleets. Also by this time the dwindling oyster schooner trade had succumbed to powered vessels and the railroad.

Ernest Ingersoll has some interesting comments about the Wellfleet schooner:

> The original cost of these fine vessels was, on the average, about $7,000; now they are not worth over $4,000 each. In summer they go on mackerel-fishing voyages, which occupy a little more than half of the year. In winter and spring they carry oysters, varying it with frequent coasting trips. Four voyages after oysters annually would probably be a fair average, and not more than a third of the vessels' yearly receipts, as a rule, will be derived from this source. They are commanded by captains of experience, and go back and forth quickly, safely, and profitably. Capt. Jesse Freeman, now one of the leading fish-merchants of the village, told me that he had sailed between the Chesapeake and northern ports 316 times before he was forty years old, that is 158 voyages. His opinion was that no cargo wore upon a vessel less (others say the opposite), and it was usually of much profit to the owners. In the spring, oysters for bedding are brought cheaper than those designed for market in winter.
>
> The crew of an oyster-vessel usually consists of two (often three) men before the mast, with a cook, mate and captain. One-third (as a rule), sometimes one-half, of the freight money goes to the owners, and the remainder to pay

The *Three Sisters* in the foreground and the *Mary Chapin* on the right in Wellfleet in 1882. They went mackerel fishing in the summer and carried oysters to Cape Cod from Chesapeake Bay in the winter and spring. Courtesy of Earle Rich.

> the men and furnish food. The wages of a mate in 1879 were $30 a month; of a cook, $25; and of a seaman, $15 to $16. Food for a voyage costs from $40 to $50. In addition to his share, the owners give the captain $15 a month.[3]

These rugged Wellfleet schooners were really deep–sea craft more at home on the ocean than on the bay or sound. Another schooner type, better suited to the relatively protected waters lying between New York and Cape Cod, was adopted by oystermen of these regions. They hauled almost everything but fish: pig iron, coal, brick, lumber, sand, gravel, granite, shells, cordwood, fertilizers, tile, horses hoofs (for glue), brownstones (for New York City homes), even horse manure.

The vessels (variously called coasting schooners, Long Island Sound freighters, carriers, runners, or simply freighters) were centerboarders as a rule, unlike their keel sisters at Wellfleet. Centerboarders possessed considerable versatility. Their shallow draft and long straight keel allowed them to rest on a beach between tides to load cargoes such as cordwood or sand for foundries, and for repairs. Such a capacity to beach gave them greater ability to get cargoes. And light draft had the added advantage of permitting the schooner to sail in shallow inlets and bays.

Steven Horkay, a New York ship broker, told a story of Fire Island Gut which points up this advantage. Jacob Ockers of Great South Bay, owner of four or five schooners around 1900, used to charge two cents extra on a bushel of oysters when going through the Gut, because the low water at Fire Island Bar (seven feet) made sailing hazardous. Often schooner captains would talk about this particular passage in Mr. Horkay's office down at the Battery:

"We had a nor'easter."

"How is the bar?"

"We made it okay but bumped two or three times."

Oysters as a rule freighted at five cents a bushel and shells at three cents a bushel around 1900.

Centerboarders always had wide decks, not only to insure stability but to contain the cargo. Oysters and other freight were preferably carried on deck instead of in the hold in order to avoid unnecessary lifting. Decks were wide enough to take the entire bulk of the cargo, with just enough stowed below for stability and ballast.

Western Long Island Sound freighters needed to be maneuverable and reasonably fast, as much of the time they worked the crowded inshore areas of Great South Bay or New York City where only a relatively small vessel could perform well. The size of an inshore freighter was therefore the result of the owner's or builder's compromise between a vessel large enough to pay its way in freight and small enough for ease in handling.

Two-masted schooners and the oyster freighters were synonymous in the eyes of the oystermen. Yet large sloops similar in hull shape to the schooners also plied the waters of southern New England with oysters. However, their immense rigs—difficult to handle, especially with a limited crew—kept their numbers down appreciably. The equally large or larger two-masted schooners with smaller, handier, easily managed sails, however, remained the favorite rig until the end of commercial sail.

Another freighter type came from the Chesapeake. The old Virginia oyster trade between Chesapeake Bay and New England that commenced shortly after 1800 enlisted schooners from both places. Those originating in the Chesapeake —the pungy, and oyster schooners of the Baltimore clipper type—were basically

The 56-foot oyster freighter *Alida Hearn*, which worked in the north but was built in Chesapeake Bay at Pocomoke City, Maryland, in 1885. Courtesy of Robert Beattie.

The 71-foot oyster freighter *George S. Page* at the Andrew Radel Oyster Company in South Norwalk, Connecticut. She was built in Astoria, New York, in 1868 and hailed at one time from Patchogue, New York. Courtesy of August MacTaggart.

identical to the northern model, yet their beautiful, long clipper-style bows and wide, square sterns stamped them unmistakably as southern.

Captains of general freighters were for the most part independent managing owners. A few big oyster companies, however, owned their own schooners. The so-called buy boats that purchased seed from the natural growthers were either company boats or chartered from individual schooner owners. Captains searched for charters themselves but often solicited the services of a New York broker who usually charged a 5 percent commission (around 1900).

The oyster freighter *Henrietta Collyer* was built in Nyack, New York, in 1880, and hailed from New Haven. Courtesy of Captain Irving DeWick.

The 90-foot freighter *J. Lloyd Hawkridge* was built in Milford, Delaware, in 1905. Most of her work was freighting oysters and other cargo in the Long Island Sound area. Courtesy of Richard Simpson.

CHAPTER 9

Powered Oyster Boats

STEAM power needed three-quarters of a century to penetrate the oyster industry or any fishery for that matter, except perhaps the menhaden. When Peter Decker of Norwalk installed a small steam plant in his sloop *Early Bird* in 1874, he ushered in a new era that revolutionized oystering. Within a decade steam power "sunk sail craft into utter insignificance."[1]

The idea was not completely original with Decker. Some fifteen years before a "prodigious bed of oysters" set New York and Connecticut in a "bivalve fever."[2] One or two steamers among 214 sailing vessels rushed to the find as if to a gold mine. This is the earliest known mention of steamers dredging for oysters though they apparently were not full-time oyster boats but rather borrowed from another service. An any rate, entire credit goes to the *Early Bird* for being the first fully steam-powered oyster boat. Initially, a boiler and engine turned the drums on which the dredge lines were hauled while sails continued to drive the boat, but shortly afterwards Decker attached a small propeller run by the same engine and the first completely powered oyster boat was created. Decker had this to say about his brain child:

> In 1869, I invented a drum with gearing attached to make easy the hauling of oyster dredges. One of these drums was placed on board of the sloop *Peri*, owned by my brother, Captain Abram Decker. In 1870, the burning of

a factory at South Norwalk left a small engine without use, and it was bought and placed on board of the *Peri* to wind the drum, and thus haul in the dredges. The following year I put a like hoisting appartus on my own sloop, the *Early Bird*, a vessel of eight and a half tons old measurement. Both sloops still used sail to propel them. The next year a propeller was added, but sails were still used to supplement the power of the boat. It was thought that propulsion by steam would prove impracticable in oyster dredging. Men wondered how I could steer the boat, and claimed that the dredges would render the boat unmanageable. This was the case with a powerful steamer, built in 1876 at City Island. This steamer was built with a very broad stern, and attempted to tow six dredges, all fastened to the stern. She proved a failure. But about the year 1874, I put in a large wheel, boiler, and engine, discarded sails, retained the same hoisting gear, put out a single dredge well forward on each side, and the problem of steam oyster dredging was solved.

It is often desirable to wash the oysters in the dredges before they are landed on the deck of the steamer. This is done by raising and lowering the dredge a short distance when the dredge is brought up near the surface. We formerly had trouble in so doing, as we uesd a positive clutch on the drum, and it was difficult to release the dredge chains. But now friction clutches obviate this trouble. The dredges used on the *Early Bird*, before the sails were taken out, weighed about eighteen pounds, and would haul, when full, about a bushel. The dredges in use on my new steamer weigh one hundred pounds, and a full bag will bring in five bushels.

At first the law allowed me to work two days in the week on the natural beds. The next year I was not allowed to dredge west of Black Rock. The next year all dredging by steam on the natural beds was made illegal.

In 1876, Joshua Levinniss, of City Island, built the steamer already alluded to. In 1877, Messrs. Albert A. Geib and William Lockwood, of Norwalk, had the steamer *Enterprise* built. This steamer is still in use, and is now owned by New Haven planters. The following year the steamer *W.H. Lockwood* was built for Captain Henry S. Lockwood of Greenwich. This steamer is now owned by a New Haven firm. The *Early Bird* was sold by Captain Decker some years ago. She was in regular use and without change till about one year ago when it was found one morning that a fire had made her unfit for future use.[3]

The Connecticut natural growthers immediately recognized the superior working capabilities of the steamers, but they also feared they would deplete and destroy the beds in time. Furthermore, power placed the sail owners at a decided disadvantage which would inevitably drive them out of work. Their complaints reached the state legislature, which in 1879 restricted the employment of power boats on the natural beds throughout the year to only one week. Continued objections led to the complete ban of steam boats on the public beds the following year. This law, similar to those on the Chesapeake and Delaware bays, was the sole force that kept commercial sail alive.

The fourth oyster steamer built—in Norwalk in 1878—and the one referred to by Decker was the popular *William H. Lockwood.* Her skipper and owner, Henry C. Rowe, the acknowledged oyster monarch of Connecticut, described her:

> She has a length of 63 feet; a beam of 16 feet; depth of hold of 5 feet; draws 5 1/2 feet of water aft and 2 1/2 feet forward. The machinery is placed well aft and the oyster room amidships; the pilot house is on the hurricane deck. She has a double hoisting engine for hauling in the oysters, and also a very large engine for propelling the boat. Iron blocks and chains are used to haul the dredges. On either side of the boat are two doors provided with a roller, over which the dredge chains run smoothly. The propelling engine is 11 by 11 inches and the hoister 5 by 7 inches.[4]

An account in the journal *Sea World* of August 4, 1879, supplied more details:

> The most efficient and convenient oyster steamer in the country, and perhaps in the world, is that owned by H.C. Rowe, of Fair Haven, Connecticut. She is housed over to protect men and oysters from exposure to storm, sun, and cold, and can work in the coldest weather. She works four large dredges and when running full blast employs 10 men, and takes up 500 bushels a day in 35 feet of water. She is a new boat, having been run about a year. Her boiler is larger and her engine more powerful than usual in a boat of her size, and she can therefore be used for towing, and can force her way through heavy ice in the winter, so that her owner is sure of a supply of oysters for his customers when other dealers may be unable with sailing vessels to get them. Especially is this greatly valuable in connection with the European trade, her owner keeping informed by cable of the state of the market, and taking up and shipping large quantities when the market is high in Liverpool and London. Besides her regular propelling engine she has a double engine for hauling dredges, which hauls all four dredges full of oysters at once and lands them on deck, two on each side. She costs $6,500. To an oysterman like Mr. Rowe, who cultivates miles of ground and takes up 7,000 bushels in a month, such a boat is of immense convenience.[5]

Those first steamers were surely a convenience compared to sail, saving tremendous amounts of time and labor. Oyster cultivators soon followed the example of pioneers like Rowe and Lockwood, but not without some hesitation. During the early 1870s, out of jealousy, fear, or tradition, they opposed the steamer on the grounds that its use, among other things, would ruin the oyster bottoms. Proper handling of the dredge did not ruin the beds unduly and by the 1880s steam proved itself completely acceptable. Oystermen abandoned sail, had steamers built, and henceforward relied solely upon power. The oyster steamboat era had begun.

Oystering pressed ahead under steam for over one-quarter of a century. Those steamer days paralleled the heyday of the northern industry. But time and events have a way of changing things: by about 1906, when one of the last and the biggest oyster steamer built—the *Standard*—was launched, that smokey, puffy era had reached its peak. A few other steamers were built at this time, notably the *Supervisor*, and older ones continued to work alongside the gas and diesel vessels that ultimately replaced them, but steamboat building had ended before World War I.

During those bustling decades the steamboat was justifiably the pride of northern oystermen. On Delaware Bay, in the Chesapeake and farther south, oystermen, being reluctant to cultivate their own naturally abundant oyster reefs as the North was doing, were content to stay with sail. The North, therefore, could and did boast of having the largest oyster steamer fleet afloat and indeed owned the biggest oyster steamer in the world, the 142-foot *Rowe* of New Haven.

Though steamers were universally accepted, only the more prosperous companies were able to afford them at first. Yet the cost of steamers in those days appears ridiculously low to us today. According to the Connecticut Bureau of Labor Statistics of 1889, they ranged from $2,000 to $4,000 depending on construction, quality, and size variations of 30 to 95 feet. Big, heavy boats, however, have always been relatively costly, and oyster steamers were often large in order to hold the engine, boiler, water, and coal and yet have enough carrying capacity for a thriving business. Ordinarily they ran from a little under 50 feet to somewhat over 100 feet overall. The average size was in the 70-foot range. A marine steam power plant required up to 50 percent more room than gasoline or diesel engines. This is not meant to imply, however, that a steamer must always be huge; the *Early Bird* was fairly small and so were others. At any rate the industry was prospering and scores of steamers of all sizes were built for companies from New York to Boston.

The well-known oyster steamer *Supervisor*. Courtesy of Hitchcock Gas Engine Company.

The first powered oyster boat, the *Early Bird* of South Norwalk, Connecticut, carried 350 bushels. Photograph from *Annual Report of the Shell-Fish Commissioners, State of Connecticut,* 1901.

The *Richard W. Law*, an enclosed or houseboat-type oyster steamer. Courtesy of Hitchcock Gas Engine Company.

These saucy little ships somewhat resembled the tugs and small passenger screw steamers of the day. Builders apparently copied their already tested and established power hull form and house structures, but early in the steamer age two main types developed that set the general style for the following half century. Although vessels, except perhaps sisterships, varied in size, accommodations, construction, and other details, they all fell into what might be called the enclosed and the open deck types. In the enclosed or "houseboat" type, well represented by Rowe's old *William H. Lockwood* and the *Richard W. Law*, another New Haven boat, the house extended—except for a short foredeck and shorter afterdeck—the full length of the vessel. The oysters were carried on the main deck inside this house structure, thereby establishing the real reason for the design—full protection for the oysters (not the men) in any weather. In many of the boats the house rose up at the rail, while in others the house sides began on deck a few feet in from the rail, thus allowing walking and cargo space around the deck outside the cabin. A pilot house was positioned on top and on the forward end of the house. Below it, out of the pilot's direct vision, stood the dredge post from which the dredges were hauled. The ordinary oyster boat had one dredge post hauling two dredges, one on each side. However, some of the bigger steamers, gas and diesel boats, carried two dredge posts, located some distance apart along the boat's centerline, that hauled four dredges. The giant steamer *Rowe* and a few others pulled six dredges on three posts—the most any boat ever employed.

The pilot could not ordinarily see the dredge post and, therefore, did not control the hoisting of the dredges in this type steamer: this was handled by a man on the deck inside. The dredge came aboard by vertical and horizontal rollers on the gunwale through gangways (wide, swinging or sliding doors on the house on both sides of the vessel opposite the post) and the oysters were piled on deck, under cover, aft of the post. The engine, boiler, coal and, on the larger steamers, living accommodations for upwards of two dozen men, occupied the space from about amidships aft. The stern was invariably of the fantail design and at the bow a round, deep forefoot curved into a plumb or backward raking stem. Plumb or nearly plumb stems afforded good visibility to the pilot when approaching buoys, etc. Freeboard forward was sufficient for the sound and other protected waters the steamers worked, but freeboard amidships was rather low. Yet the sheer line was graceful and did not differ greatly from other steamer types.

The open deck type carried oysters on a clear open deck exposed to the elements. The steam plant was located in approximately the same place as on the houseboat type, but the space from the pilot house to the stem was now relatively clear and the pilot house was farther aft. Oysters were stored on this foredeck and under the pilot house—if it happened to extend out from the main house—and with the aid of portable sideboards they were piled along the side decks as far as about the quarter deck—if there was one. The dredge post remained in the same forward position on deck but was now, of course, entirely exposed and in full view of the pilot, who was therefore able to control both vessel and dredges. Pilots extolled this arrangement because it gave them a positive, sensitive feel of the entire dredging operation; they could see the motion of the boat aft and judge the rate of turn better than on the houseboat type. The hull lines and gear were the same on both. The *Henry J* built in 1882 is a fine example of an open deck oyster steamer.

Throughout the steamboat era boats increased in size with engines and hoisting machinery undergoing steady refinements. Though steam proved far superior to sail and was a tremendous boon to the industry, nevertheless it possessed so many inherent disadvantages that efforts were continually directed toward replacing it with other forms of power. Thus an engine suitable for very small boats and more modest pocketbooks was welcome. The naphtha, electric, oil, kerosene, and gasoline engines then in the experimental stage all offered some promise and oystermen tried them with varying degrees of success and acceptance, but the rapid improvements in reliability, power, and performance of the gas engine soon scored above all others. It was the best substitute at the time for the steam engine, and its advantages were numerous and telling. Less expensive all around, the engine occupied from about one-quarter to one-half of the space the steam engine required. It cut down the size of the crew, for it needed neither fireman nor licensed engineer. Starting was instantaneous, the simple, easily filled gas tank eliminated the long costly stops for water and coal and the waits for the engine crew to fire up, and no time-consuming, irksome boiler repairs and official annual engine and boiler inspections were necessary. Although in retrospect those early make-and-break ignition engines were sometimes "dogs to start," they nevertheless had decided advantages over the steam engines.

The new unit altered the appearance of the oyster boat somewhat by eliminating the huge house structures of the steamers. The relatively small, lighter engine could now be located farther aft completely below deck under a short trunk cabin, leaving a long, spacious foredeck for the dredge post and oysters. The pilot house stood on the trunk cabin or projected forward and above the engine room in some fashion. The cabin contained living accommodations, a galley and, of course, enclosure for the engine. Frequently a mast with gaff and boom was stepped forward of the dredge post (initially the mast served as the dredge post as well) and perhaps another one aft, ketch fashion, at the cabin. They were intended to be used for steadying sails in bad weather, in case of engine failure, for hoisting purposes, and sometimes for increasing speed. The *Columbia*, for instance, flew a jib on the long runs from Milford to Cape Cod, thereby adding two to three knots to her speed. Except for its extreme compactness, the house configurations of the gasoline-powered boat and the open deck steamer were basically the same; both gave the pilot complete charge of boat and dredge.

A significant characteristic of the gasoline engine was its adaptability for installation, with slight alterations, aboard practically any existing sailboat. Thus the auxiliary was born or, with sails and spars removed, a strictly power

An open deck-type oyster steamer, the *Henry J.* Courtesy of Harvey P. Treat & Sons.

The *Columbia*, one of the first gasoline-powered oyster boats. Courtesy of Emil Usinger.

boat created. An excellent powered oyster boat could thereby be almost instantly produced at a fraction of the cost of a new one; consequently, gasoline–powered boats became accessible to far more oystermen than the steamboat ever had.

The gasoline engine was an almost immediate success and from 1900 to 1906 it fostered, during those peak years, a boom in oyster boat building. Yards in Tottenville on Staten Island, in Greenport, Patchogue, Port Jefferson, South Norwalk, Bridgeport, Stratford, and New Haven turned out more oyster boats than ever before. The new century held bright promises for wooden boat builders. Except on the natural beds where the law perpetuated sail, steam and the internal combustion engine had practically displaced sail by World War I. The wooden gas boat ruled the coastal waters. Most noticeably, Great South Bay, never partial to steam—in fact, early New York laws did not permit dredging under power—yielded readily to the gasoline engine. Actually, big steamers were more of a nuisance than a help there since the bay was restrictively shallow. The beds were also generally within sight of the oyster houses and a large capacity boat was not necessary. A gas boat could be built shorter with less draft than a steamer, yet hold a sufficient amount of oysters for the particular trade requirements of the bay.

At the turn of the century, therefore, the versatility of the gasoline engine and the old steamboat offered oystermen four types of powered oyster boats to choose from: the steamboat, the gas boat, the conversion (from sail), and the auxiliary. Choices depended upon capital resources, conditions of the industry, and the oysterman's needs.

Despite the presence of the gasoline engine big steamers continued to be worked by the larger oyster growers. The early marine gasoline engines were not sufficiently developed for the big boats the growers demanded. Connecticut men, always the leaders in oyster cultivation and in number of steamboats owned, expanded at this time to Cape Cod, Rhode Island, and the Greenport area and required capacious, fast boats to transfer paying cargoes. Only powerful steamers could break through the thick harbor and bay ice apparently so common in those years. They operated all year in any weather, dredging and transferring oysters long distances to packing plants or to New York and other markets. The big steamers were suitably designed to accommodate one or two dozen men on those two- and three-day trips.

Only the steamer provided the oystermen with the needed qualities of a big boat, and this seemed to hold true throughout the 100-year history of the powered oyster boat. With gasoline and diesel engines offering other superior

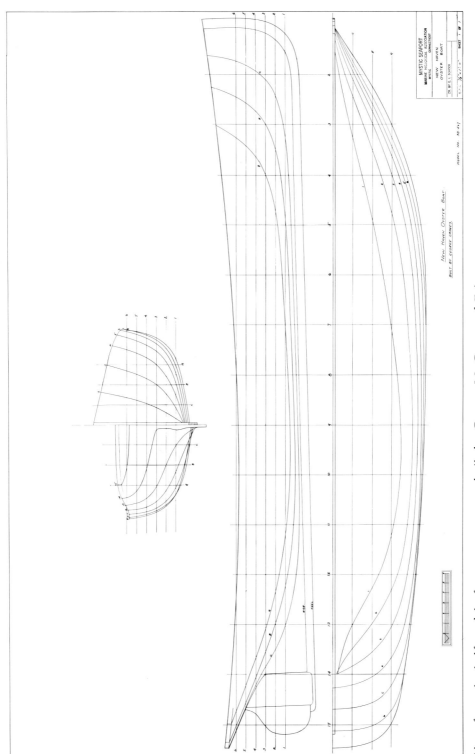

New Haven Oyster Boat

Built by George Graves.

Lines from the half model of an oyster steamer built by George M. Graves of Fair
Haven, Connecticut.

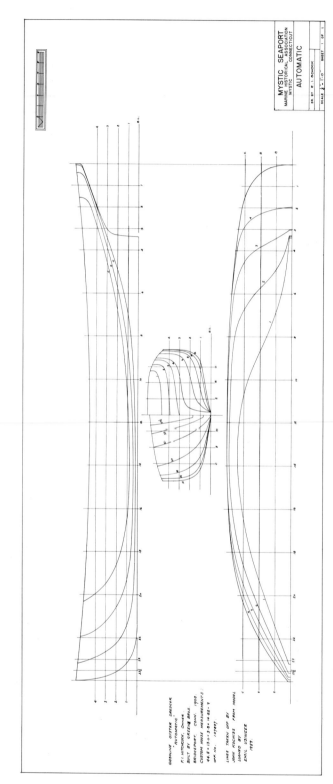

Lines from the half model of the gasoline-powered oyster boat *Automatic*.

qualifications, the giant boats nonetheless stuck to steam. It is not surprising that the biggest boat specifically designed for the oysters business, the 102-foot *Standard*, was a steamer.

A few steamboats operated right up through World War II. Eventually, they, too, succumbed to the ravages of age or conversion to diesel power. The *Louis R* was the last oyster boat in the North to use steam, converting finally to diesel in 1961. Up until then, her constant supply of steam had been very useful for killing starfish.

To large numbers of oyster growers big steamers were not necessary and, indeed, were a decided inconvenience. Smaller companies and, to an extent, larger ones also enthusiastically welcomed the gas boat. From 1896 on, countless gas boats were built all with the same general superstructure configuration: clear deck forward, cabin and pilot house aft. At first the hulls were similar to the sometimes yacht-like lines of the oyster steamers. Then they became more burdensome and the forefoot was cut away in order to allow the boat to ride up on ice and by its weight break down through it—instead of cutting through as the steamers did: the sisterships *Albert* and *Earle* were the first to have this type of bow.

A host of marine engine manufacturers deluged the market offering models to suit nearly any oysterman's requirements. Some of the popular engine makes of these days were Globe, Automatic, Hitchcock, and Wolverine. When diesel arrived the Fairbanks Morse, General Motors, and Caterpillar engines were commonly used. Incidentally, boat owners often changed engine makes as old plants wore out or newer models appeared.

After boats were built and in service they frequently underwent drastic alterations. The boom years at the turn of the century placed unexpected demands on oystermen and they, in turn, found their boats inadequately small. Instead of building another one, they often cut the old boat in half and lengthened the midsection. Besides enlarging the boats, repairs were inevitable on those wooden hulls; most oystermen, however, maintained their boats in good condition. This, coupled with the fact that they were usually quality-built originally, is why some boats afloat in 1974, such as the *Medea* and *Commander*, are around seventy years old.

Gasoline-powered boats at the turn of the century ranged in size from 30 to 80 feet. An interesting and informative description of the average oyster boat appeared in the (c. 1908) catalog of oyster dredge machinery of the Coulter & McKenzie Machine Co. of Bridgeport, which specified for gasoline-powered oyster boats the following dimensions:

. . . as a popular size outfit that can be built at a reasonable price, complete, ready to work.

Forty to 60 feet long over all, 12 1/2 to 16 feet beam, 4 1/2 feet deep, drawing about 34 inches when not loaded, complete with engine room and pilot house, wheel, rudder chains, anchor and lights, fitted up with berths, 16 to 25 Horse Power Gasoline Engine of most improved model for the purpose, propellor wheel, shaft bearings, etc., tanks and pipes complete.

The Thwartship style of Hoisters are more generally used than other styles, and a complete outfit (outside of the Gas Engine), consists of the following items:

The Extension Shaft forward end of Engine, which is usually furnished by the engine builders. Clutch connecting Engine with Hoisters. The set of Hoisters, with cut bevel gearing. Friction Screws, Babbitted Bearings, and all connections to same. Two Drum Idlers with Bearings, Shafts and Collars. Two Post Sheaves and Bearings. Two Deck Irons, complete. Two Post Hauling Blocks. One Post Forging. Two Chain Claws with Staples and Chains. Two Hauling Chains of best make "short link" style and with large link in each end of each length, dimensions suitable for depth of water desired. Two Dredges with tooth blades. Clubs, Chain and Cord Bags. Complete set of Side Rollers for both sides of boat, all necessary Bolts, Screws, etc., to install the outfit.

The prices of a complete outfit vary, according to details and materials used, style of Hoisters, location and where the machinery is installed.

We advise putting in the largest Hoisters that the engine will properly care for.

Such a boat can easily make 8 to 10 miles per hour when not using the hoisters.

The hoisters can be attached instantly. One man pilots the boat, runs the engine, and hauls the dredges, all worked from the pilot house by means of levers, etc.

The pilot has full control of the men on deck, and 150 bushels per hour is considered a good catch where oysters are plentiful, and 400 to 600 bushels is capacity of boat.

Where the oyster grounds are not too far away, it is customary to get two loads a day.

A typical small powered oyster boat of the 1910 to 1940s era. Note the dredge post and rollers. Courtesy of Bluepoints Company, Inc.

The oyster freighter and buy boat *B. F. Jane*, shown here planting oyster shells off New Haven in 1938, was originally a two-masted schooner. Courtesy of Shellfish Institute of North America.

Besides the steam boat and the gas boat, the oysterman's third option was to convert from sail to power. Schooners and big sloops were still in use when the gasoline engine appeared, so to compete with companies owning power boats, the sailing oystermen were forced to turn to power. Some tried to get along with sail or a small auxiliary engine, others sold their sailboats and built power boats, but many chose the least expensive course—conversion.

Comparatively little alteration was necessary. A pilot house was built over the trunk cabin aft and the engine, hoisters, post, rollers and other equipment installed. In the case of a schooner, the sails and mainmast were removed and the bowsprit and foremast shortened or discarded. A quite servicable and often sea-kindly power boat resulted. Three boats of the J. & J. W. Elsworth Co. of New York, the *Commodore, Ensign,* and *Captain,* were among the first sailboats to be converted.

Another common practice was to buy a used ferry, tug, or power yacht and convert it to an oyster boat, usually retaining the old engines, but refitting them for the trade. The *Rowe* and indeed most H.C. Rowe & Co. boats were conversions from other services.

The fourth type of powered oyster boat was the auxiliary. At first, a small 6 to 10 h.p. gas engine was installed in the cabin of a 25- to 35-foot sailboat. The sails and rigging were kept and power was employed strictly as auxiliary to the sails in light airs and for maneuvering in and out of harbors. The auxiliary appealed almost exclusively to the natural growthers or the small private oyster grower. Since the advent of steam power most states had prohibited its use on the public beds—either for propulsion or for hoisting dredges—while dredging, both to conserve the seed supply and because the few who could afford engines would possess undue advantages. In Connecticut, after some delay and debate, the law allowed engines and propellers aboard sloops as long as they were not operated while dredging. The benefits of auxiliary power were obvious to all oystermen and few Connecticut natural growth sloops were without it by the mid-1920s. From the beginning of the century to the 1960s these four boat types comprised the bulk of the power oyster boat fleet in the North.

There were some other working types, however. Oystermen knew that the common boat and dredge, even under ideal conditions, was only partially effective. Consequently, men of imagination strove to improve boats and harvesting techniques. As a result, a paddle wheeler, a few power scows, a trimaran, and a baby submarine spotted the fleets of conventional boats and added a bit of interest and hope for the industry.

The aptly named *Curiosity* of Great South Bay was one of the first of these unusual craft. According to a contemporary account she was a side wheel dredge boat designed by Captain Charles S. Mott and built in Patchogue in 1894. She was "the most peculiar craft in the bay. She carries a crew of six men, and has a capacity of 1,500 bushels of oysters."[6] She probably lost most of her curiousness when her paddle wheels were removed and she was converted to a regular gas boat with screw propeller in 1910.

Another oddity was the scow *Peconic*, built in 1907. At the time, it was reported: "A novel oyster boat, or rather a scow, is being constructed at the Greenport Basin & Construction Co. yards for Fred Lewis & Co. comprising Fred Lewis, Jacob Ockers, Wm. J. Mills, and Fred Ronik. The scow will be used for conveying oysters from adjacent waters through the canal to the Great South Bay, and will be 60 feet long, 17 feet wide on deck, 16 feet along the bottom, 4 feet deep aft, 3 feet amidships and 3 feet 9 inches forward. These unusual dimensions are believed to be the most favorable for a boat to get through the Shinnecock Canal, oyster laden. The craft will be equipped with twenty-four horse-power in the form of twin screws, Greenport motors."[7] The *Peconic* and other powered scows—the *Montauk, W.W., Emma Frances*, and *Admiral*, for instance—did yeoman service for the Long Island oyster companies for many years.

Perhaps the most promising vessel—machine might be a better word—was N. A. Lybeck's "oyster harvester and cultivator," the *Dark Horse*. Built and demonstrated just before World War I, it was designed to scoop oysters off the bottom mechanically and to convey them continuously to the deck. *The Fishing Gazette* in 1913 reported the following:

> The "Dark House" is really three boats securely bolted together side by side. The bow of the central hull which contains the engines and machinery reaches only to the mid-ship section of the two on the outside. This leaves an open space between the two outer hulls in which a long carrier is lowered to the bottom. A scoop on the lower extremity of this carrier or conveyor is provided with fingers which pick up objects it meets and carries them to the conveyor which in turn elevates them and deposits them on the deck. A three-cylinder, 40 hp gasoline engine turns the screw projecting from the center hull. Twin rudders on the two outer hulls guide the craft, being connected with the wheel in the pilot-house. A second gasoline engine of 4 hp operates the dredging machinery. . . . The deck of the "Dark House" has the appearance of an ordinary vessel, 45 feet long and 22 feet beam from which a section of the bow has been cut out extending amidship. . . . Oystermen as well as all

seafaring men are always prejudiced against new fangled notions and the innovation of Capt. Lybeck will meet with opposition from this source until he has fully demonstrated that he can do just what he promises.[8]

Apparently Lybeck's promises were not fulfilled, although the boat was satisfactorily demonstrated at Bridgeport in water up to ten feet. Neither did it achieve the inventor's lofty hopes of revolutionizing the industry. The contraption lay abandoned in Sayville, Long Island until 1918 when it was finally sold for junk.

Another vessel also expected to revolutionize the industry was championed by Connecticut's pioneer submarine designer and builder, Simon Lake. Soon after he began building submarines in the 1890s, Lake envisioned mother ships connected to subs that could crawl along the sea bed gathering oysters, or anything else, through openings in the bottom. In 1932, after concentrating his efforts on war subs, Lake built and tested his last submarine, the *Explorer*, a 22-foot experimental craft. During its construction, he predicted: "I expect to try this boat out on all types of work; the gathering of food shellfish from the bottom; taking of submarine pictures and movies; location and exploration of sunken cargoes; the gathering of pearl oysters and clams and the garnering of sponges. When she has proven her efficiency at these jobs, bigger boats will be built with special equipment suited to the particular job for which they are designed."[9] Like Lybeck before him, Lake's dream failed to materialize. While the *Explorer* did dive for sponges off the Florida coast with some success, it was not accepted by the sponging industry. Lake also tried to locate sunken ships with it, such as H.M.S. *Hussar*, which sank in Hell Gate in 1779. Unlike the *Dark Horse*, however, the *Explorer*, although abandoned for years, was fortunately rescued from a park in Milford and placed in the Museum of Art, Science and Industry in Bridgeport. There in the city where she was built, she stands to remind us of Lake's genius and his unrealized hopes for the oyster industry.

Conditions and events were always changing the industry and the boats as well. Although less than a dozen boats were built in the 1920s, during this decade a silent revolution was being waged in the engine rooms. The diesel engine, slumbering since the 1890s, developed into a superb marine engine and did to the gas engine what it had done to steam and steam to sail. Gas, steam, and the remaining sailing boats switched to diesel as to a new religion, and the handful of boats built after 1921 were mostly diesel powered.

This time the changeover was not nearly as visually dramatic. Nothing was altered on the boats except the engine, which occupied about the same volume as the gasoline engine and at first glance looked similar to it. The advantages of diesel over gasoline and steam were, however, striking. The diesel engine initially costs more than the gasoline engine but operates for less. There is no ignition or carburetor problem and, most comforting of all, little or no fire risk.

Most gas boats eventually converted to disel: one of the first in Connecticut was the steamer *Medea*. But natural growthers generally could not afford the extremely high cost of the few small diesels then available, and therefore stayed with gas.

Except for the diesel engine, the oyster boat underwent no major alterations during the two decades between the world wars. One minor feature, however, did appear on some boats. The *Clara C. Raye*, the *General*, and the *Harvester*, with the old *Columbia* following later copied the fishing dragger's whaleback bows and enclosed the foredeck up to the dredge post for crew and cargo protection—a hark-back to the old-time steamers. Although the gas and diesel oyster boats had looked pretty much alike since 1900, all were different in details. Refinements, improvements, and modifications of hull, components, and materials progressed, along with marked improvements in hoisting gear and dredge design.

But one other condition did change. The wooden shipbuilding era had about ended in southern New England. First iron, then steel, replaced wood in ships, although only a couple of steel oyster boats ever existed. After 1930 proportionately more oyster boats were built outside the New York-Connecticut area than at any other period, with only Maine and, to some extent Massachusetts, continuing to build in wood. Two of the larger oyster boats built in the 1930s, the *General* and her sistership the *Harvester* were both built of wood in Maine in 1938. And two of the last conventional style wooden oyster boats, the sisterships *Greenport* and *Milford*, were also built in Maine in 1946.

The years after the rather languid depression period saw events inevitably reshaping the entire industry. The great hurricane that ripped through New England in 1938 inflicted heavy financial losses on many oystermen and left the Rhode Island oyster industry nearly prostrate. Following closely on its heels, World War II thrust tremendous pressures on the already weakened industry. Most significantly, the war displaced manpower. Yet after the war conditions did not improve very much. The struggling oyster business offered relatively low wages and thus attracted few newcomers, and shore industries, with their abundant enticements, easily drew men away from their old occupa-

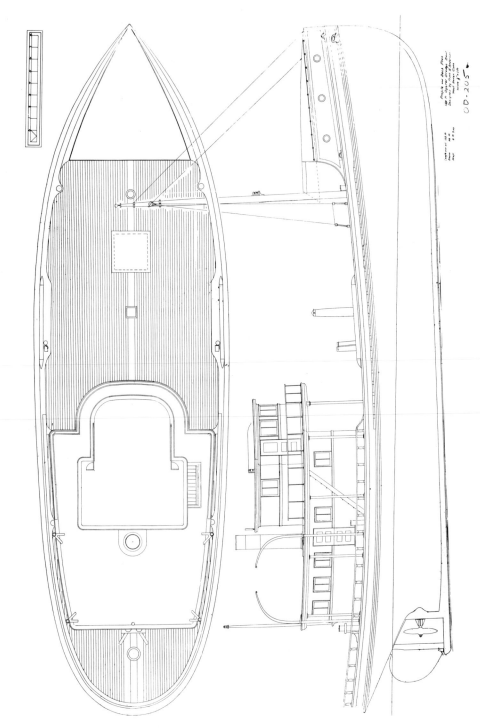

Outboard profile plan of the *Clara C. Raye*, designed by Frank Anderson.

tions on the water. Faced with these acute problems, more economical ways were sought to operate boats and oyster shops.

One solution to the high cost of hand labor was found in mechanization. Before World War II the average boat carried two dredges and a crew of four or more men. A large crew was absolutely necessary under the traditional dredging methods employed. In this system the dredge was hauled to the rollers at the rail by means of hoisters and blocks at the dredge post. The heavy dredge never went much beyond the rail: it was dumped by the combined physical efforts of three or more men, the oysters were shoveled away to the oyster heap, and the dredge was heaved overboard—again by muscle power. The laborious, inefficient operation, largely a carry-over from the sailing dredges, had been hardly questioned or challenged before. Now it was.

In the 1930s, H. J. Lewis, a noted Connecticut oysterman (who was drowned in the 1938 hurricane) worked unsuccessfully on a radically new one-man boom rig with a bottom dumping dredge. He was not able to remove the bugs and nothing came of it. But at the war's end Captain Fred Lovejoy of East Norwalk cleverly devised the thoroughly practical boom dredge rig used on almost every dredge boat today. The rig looked and operated much like the derrick and scoop rig of land contractors, and consisted of two booms pivoted at or on the dredge post, one for each of the two dredges. Each boom and dredge operated independently. Under the pilot's and deck hand's control the boom with dredge was swung outboard clear of the boat and rail. By a separate chain system the pilot lowered the dredge to the bottom, allowing it to drag along the bed in the traditional manner. When full, it was hauled up and directed inboard over any point on deck. The dredge, now built like a rectangular basket instead of the old iron, chain, and cotton net design, easily released its load when one man tripped a lever at the bottom of the dredge. No shoveling was necessary, for the oysters were delivered directly to the oyster pile. The beauty of this boom rig lay in its controllability and the fact that the heavy dredge never touched the boat. (It did have one fault, however; under rolling conditions in heavy seas the boom had a tendency to become unmanageable.) Most beneficially, it required only one man in the pilot house and one man on deck to operate it. Lovejoy first installed the rig on his *Ellen J* and about a year and a half later Frank Flower of Bayville, New York, made one for his *Ida May*. Other boats were converted and the old dredge post went the way of most old things. And even the boom rig seems to be undergoing an evolution. The hydraulically controlled booms on the *Captain* and some other boats owned by the Long Island Oyster Farms Inc. have been shifted away from the centerline and closer to the gunwale.

To save more labor costs and work, self-loading and unloading machinery was added to a number of oyster boats right after World War II. The *Twin Harbors* was one of the first to use a conveyor belt system as well as the boom rig. And today the Long Island Oyster Farms unload their dredges directly into pens on deck, which later are removed from the boats by a crane, then to the plant by fork lifts.

Besides the dredge—either the old or bottom dumping basket type—no other mechanical means of raising oysters off the bottom has been applied in northern waters. A device known as the Brown oyster harvester, somewhat similar to Lybeck's machine and to one used in Great South Bay to harvest clams, is used in the Gulf oyster industry. In common with Lybeck's, the Brown machine was limited to very shallow water and, therefore, is not generally applicable to the deep water oyster farming methods of the north.

After World War II, four or five conventional oyster boats were built with boom rigs instead of dredge posts, and conveyor systems were put on some boats, but all in all, the common dredge boat was still fundamentally no different in appearance and hull shape than before World War I.

The dredge, in any form, has built-in deficiencies. It cannot operate continuously over the beds because it must be hauled aboard when full. Therefore, areas are left undredged. On scattered grounds it may miss oysters. Furthermore, when poorly operated, it will crush and kill oysters. When worked properly under favorable conditions it is only fairly effective. Realizing this, and with soaring operating costs to add to the problem, oystermen looked for other ways of harvesting. A hydraulic dredge for raising oysters, reminiscent of one of Simon Lake's ideas, was tried for the first time in the 1940s on Frank Flower's scow the *Pine Island*. The simplicity of the gear was amazing: some hose, blocks, belts, and a small centrifugal pump were arranged to lift the oysters off the bottom. Though initially developed to catch oyster drills, it proved very successful in gathering small oysters and set.

In 1947, H.C. Rowe & Co. purchased a used boat—an army freight supply vessel that saw service in the Pacific theater of war, renamed her the *Rowe*, after their old *Rowe*, and converted her to a hydraulic dredge. A nozzle in the form of a 6-foot dredge blade was fitted at the end of the suction hose. As the blade was raked along the bottom, oysters and all other material were forced by water in motion up the suction hose onto a screening conveyor. The new *Rowe*, like the old one decades before, dredged and transported oysters safely, under

The suction dredger *Quinnipiac* of New Haven used mainly for cleaning ground and catching oyster shells, gathering as many as 200,000 bushels of shell a season. Courtesy of National Marine Fisheries Service.

cover, to oyster houses over 100 miles away. The F. Mansfield & Sons Co. bought an army vessel, renamed her the *Quinnipiac* and converted her to a hydraulic dredger. Although far from a handsome vessel, she is a most successful oyster boat with a suction gear and efficient conveyor system for handling and unloading, and in 1973 she was owned and operated by the Long Island Oyster Farms out of New Haven primarily for cleaning oyster beds.

Later, another oysterman, Waldron Bayles of Oyster Bay, bought the old steel ferry *Sea Gate*, converted her to a suction dredge. and renamed her the *Seawannaca*. Flower converted another vessel, the New Jersey freighter *Norman L. Jeffries*, into a suction dredger but she also has a regular boom rig aboard, making her a little more versatile than the others.

As of 1973, four hydraulic dredgers were working in the North: Long Island Oyster Farms's *Quinnipiac*, the ex-freighter *Charles W. Lynde*, Frank M. Flower and Son's *Pine Island*, and the *Norman L. Jeffries*.

Today the northern oyster fleet consists of a small varied assortment of ancient and near ancient craft. No known conventional style oyster boat has been built in the last twenty years. Newer types might yet appear but the prospects of building a wooden, conventional dredger are remote indeed. Eras come and go and now the wooden oyster boat age has passed. The hatcheries and a reviving industry may exert some force upon the character of the future oyster fleet, but at least the diesel engine era still remains in full bloom.

CHAPTER 10

Oystering on the Natural Beds

INCE the beginning of oyster farming in the mid-nineteenth century, many Connecticut oystermen, realizing the value of seed, and that Long Island Sound seed produced the only consistently successful "plants" for the northern industry, specialized in growing it. Connecticut gradually blossomed into the leading oyster seed growing state in the North. As the industry in New England began its rapid decline before World War I, Connecticut assumed almost full responsibility for supplying the needed seed not only for itself, but for its neighboring states.

For the most part this seed was raised by the companies on their private beds off the Connecticut shore, but much of the best came from the state's and towns' natural beds. The remarkable fact is that those beds never exceeded 5,805 acres or 9 square miles: a tiny area when compared to the 76,000 acres, or 119 square miles of natural beds in Delaware Bay, and the colossal 566,000 acres, or 885 square miles, in Chesapeake Bay.

The workers on these natural beds—a small group of never more than 1,000 men known as "natural growthers" who carried on a tradition of sailing and oystering ways harking back centuries—were the last commercial oystermen to use sail north of New York.

Natural growthers and the sailing oyster boat are inextricably linked. For a short time in the 1870s oystermen flirted with power until the State of Connecticut in 1881 prohibited its use on the public natural beds. Thus the law gave the little man who did not have the money to buy a motor boat, or even a motor for his sailboat, the opportunity to oyster profitably on a more or less equal footing with others also using sail. Everyone hauled the dredges by hand, again giving everyone an even break. And sail got a new lease on life and remained commercially active as long as the natural beds produced seed, that is, up to the 1950s.

In the early part of the nineteenth century the natural growthers worked on the numerous naturally productive inshore areas along the Connecticut coast, particularly from the New York line to Guilford. As time went on much of this inshore property was staked out and designated as private holdings. In 1881 the newly formed Connecticut State Shell-Fish Commission identified the location of seventeen natural beds within state jurisdiction that were open to public dredging, and it was here and on some town-owned ground that the natural growthers were allowed to work. These state-owned public natural beds, as recorded in the First Report of the Shell-Fish Commissioners in 1882 and in the 1894 report, are as follows:[1]

NAME OF BED	LOCATION	1881 ACREAGE	DEPTH	1894 ACREAGE
Portchester	Byram	300	6′–18′	218
Cormell Reef	Greenwich	—	—	15
Great Captain's Island	Greenwich	200	5′–30′	152
Field Point	Greenwich	200	7′–10′	84
Greenwich Point	Greenwich	300	50′–60′	403
Gravelly Bar	Stamford	50	9′	—
Shippan Point and Westcott's Cove	Stamford	450	6′–20′	—
Roton Point and Fish Island	Norwalk	300	1′–14′	307
Ram Island Bay	Norwalk	50	5′	—
Light House and Old House	Norwalk Harbor	75–100	9′–13′	—
Calf Pasture	Norwalk	600	1′– 6′	—
Fairfield	Southport	125	4′–12′	—
Fairfield Bar	Fairfield	200	3′–13′	1237
The Dumps	Bridgeport	100	21′	—
Bridgeport-Stratford	Bridgeport; Stratford	1200	18′	3389
Stratford Point #1	Stratford	50	?	—
Stratford Point #2	Stratford	75	?	—
Pompey	Off Housatonic River	350	21′	—

It will be noted that nine natural beds disappeared from the list between 1881 and 1894. Some of these were totally depleted or, like others later on, parcelled out and leased to individual cultivators and oyster firms. The loss of the natural beds to the big companies was one of the reasons behind the age-old antagonism between the natural growthers and the cultivators. Natural growthers believed the companies would eventually gobble up all the natural ground leaving them with nothing from which to make a living. Through the years some men justified their occasional poaching raids on cultivated beds on the theory that they were originally natural and, therefore, somehow legally or at least morally still public property. Oyster police were organized to prevent this poaching as well as outright stealing. Many of the bigger companies maintained watch boats that anchored on their beds all day and occasionally at night, for some natural growthers "moonlighted" on what they called the "steamboat grounds." The H. J. Lewis Oyster Co. of Bridgeport once used the sloop *Helen* and the small schooner *Artemesia*, but later employed steamers as watch boats.

Through the years two or three natural beds, such as the Savin Rock Bed, were added to the list but these and some of the old ones were later dissolved, leased, or merged with others. In 1930 only four of the original were productive and by the 1950s only two were worked—the Bridgeport and Stratford beds. Since these beds are contiguous their separation was rather uncertain, especially while dredging. The phrase "Bridgeport bed" will therefore include the Stratford bed as well.

The history of the Bridgeport bed is one of fluctuation between complete exhaustion and bountiful harvest. Prior to 1850 it was very productive but shortly thereafter it became depleted, being of little value until 1867. As a citizen of South Norwalk commented:

> The Bridgeport bed was discovered [actually rediscovered] in July, 1867. Then it extended from Black Rock harbor to Point-No-Point, at least four miles, and was from one-half to one mile wide, covering about three thousand acres. Capt. Samuel Byxbee, Joseph Coe, and William M. Saunders were the first to go on it from this town. In one drift, in a light breeze, they caught over 300 bushels of seed. Capt. J. Levinness, in going across the bed three times, took 1,000 bushels. Capt. Barnes piled the deck of a fifty-ton sloop in one drift. Catching seed there was a constant letting go and hauling, and men became so exhausted they fell down from sheer fatigue. At one time 450 sails were counted at work on the bed and they had plenty of room. That number of vessels could not be set on three acres, place them side by side. Now the bed does not actually cover 40 acres, and is in small patches, scattered over the ground of the former bed. It has been worked almost to death, and it only needs one season of steamers to exterminate it entirely.[2]

Gradually, within a couple of decades, the Bridgeport bed regained its former life and continued to support many oystermen. In 1900 alone over 300 sailboats dredged these 3,389 acres, surpassing any commercial sailing fleet in numbers anywhere in the state and possibly in New England and New York for an area of comparable size. After 1900 the bed experienced exceptional sets, but also disappointing failures. During the World War I years no set occurred, which slackened business somewhat, though the bed was worked for older oysters. Finally the 1938 hurricane, subsequent tropical storms, and lack of spawners caused the complete annihilation of this as well as of many private beds by the 1960s. But to the opponents of the public oystering system, failure of the natural beds was due to local and state politicians who refused to change antiquated, harmful, harvesting laws. The law, therefore, sanctioned plunder of the natural beds, and thus natural growthers took but did not give. Oysters, the opponents further claimed, did not have time to renew or reestablish themselves.

In the late 1960s oysters set again on the old bed. By 1970 a half-dozen men, after years away from oystering, dredged there. But, alas, sails were now gone and power propelled their odd assortment of boats. A state law passed in 1969 under pressure from the natural growthers themselves permitted the use of power for propulsion while dredging. Hauling dredges by hand was still mandatory, but it will not be long before power will be allowed for this operation also. Then, the last vestiges of an ancient skill will have disappeared forever.

Since the Bridgeport bed was the largest and most prolific in Connecticut the bulk of the natural growthers worked it and lived nearby. Some from ports farther away laid over in Bridgeport for weeks at a time while working, and a few took the train home on weekends to be with their families. Some lived aboard their boats all season—usually those who made the sloop their home anyway. In the 1880s and 1890s a large fleet moored in a spot deep in the harbor near the railroad station, called by the oystermen the "pen."

In the next fifty years they moved to picturesque Henry Street or dispersed throughout the various nooks and inlets of the harbor. Since Bridgeport was the hub of the natural growther fleet, it remained the last stronghold of commercial sail north of Chesapeake Bay.

Hard, honest work, in sun, rain and snow marked the life of a typical full-time natural growth oysterman. From fall to spring he pulled heavy dredges, tended sails, managed his boat, and delivered his cargo—always outside, exposed to the winds and waves of Long Island Sound. At the end of the season

Lunchtime aboard the oyster sloop *Bernice C* on the Bridgeport natural bed. Courtesy of Robert Prindle.

Oystering on the Bridgeport natural oyster bed in 1941. Among the boats is the Chesapeake Bay skipjack *Dorothy G.* Courtesy of National Marine Fisheries Service.

he outfitted his battered sloop again for a summer's work of sword fishing, fishing parties, freighting farm produce between Long Island and Connecticut, and perhaps a workboat race or two. Then the long hard cycle began again in September. The season was set by state and local law and through the years varied considerably. Usually it extended from fall through spring. In 1971 it ran from September 20 to July 20, but during this year the State Board of Health intervened and shortened the season.

The oysterman's work was always tough but physically and emotionally rewarding, and his good health and vigor carried him through to a ripe old age. He was justly proud, for as a free-lance oysterman he was completely independent and accountable to no one but himself.

He usually owned his own boat, hired a crew of from one to six men, harvested oysters on the public ground, and sold them to the oyster companies. He ordinarily did not own oyster ground and did not cultivate oysters as the oyster companies did. He was comparable in a sense to the man who might earn a living by scouring the countryside for wild strawberries. However, some of the men, especially the full-time oystermen like the Chards of Greenwich, the Stevenses of Rowayton, Fred Lovejoy of East Norwalk, and the more contemporary George Chase, Jr. of Milford, and Bill Ciaurro of Bridgeport did own oyster ground and dredged for their own seed on the natural beds.

The natural growther was a crack sailor and an expert oysterman who

The *Eaglet* on a drift on the Bridgeport natural bed. Three men working five dredges was most common. Photograph by the author.

Oyster boats on the Bridgeport natural oyster bed in 1941. Courtesy of National Marine Fisheries Service.

frequently learned his trade as a boy on the deck of his father's sloop. Fathers and sons, uncles and even grandfathers worked together on the same boats year after year. And when the father retired, his son continued to work the old sloop. In this way and with loving care boats lasted two and sometimes three generations.

These career oystermen formed the small but strong core of natural growthers. The balance of the total group were part-time oystermen. At the beginning of the oyster season when the pickings were best, Bridgeport factory and office workers left their work on vacation time for "a bit of fresh air and a quick buck." Ash Bond, the well-known Bridgeport oysterman around the turn of the century, sometimes took on waterfront bums to get them off the docks, but they seldom lasted more than a day. Tradesmen—in particular carpenters and mechanics who did not have work all the time—oystered between jobs. As a rule many part-timers crewed for someone else; others owned their own boats or clubbed together and rented a sloop. Dan Sprague of Bridgeport, for example, owned thirteen sloops and let them out on shares. Though the incentive to oyster was great, the part-timers sometimes showed little interest in improving or changing conditions for natural growthers. At those times, they tended by their lack of deep concern to misrepresent the feelings, desires, and even character of the career oystermen.

Although natural growthers were remarkably free agents, they all had to comply with a few simple regulations. As far back as colonial days oystermen were subject to state and local restrictions of one form or another. The laws evolved gradually over the years until the early 1900s. From then until the 1960s no major revisions were made. The following laws are from the *Laws Relating to Shell-Fisheries* of 1969 with comparative notes in parentheses from quite similar ones enacted in 1900:

> Sec. 26–212. Licensing and numbering of oyster vessels. No person shall take or gather oysters from any natural oyster bed in the exclusive jurisdiction of the state in any boat or vessel unless it is licensed and numbered in the manner hereinafter provided. Any person desiring to use any boat or vessel for such purpose may make written application to the clerk of shell-fisheries, stating the name, owner, rig, general description and tonnage of such boat or vessel and the place where it is owned, and said clerk shall issue to the owner of such boat or vessel a license to take and gather oysters from the natural oyster beds in the exclusive jurisdiction of the state for the term expiring on the next succeeding twentieth day of July, unless sooner revoked, upon the payment of fifteen dollars ($2.00) for a vessel or boat of under five gross tons

and over twenty-five feet in length overall and, for a vessel or boat exceeding five gross tons, three dollars ($0.50) for each additional gross ton, custom-house measurement, and, for a vessel or boat twenty-five feet overall or less, eight dollars; provided, before such license is granted, the owner or master shall prove to the satisfaction of said clerk that such boat or vessel may legally be used on work on the public beds of the state, that the captain and crew of such boat or vessel have been residents of this state for one year next preceding the date of such license and that the dredges and other contrivances do not weigh more than thirty pounds. Each boat or vessel so licensed shall, while at work upon any of the natural oyster beds of the state, display, upon both sides of the peak of her mainsail, the number of such license in black figures not less than one foot in length and the coat of arms of Connecticut painted or stenciled upon cloth of suitable and uniform material, to be attached or stitched to the sail. Said clerk shall furnish such numbers and coat of arms when the license is granted. When any boat or vessel so licensed is sold to a resident of this state, the license shall be transferred at the office of said clerk. Any license granted to any person who, during the period for which such license is granted, removes from the state shall be revoked. The sale to a nonresident of any boat so licensed shall operate as a forfeiture and revocation of the license, and the license certificate shall be surrendered to said clerk. (1949 Rev., S. 5044)[3]

One old law from the last century handed down in the same form and carrying the same penalties permitted work during daylight hours only. As oystermen used to say, "You can't throw a dredge until sunup and can't throw a dredge after sundown."

The law, therefore, established the oysterman's working day. Before sunup, men and boats sprang to life. Almost as one, the sloops were off scrambling for a favorable position on the beds. Like the piecework of the factory many oystermen knew so well, they were in a race: the more they caught the more cash in their pockets. But before earning a cent they had to reach the beds. These were a scant mile or two outside the harbor breakwater, but it was often a long, slow sail out. Before the days of auxiliary power and in the lazy days of September boats often took all morning to reach them. The light contrary airs might last all day while men lolled around the decks, boats drifted with the tide and sails hung limp. Near sundown a squall might hit with a shift of wind to the northwest and the inevitable hard thrash back in would follow. To beat the wind's vagaries, a long sweep was sometimes used off the stern of the sloops as on the *Henry Ruppel,* or with oar locks placed somewhere aft of the chain-plates as on the big sloop *Harp.* (Incidentally, oystermen said with pride of the

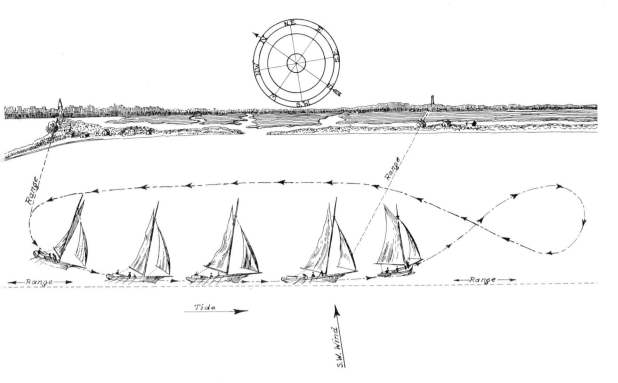

Oystering under sail. Drawing by John Leavitt.

Harp "she died a virgin," for she never had an engine.) In the old days during a calm old-timers walked their sloops along the shore with a long line, like a horse pulling a canal barge. This is perhaps another reason the shallow center-board hull was adapted for oyster boats.

Fortunately it was not always calm. With fall came the heavy northwest winds, and boats flying jib, main and gaff topsails raced like yachts to the beds in jig time. After 1921 boats were allowed to motor out to the oyster beds, oblivious to calms and wind direction. Upon reaching them engines were stopped and sails, which were hoisted while running out, took full command until quitting time.

The Bridgeport natural bed was irregular in shape, running contiguously for about four miles in an east-west direction and extending no more than two miles out from shore. Southwest winds prevailed in the fall, spring, and summer and blustery northwest or northeast winds hung out during winter. Under the sea oysters grew all over the bed. In some places they were found in the hollows of gullies known as "dreens," which—formed for the most part by storm and wave action—ran in any direction but usually paralleled the path of the tide and the length of the bed, that is east to west. Here the row of oysters in the gullies were referred to as "a streak of oysters in a dreen."

At the grounds, the oystermen felt out oysters and dreens with his dredge. If he already knew where they were, he found them by previously established ranges—directing straight lines formed by aligning by eye his boat offshore with two prominent objects on land such as a church steeple and a tree or light-house. Ranges were "snapped" or fixed to establish locations of dreens, drifts, boundaries, and objects lost overboard. To enable him to retrace the same path over the oyster bed a skipper noted two ranges, one on each end of a run or drift, and a third range for the direction of the run. On areas of no dreens the skipper simply dredged in the direction of the tide, fixing his path by ranges.

Dredging under sail was more drifting than sailing: the sailing oystermen of Long Island Sound and vicinity let the tide help rather than hinder them. For instance, working on an ebb tide (running to the eastward) with a moderate southwest wind was a typical situation. The sloop began its drift, or path, across the bottom of the bed upwind at the western end. The boat followed the tide toward the East with the centerboard more or less down, the bow headed roughly south, and the southwest wind over the starboard side. To minimize forward motion, the mainsail's leech was free to flutter while a portion only of the main filled in order to keep the bow up into the wind. The jib was trimmed just short of luffing. The jib functioned like the throttle of a car by controlling the speed of the boat and both sails and a properly adjusted center-board maintained balance. In this subtle equilibrium between tide and wind, centerboard and sails, the skipper allowed the boat to drift with the tide yet did not permit the wind to blow it off the drift. To aid the skipper the mainsheet was cleated just aft of the steering gear, and the jib sheet and centerboard pennant cleated on the cabin top all within his easy reach.

The dredges were dropped one by one, aft dredge first, over the windward and, in this case, starboard side. The sailboat was now dredging. On a 30- to 40-foot boat, the crew consisted of the captain and two men. As a rule the three men worked five dredges; the captain steered but also tended one dredge and doubled up on another with one of the men. With a good fresh breeze six to eight dredges might be used though it was not common. Under these conditions Captain Lovejoy had ten dredges overboard on his sloop *Sarah L* with only three men aboard.

When the dredges were full the skipper let the jib sheet flow and the sloop slowly came up into the wind and slowed down. The dredges were all hauled aboard by hand, aft one first usually, and the contents dumped on deck. Then they were heaved overboard again and the dredging continued. Occasionally oysters were so plentiful that there was a constant "heave and haul." Ordinarily, under expert handling, two to six hauls per drift were made on "good stuff." The length of the drift depended upon bottom conditions and went as far as the

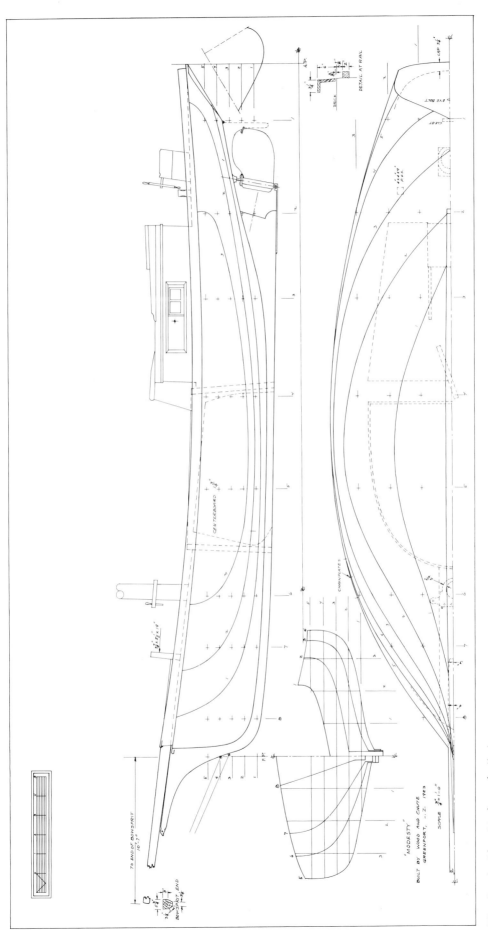

The South-sider *Modesty*, built in 1923

oysters were located but not necessarily the full length of the oyster bed. Drifts generally ran from 300 to maybe 1,000 feet on the Bridgeport natural bed.

At the end of a drift and with all dredges aboard the sloop, the jib was hauled in, the main then filled, and the boat gathered headway. When proper speed and momentum developed, the helm was put down hard-a-lee and the vessel came about slowly amid a clatter of slatting sails, creaking blocks, and slapping lazy jacks. The sails filled again on the other tack and the sloop streaked back—never to windward but always under the sterns of the rest of the fleet—to the ranges at the western end of the bed. While "sailing back on a drift" the crew culled, threw the trash overboard, and shoveled the oysters in the hold or on deck someplace. The run back was so quick at times that culling continued during the next drift. Upon reaching the ranges, commands were given, the boat came about, the dredges were thrown and the dredging cycle repeated. Except for a possible short time out for lunch when, as the oystermen would say, "we layed (anchored) to our dredges" the boats went through the same circuit all day long—drift and sail back on a drift. Or when oysters thinned out on drifts, boats broke away from the bulk of the fleet and searched for better sites.

The scene was animated, with men yelling and pulling dredges, and boats sailing or drifting all in apparent confusion. Yet it was not chaos: each boat was under complete control at all times; they had to be on that relatively small, crowded, busy public bed. Though every boat was not at the same phase of the dredging cycle, all drifted parallel courses with the tide, kept proper speeds, and tried to avoid collisions. A boat's correct relative position within the fleet was important to the smooth functioning of the fleet. And no one consciously violated this unwritten principle without expecting some sort of reproach or curse thrown at him.

The Bridgeport natural bed was only 7 or 8 feet deep near shore, and out "on the line"—the offshore side—the depth did not exceed 28 or 30 feet. The dredgers generally worked about one-quarter of a mile offshore, so the 8- to 12-fathom dredge line commonly used was sufficient. Length or "scope" of a dredge line overboard varied according to the water's depth as well as the condition of the bottom, so an experienced oysterman maintained the proper scope at all times.

The dredge line was tied to the dredge with a fisherman's bend. Near the other end of the line at the boat, a few loops of twine ran through a scupper and around the rail served as a becket and safety valve, so to speak, to which the dredge line was slipknotted. The unused length of line ran from the becket forward near the mast, out of the way, and the tail end was tied to a wooden buoy. In case the dredge hung up on anything, the becket easily broke—instead of the rail—and the rest of the line and buoy were quickly thrown overboard. The buoy marked the location of the lost dredge, to be retrieved on the next drift.

It was possible but not customary to dredge 100 bushels in a couple of hours. The catch really depended upon variables such as the wind and how thick the oysters were on the bottom. Usually two or three days were needed to load a 100- to 300-bushel sloop, yet the big oyster sloop *Ann Gertrude* once loaded 252 bushels in one day, and at another time she took five days to load and put out 1,029 bushels to the buyer. Actually, a full load was not necessary— just enough bushels to make a profit. On the bigger boats with wide decks and a hatch over the hold, oysters were usually left on deck and over the hatch, only enough for ballast going below. Rather than fill the hold, removable sideboards were built aft near the cabin so more could be carried on deck. In cold weather, however, they were stowed below and covered with carpets and tarps, and at night in port the warmth from a lantern was enough to keep them from freezing.

On the day the buyers were expected oystermen kept a sharp eye on the horizon all afternoon for their appearance. When they were already in port, the dredgers nervously waited for the first boat to quit at the end of the day. In any case, the first boat with a "jag" (load) made a break for it under full sail to the buyers anchored somewhere in Bridgeport harbor or near the beds. As if a starting gun had gone off at a yacht race, everyone upped dredges, sailed (or powered) in and maneuvered for a favorable unloading position at the buy boat. The first boat at the buyer tied up alongside and "put out" (unloaded) and then slipped away. The others, as they came in, tied abreast of each other, building up sometimes to seven deep on either side of the buyer. Though they unloaded two at a time, the end boats had a long wait.

Loads were "busheled out" and measured off by a tallyman on board the buy boat. Oystermen unloaded their own boats using old bushel baskets supplied by the buyers. Natural growthers called these "hampers" because they were often slightly bigger than a regular bushel (to the advantage of the buyer, of course). The oysters were shoveled into the baskets, lifted to the coaming, then lifted again to the deck of the buy boat. When a load was delivered direct to the oyster companies, an experienced, respected oysterman might be permitted to "call a load"—that is, to estimate the number of bushels he was carrying. Then the oysters were shoveled out of the sloop to the companies' dock, boat, or oyster bed. Before the days of income tax, oystermen bought and sold for cash or on their own word and kept no receipts or records.

However, not all the natural growthers sold to the buyers in port. Some made verbal commitments with certain companies to sell (and run) to them only. Set and seed oysters sold for about 30 cents a bushel in the early 1900s. A basket hoisted to the masthead of a buy boat meant it would pay 5 cents higher than the prevailing prices, or more often that the buyer was ready for business. Priced fluctuated, however, and the buy boats bid against each other. By 1973 the price had shot up to $3 a bushel, though the oystermen had to deliver the oysters, for no buy boats were left.

In the late fall when cold weather set in the buyers quit Bridgeport, and so did many of the natural growthers, who went back to the factories and trades, leaving only the old-timers and career men hanging on. In the worst weather the sound offered, they sailed their cargoes once or twice a week to the buyers' docks or beds—to Oyster Bay, Greenport, New Haven, Norwalk, or to anyone who would buy. Some of the bigger sloops, such as the *Dora Dean* out of Cos Cob, worked on the public beds in the fall and later in the season hauled mature oysters to the New York markets.

On Saturdays, or after unloading, the skipper divided his earnings. Oystermen always worked on the share system. As a rule, in a crew of three men, the boat got $1/4$, the captain $1/4$ and the two hands $1/4$ each. With two men the boat received $1/3$, the captain $1/3$ and the hand $1/3$. On a four-man basis, the boat got $1/5$, the captain $1/5$, and the three crewmen $1/5$ each. In a good season it is no wonder that oystermen made a handsome haul. In the early 1900s alone, when a dollar went a long way compared with today, oystermen cleared $800 to $1,000 apiece a season.[4] Yet, due to the frequent failure of sets, oystermen usually experienced either a "feast or a famine." And often they spent what they made in the fall and winter on their boats in the spring and summer. No one ever got rich working on the natural beds.

Full-time watermen seldom left their oyster sloops idle for long. As relief from oystering, freighting, and fishing they raced their boats during the summer wherever workboat races were held. As an additional incentive, the cash prizes given were enough to keep men busy at making their boats go faster, either in their own races, or the occasional workboat races sponsored by the Black Rock Yacht Club in Bridgeport and the elegant Larchmont Yacht Club in Larchmont, New York.

Perhaps no oysterman was more famed as a racing champion than Captain Bill Lewis of Bridgeport and Stratford. He sailed his yacht-like 32–foot 6–inch sloop *Amateur* to victory so many times that she gained the reputation of being one of the fastest oyster sloops on Long Island Sound.

Bill Lewis was not the only skipper with a fast, shipshape sloop. In the early part of the century Captain Sid Wilsey of New York won a close race at Larchmont in his 45-foot Elsworth-designed sloop *Watson* over, among others, the speedy 600-bushel sloop *Grace Mackey*. He was not awarded the prize, however, because her bright spars and beautifully kept hull and sails convinced the race committee, in spite of his protestations, that the *Watson* was primarily a yacht. And although any rig and sail combination was acceptable, she flew a jib topsail as well as a gaff topsail, then a rather outdated sail combination for oysterboats.

Workboats races, natural pride, tradition, and competition to reach the buyer promoted a keen interest in fast boats and in whatever might improve them. These were the days, before the turn of the century, of the yacht-like sail plan, the gaff topsail, big jibs, fine lined hulls, and the converted sandbaggers. To an oysterman, his boat was his kingdom, his work, and often his home and sailing was a way of life. Speed was highly desirable in a sailboat, but delays of hours or days meant little, for this was a part of that life.

Not until 1903 did the old ways begin to change. The motor compressed time, and delays that could be avoided by motoring were now irritating, let alone expensive, competitively speaking. Time ruled and patience lost its virtue. Further refinements in sail plan eventually ceased and the motor assumed a prominent place in oystermen's thinking and planning.

Though the motor was allowed in the boat by law, curiously enough the propeller could not be left on while dredging, thus creating somewhat of a problem. Still the auxiliary engine appealed especially to the natural growther living a distance from Bridgeport and those owning oyster grounds. Traveling time was shortened and the engine could be employed on their private beds without restrictions. But an engine on the natural beds without a propeller was almost useless. Men living south—in Greenwich, Stamford, Norwalk—gladly motored to Bridgeport, where they beached their boats and removed the prop. On the next tide they sailed to the public beds and worked there until loaded. Since they could not safely beach a loaded boat to put the prop back on they were compelled to sail the load to the buyer or home. Captain Fred Lovejoy was the only one to beat the foolishness of the propeller ban by devising a unique method of reaching the prop from inside the boat for removal or installation while afloat. He kept the design, which was similar to the present-day outboard motor well, secret for many years, all the while baffling other oystermen and the oyster police. He was often boarded while at anchor on the bed by the puzzled police, who could not believe it could be done, and always probed the end of the propeller shaft with a long stick for the prop.

Eventually, pressure from oystermen for removal of this unreasonable ban forced a change in the laws. As late as 1921 the propeller was finally permitted on the shaft at all times but the engine still could not be run while dredging. Then, within a few years, nearly every sailboat was powered.

Yet sail survived until the 1950s, when oysters on the great Bridgeport natural bed gave out and the law perpetuating sail remained on the books unchallenged—a dead issue. In the late 1960s the old exhausted bed revived, but unfortunately, no serviceable sloops remained to work it. Through the persistent efforts of the last of the breed of natural growthers, the state dropped the power restrictions, and less than a dozen old-timers and a few young men worked the long-abandoned bed again, this time in a bizarre mixture of powered scows, skiffs, and one converted sloop—the venerable *Henry Ruppel*, with George Chase, Jr. skipper once more.

CHAPTER 11

Shelling in the Housatonic River

SHELL mounds found along the river bank of the Housatonic in Stratford gave ample testimony of pre-Columbian oyster repasts. Indians, taking advantage of the abundant fish and shellfish, had gathered there for generations for their feasting and left the empty oyster shells along the water side. The sheer abundance of these oysters, that ran some two to three miles up river, also supported a small community of oystermen who lived in a quaint sea-hut village on the Milford side of the river mouth. Even today the river continues to produce oysters and, until 1971, when a law went into effect allowing the use of hand dredges in the Housatonic, was about the only place left in Connecticut where they were still tonged by hand.

While the river has been most bountiful, countless millions of oysters were left untouched and remained where they set. Reaching back to prehistoric times well before man arrived, oysters spawned, set on old empty ancestral shells, reproduced, and died, and the life cycle repeated itself over and over again. And all the while empty shells of the dead oysters kept piling up in the river bed and creeks along the marshy eastern bank.

Man certainly relished the oyster, but regarded its empty shells as nature's debris. Some use was made of the shells, however, in road building, for land fill and fertilizers, and they were even burned and converted into lime for masonry work. But no one utilized the ancient Housatonic oyster shells buried under the river and creeks until the era of oyster cultivation in the later part of the nineteenth century. Then the spreading of shells as cultch on the beds prior to spawning became a most important step for the oyster farmer. Instead of discarding shells after shucking as before, oyster companies now covetously saved them outside their shops where they dried out, ready for planting. The huge piles soon became a distinguishing feature of northern shucking plants.

But there always seemed to be a need for more shells, and finally Connecticut oystermen thought of those long dormant shells at the bottom of the Housatonic. Out of this need, a unique, purely local occupation known as "shelling" originated in Stratford. Though it supported a relatively small group of men— a dozen or two at any one time until the near demise of the oyster industry in the 1950s—it was a valuable and important source of shell cultch for the northern oyster growers.

According to some oystermen, the spawn, in searching for something to set on, seemed to prefer these shells to all other surfaces. The Housatonic shells were not only clean and soft, but they were friable, and after a year in the water as cultch they completely dissolved, leaving a single, unattached oyster—the ultimate goal of the oyster cultivator. Also, on an initially soft bottom, a layer of these shells created a hard, firm bottom—another highly desirable feature.

In the beginning, oystermen calling themselves "shellers" or "shellermen" tonged the shells from Stratford-built sharpies and skiffs in the river below Smith's Point. Later they found that Nell's Island and the area between Smith's Point and Nell's Island were rich hunting grounds. The shellermen tonged in eight to sixteen feet of water down through the dirt and mud. Test borings made during the construction of the Stratford breakwater revealed oyster shells at a depth of eighty feet.

The work was hard but the flowing tide helped somewhat to wash the loaded tongs of mud and sand. A sharpie load of sixty bushels was considered a good day's work. The shells were shoveled off the sharpies into wheelbarrows, wheeled on 2 x 12 inch planks to the banks of the river, and dumped into piles on the adjacent meadows. Each shellerman had his own storage pile or shared with someone else. When the planters arrived in the spring and early summer, the dried shells were lifted with coke forks from the storage mounds and wheelbarrowed directly to the shallow draft schooners hard by the marshes. The loaded schooners sailed to the oyster beds in the sound or elsewhere and the shells were shoveled overboard just prior to the spawning season.

This old, laborious procedure lasted until 1908 when power was introduced to the business. Digging by hand out of the bottom stopped, and another

Housatonic River shellerman wheelbarrowing shells off scow on the left. On the right, a shell kicker. Courtesy of August MacTaggart.

Piling shells on the meadows along the lower Housatonic River. Courtesy of Fred Goodsell.

Loading the schooner *Sarah Maria* with Housatonic River oyster shells. Courtesy of Fred Goodsell.

technique called "shell kicking" developed. Apparently not used anywhere else in the oyster world, its ingenuity eliminated a great deal of the hard work and increased production manyfold. The backwash of a boat's propeller was utilized to loosen and "kick up" the buried shells into underwater mounds which were then easily tonged. A boat referred to as a "kicker," usually an old sandbagger, work sloop or any wide boat with a stern affording a free flow of water was employed. It was specially equipped with a shaft set at a steep angle approximately 2 1/2 inches to the foot to permit a more direct water thrust at the bottom. In addition, water-filled barrels or tanks weighted down the stern, further increasing the rake of the shaft. At first 4 to 6, then 10 to 12 h.p. engines provided the kick, but gradually the horsepower rose to 150.

Before kicking began, the boat was carefully positioned over the area to be worked. An anchoring line ran from the bowsprit end ahead to or near the bank. Also from blocks at the end of the bowsprit two holding lines, to stop forward motion, fanned out aft of the boat for upwards of 300 feet. As the kicker pivoted at the bow under rudder control, the propeller washed and dug a semi-circular trough between the two holding lines. When the kicker finished an area, the washed shells, now almost surfaced along the ridge of the trough a few feet aft of the stern, were easily tonged into the 30- to 40-foot-long anchored scows. From these they were wheeled, as formerly, onto the storage heaps on the nearby meadows. In this way immense quantities of shells accumulated. At one time 400,000 bushels were stored on Nell's Island alone. On rare occasions they annoyed nearby residents with an offensive odor, for in the days before the power boat the sharpie tongers sometimes piled live mussels on the meadows along with the shells. These rotted during the year and caused complaints from Stratford people when the wind was right. However, the kicked shells were more or less sand-blasted and therefore carried no odor.

In June and July when the buyers came, the shells were transferred again by wheelbarrow to the oyster company's big scows (60 to 80 feet long, and around 20 feet wide) and schooners. The powered oyster boats and occasionally tug boats then towed the scows to the planting grounds out in the sound where they were shoveled overboard as before. Later, on some boats, they were washed overboard with fire hoses. In the 1930s Leroy Lewis of the H. J. Lewis Oyster Co. designed an endless bucket for the *Oyster Harvester* to unload shells. Though it saved much work, only one such device was ever built.

The oyster plants and companies contracted the shellermen in the fall for a specific number of bushels to be delivered by the following fourth of July. Shellermen then worked nine months of the year, from March to November, stockpiling the contracted amount. A hard-working, three-man crew could kick, tong, and unload 400 to 1,000 bushels a day depending upon the shell quantity on the bottom, the tide, and the weather. Payment was by the wheelbarrow unit of four bushels capacity—the wheeler getting a few cents and the contractor the remainder. In the 1880s shells sold for from three to six cents a bushel or twelve to twenty-four cents a wheelbarrow. In the 1930s the price went up to around forty cents a wheelbarrow load.

The planting scows or barges were invariably owned by the companies, whereas the schooners that also carried away the shells were generally chartered. Some companies owned one or two schooners, however, for shelling and for buying seed oysters. The independent schooner captains considered the shelling season a short, two– to four–week fill-in job, and seemed more irked than pleased by it. As Captain Wakely of the schooner *Blanche* often said when loading Housatonic shell, "Let's get these shells out of here. When they start to dig potatoes on the other side—Orient Point—here I come!"

About two dozen men shelled the river after World War I. Almost to a man they earned a reputation of being responsible, sturdy, and hard-working watermen. They owned sharpies in the old days and kickers and scows later on. The Goodsells of Stratford were typical of these men and their popularity was well earned. The late John Goodsell, a riverman throughout his life, worked seasonally at clamming, catching bait, trapping, fishing, shelling, and natural growth oystering. In the late 1890s he shelled in a sharpie and later installed power in an old 24-foot boat, the *Lena*, and then on the 30-foot keel fishing boat, the *Victoria*, kicking with her until his sixty-fifth year. His son Fred followed in his father's footsteps and both Goodsells oystered all year on the Housatonic and the sound. The work on the river was hard but apparently rewarding, for Fred Goodsell claimed, "I never felt better in my life tonging and working the river."

Shelling, like so many other aspects of the oyster industry, is a thing of the past, though countless shells still lie buried. Perhaps there will be a revival of the business now that oystering seems to be on the rise, but the prospects look dim, for at present the few oyster companies in business supply their own shells.

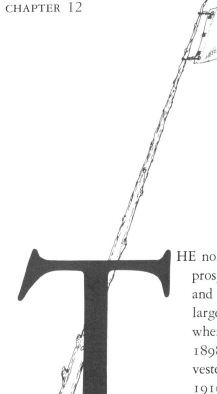

CHAPTER 12

Oystering in the 1970s

THE northern oyster industry experienced its most prosperous and productive years between 1885 and 1910. In 1888 Connecticut maintained the largest area of privately held oyster ground anywhere—86,761 acres. Production peaked in 1898 when over 15,218,614 bushels were harvested, amounting to $1,249,071. Then, from 1910 to the 1960s the Connecticut industry was marked by repeated set failures, with the effect felt not only in that state but also in those regions dependent upon its seed. By the 1950s and early 1960s her oyster industry had nearly disappeared. Ever-diminishing returns due to these set failures, storms, pollution, and other factors forced most oystermen out of business.

In spite of all kinds of setbacks, oystering survived in Connecticut. In 1972 about a dozen natural growthers continued to work the Bridgeport and Housatonic River natural beds. One firm opens oysters today—Bloom Brothers (Norman and Hilliard)—and carries on an active business in South Norwalk in the building formerly occupied by the Talmadge Bros. Inc. Long Island Oyster Farms, Inc., a branch of the New York firm, maintain vessels, shore property, and seed and holding beds in New Haven. They specialize in growing seed for transplanting to their other grounds off Long Island, for they have only minor market grounds in Connecticut. Others working on a smaller scale are

Captain Lawrence "Snakes" Malloy of New London, Joseph and Frank Dolan of Guilford and Shellfish Inc. of Clinton.

In Rhode Island the business soared to its highest production in 1912. Then decline set in—with the assistance of man and nature—as rapidly as prosperity had rushed in only a few years before. The set, which had been regularly taking place for about fifteen years, suddenly stopped in 1914, never to occur again to any significant extent. After this, most of the seed came from Connecticut and elsewhere as it had in preceding decades. To add to the trouble, heavy starfish attacks reminiscent of the 1860s periodically induced heavy losses on oyster crops. And most importantly, industrial waste spewing out of the burgeoning industries ashore destroyed hundreds of profitable oyster grounds in upper Narragansett Bay and the Providence River. Unfortunately few people besides the oystermen cared about the state's oyster resources. Legislation and some protestation—reminiscent of our ecology movement today—had no effect, and the oyster growers fought desperately for their existence. Some of the recently arrived Connecticut men searched for oyster ground elsewhere and found it at Greenport and Staten Island.

Troubles multiplied. Severe winter storms damaged boats and beds in the 1930s. The great hurricane of 1938 silted beds and put an end to about 80 percent of them, inflicting incalculable loss on vessels, shore property, and equipment. Within hours the industry was practically obliterated. A few companies managed to survive, but World War II placed a heavy drain on manpower and entailed a serious work slowdown. Despite all this destruction, oysters set again in the Pawcatuck River below Westerly from 1945 to 1955, promising some hope. But Rhode Island's oyster industry never regained the prosperity and glory of the early 1900s, and since the 1960s extremely few oysters have been harvested commercially in its waters.

Massachusetts followed the other states in their downward trend. After World War I sets continued to fail, the scarcity of seed shot prices up, and the demand fell. Oystermen just hung on or eventually went out of business. In 1973 at Wellfleet only fifteen legal grants of 65 acres are active as compared to 387 grants covering an area of 2,400 acres in 1907.[1]

Only a half–dozen individuals gather the natural set at Wellfleet, transferring it to these beds for growth, and producing from 1,000 to 5,000 bushels yearly. At West Chatham one man, John Hammond, oysters, but on a part-time basis only. He beds three-year-old Long Island Sound oysters from Norwalk and New Haven in the spring and harvests them in the fall and winter, in much the same way as oystermen 100 years ago. The Cotuit Oyster Company, owned by

Long Island Oyster Farms, Inc., also beds Long Island Sound and Peconic Bay oysters. Here, after a short period, the foreigners acquire the renowed Cotuit flavor. Cotuit and Chatham apparently have never been able to catch set, but at Wareham and around the head of Buzzards Bay there has always been a noted natural setting ground. Yet even here, oysters set so infrequently that oystering on a commercial basis is far from profitable. Some experimental work with growing Fishers Island set is being conducted by the Aqua Dynamics Corporation of Wareham, Massachusetts, and it is hopefully expected to prove commercially successful.

With most of the life kicked out of the industry in New York the lowly oyster has retreated to Long Island's eastern end where, thankfully, remarkably clean and pure waters still exist. Long Island Oyster Farms Inc. maintains beds and a processing plant at Greenport and John L. Plock runs the Shelter Island Oyster Co. at Greenport and Southhold. At Fishers Island the Ocean Pond Corporation conducts a salt pond oyster operation. The only other places in New York where oysters are grown commercially are on the north shore of Long Island, where Long Island Oyster Farms Inc. operates an oyster hatchery at Northport, Frank Flower's oyster business at Bayville and the Andrew Radel Oyster Co. at Oyster Bay.

As we have seen, the northern oyster industry slid from its production high at the beginning of the century to relatively nothing in the 1960s. Since then, however, the trend seems to be upward, with new forces working outside and within the industry to slowly reform it. Among these are a realization of our responsibility as a part of nature and the knowledge that if we continue to alter the ecology we will drive ourselves and other living things out of existence.

Quite remarkably nearly everyone today from the school child up is aware of and ready to do something about preserving our natural environment. Domestic discharges have been almost completely halted in the coastal cities and in many towns in the Long Island Sound area. Industries are being forced by alarmed, concerned citizens and authorities to control their harmful discharges. Landfills along the wetlands are under strict control, and through local, state, and federal efforts the wholesale, thoughtless destruction of our marine environment seems to have slowed down. There is evidence that Long Island Sound is becoming cleaner—at least the rate of pollution has altered. And it is hoped the pollution factor, a major cause of the destruction of our best near-shore spawning grounds, may soon be eliminated and become a thing of the past.

A tendency to shift from adulterated to more natural foods may also help the industry, and perhaps the highly nutritious oyster will be rediscovered in the north and midwest, especially by the young. A recent push by the Shellfish Institute of North America to attract attention to the oyster reflects rather succinctly the current thoughts on life and love. One of their free car stickers reads: "Eat fish live longer. Eat oysters love longer."

Another factor which may help the industry is the drive to sell oysters during the R-less months of May through August. Traditionally oysters left the menus then to return during the remaining months with an R in them. (Immediately before spawning oysters are full of spawn and not attractive, and just after spawning they appear thin and poor tasting.) Now, as a result of the new aquaculture techniques practiced, particularly by Long Island Oyster Farms, oysters can be harvested and shipped all year round yet retain their quality, plumpness, and succulence.

Although the industry is relatively small, an interesting internal development has occurred: the oystermen's basic approach to oystering has changed; while some still rely upon nature others are looking to science and its new art of aquaculture. At the turn of the century the northern oyster industry and indeed the entire American industry were united in their reliance upon nature. Each of the hundreds of oyster companies either depended wholly upon natural set or upon cultivated oysters. That is, they planted cultch and hoped nature would cooperate with a good set. Those that continue to follow this well-established technique claim you cannot raise oysters as cheaply as nature in spite of its unreliability. One bushel of natural seed, bought for $3, may produce ten bushels of market–size oysters selling for $18 a bushel. One bushel of hatchery seed oysters may cost $10! The former oystermen maintain that one good set can make up for those years with no set. Primarily all you need, they say, is cleaner waters and good management.

The Bloom Brothers echo this view. They generally buy seed from the natural growthers and cultivate and harvest it by time-honored techniques. Only when natural seed is not available do they use hatchery seed from Edward Fordham's shellfish hatchery in Stratford. Two or three shuckers open the Bloom's oysters by the cracking method—a far cry from the 200 to 250 shuckers employed decades ago by their former next door neighbor, the Andrew Radel Oyster Co. The oysters are cleaned and washed in blowers, then canned. Many are also sent in the shell in gunny sacks. All aspects of the Bloom Brothers' operation are, of course, under the eye of local, state, and federal health agencies, and their product is not only considered sanitary but also of exceptionally fine quality.

Captain Joe Laucher and crew of the Aquaculture Division of the Connecticut State Department of Agriculture buoying newly leased oyster grounds from the *Shell Fish*. Photograph by the author.

Those who run their business on scientific principles take the opposite view. They believe you cannot base a modern oyster business upon the uncertainty of natural setting, and have, therefore, turned to the hatchery for their necessary seed. Long Island Oyster Farms, a sudsidiary of the Inmont Corporation of New York, is the leading proponent of this approach. After acquiring a number of floundering small oyster businesses in the Long Island Sound area, they went into operation in 1970 with a new hatchery in Northport, a processing plant near Greenport, and seed and holding beds in New Haven. Production of their scientifically grown oysters begins in their unique plant in Northport. Here in the hatchery adjacent to the Long Island Lighting Company certain oysters are selected for their superior breeding qualities, shape, and resistance to disease. In laboratory breeding tanks they are stimulated to spawn. Then the oyster larvae are fed by special algae collected from sea water and grown in glass containers. The larvae here grow into single, cultchless oysters— a highly desirable and economical feature first developed on a commercial scale in California in 1967. After about six weeks in the hatchery, where they experience a remarkable rate of growth due to the strict control of temperature, food, and other environmental factors they are placed outside in screen trays and suspended in a lagoon. To maintain a warm environment, which insures continuous growth all year long, the heated sea water (85° F) discharged from the Long Island Lighting Company's plant condensers is utilized—another financial benefit. In the warmth and safety of this "nursery" the oysters are carefully introduced to natural waters, protected from their natural predators, periodically cleaned, and sorted for size.

After reaching planting size they are again shifted, this time to the traditionally maintained beds in the open bay waters at Northport, Huntington, or Greenport for maturing. Market size oysters are finally dredged and sent, mostly to hotels and restaurants, in the shell, or processed, cooked, and packaged frozen at the Greenport plant. The specialities here are flash–frozen topped (garnished) oysters on the half shell ready to be eaten within minutes of heating. These include such delicacies as oysters Rockefeller, Provençale, Bienville, and Mornay.

Fortified by time, technical skills, and a goodly dash of money Long Island Oyster Farms Inc. have overcome the complex engineering problems always associated with hatcheries. Unlike the natural cultivators, they claim to grow oysters on a reliable and predictable schedule with control of growth and survival. Due to selective breeding, hatchery spawning, and warm water incubation the time from spawning to market size has been cut to two and one-half years—half that of naturally bred oysters. Furthermore, the firm applies efficient, modern techniques to dredging, unloading, shucking by machine, and packaging. Yet in spite of its apparent success, it still does not always have to rely on the hatchery. From all observations and impressions much if not most of its product to date actually originates as naturally propagated seed on the firm's cultivated beds off New Haven.

Through the years a number of commercial hatcheries have appeared on the scene but only three, besides the Northport one, now operate north of New York. At Bayville, Long Island, Frank Flower runs his in connection with a regular oyster business. John L. Plock, head of the Shelter Island Oyster Co., produces hatchery seed in Greenport for transplanting to his salt pond in Southold. In Connecticut, Edward Fordham conducts a small hatchery, the Shellfish Laboratories, in Stratford, from which the Bloom's draw set when needed.

Another approach to the problem of oyster failure and scarcity has been

Inside the Long Island Oyster Farm Hatchery in Northport, Long Island. Rows of larvae tanks contain young oysters that have spawned and are at the swimming stage. These are fed specially grown algae in a scientifically controlled environment, with emphasis on proper temperature and water purity. Courtesy of Long Island Oyster Farms, Inc.

the use of salt water ponds for the propagation of oysters. The Ocean Pond Corporation of Fishers Island, New York, has been the most successful in this endeavor, and has been producing seed oysters in their pond since 1961. Before that time oysters were not grown on the island at all, but when the 1938 hurricane broke through a barrier beach on the island it exposed a fresh water pond to a unique tidal situation. Salt water from the sea now flows through the break only during the two highest tides of the month instead of on a daily basis. Fortunately a favorable salinity level for oyster breeding is maintained naturally in the pond and, furthermore, the larvae are blocked most of the time from escaping to the open waters. The shallow pond waters also warm up at least a month earlier than Long Island Sound.

When larvae are detected in the pond, nylon strings of scallop shells, acting as cultch, are suspended in the water from rafts. After the oysters reach 1/2 inch or so, which may take from three to eight weeks, the strings of scallop shells and attached oysters (five to ten per shell) are taken out. Since lack of a good supply of food limits their growth here, they have been sent to oyster growers as seed, but now that the Ocean Pond people are associated with the Aqua Dynamics Corporation of Wareham, where much oyster research has been done, their seed will be trucked there primarily, suspended again in twenty feet of water, held for two to three years, then harvested. Plans have been made for these "off-bottom" raised oysters to be marketed opened, frozen, or in the shell.

The hatchery, and in certain respects the salt water pond, are the current controlled approaches to oyster breeding. Although the theoretical and, to some extent, the engineering problems of the hatchery have been solved, it is still in the pioneering stage and not yet widely adopted. Yet the history of oyster research reaches as far back as the middle of the last century when scientists were trying to understand the causes of the industry's deterioration. Most if not all of the research, however, was conducted under the auspices of academically or governmentally supported agencies not dependent upon profits. It has been difficult for private, commercial concerns to devote much time and money to research, for they must realize some profit for their efforts and there is little of that during periods of experimentation.

Modern scientific oyster study began in France with the governmentally supported researches of M. de Bon and M. Coste in the 1850s. Credit in America is given to Professor William K. Brooks of Johns Hopkins University as the pioneer researcher who, in 1879, was the first to succeed in raising oysters in the laboratory to the larval stage. Among other early workers in the field were Lieutenant Francis Winslow of the United States Navy, Professor John A. Ryder of the University of Pennsylvania, Dr. Julius Nelson of New Jersey, and Dr. David L. Belding of Massachusetts. Although these and others made vast contributions to our knowledge of the oyster none, however, were able to go beyond Professor Brook's larval stage. Their main problem was inability to change the water, which brought in the fresh food, without losing the larvae. It wasn't until 1920 that William F. Wells and his assistant Joseph B. Glancy, working for the New York State Conservation Commission, succeeded in carrying the larvae through to the setting stage under controlled conditions.[2] By

Aerial view of the Aquaculture Division, Connecticut State Department of Agriculture (at water's edge), and the National Marine Fisheries Service Laboratory (upper portion of photo) at Milford, Connecticut, the center for Connecticut's oyster administration and research. Photography by Charles A. Borrmann, Jr.

using an aerating system and centrifugal apparatus at the Bluepoints Company, Inc. in West Sayville, Long Island, they set the pace for subsequent hatcheries.

The leading laboratory for oyster research in the North for the past forty-one years has been the National Marine Fisheries Services Laboratory at Milford, Connecticut, under the control of the National Oceanic and Atmospheric Administration (NOAA) in the United States Department of Commerce. Formerly known as the Bureau of Commercial Fisheries Biological Laboratory of the United States Department of the Interior, it was established in 1931 to study the biological problems of Connecticut's oyster industry. Under the able leadership of its first director, Dr. Victor L. Loosanoff and its second and present director, Dr. James E. Hanks, the laboratory has made significant contributions to our knowledge of shellfish life. In particular it has developed standard methods of rearing molluscan larvae, made commercially feasible techniques of oyster seed production, devised methods of predator control, and studied the effects of pollutants on shellfish. Most of the commercial hatcheries have drawn heavily upon the laboratory's theoretical work, and many scientists from Denmark to Thailand have been trained there in laboratory culture techniques. In the past the laboratory has concentrated on oyster and clam research and has aided and advised the northern oyster industry. Today, with the increased national concern for our environment, it takes a broader view and aims at the preservation of the fishery resources in general.

Now with two different approaches to oystering current the question arises: will the natural or scientific oystermen prevail in the future? Unless the high cost of operating a hatchery is cut drastically, it appears that its widespread use will be as limited as it is today. As one old oysterman put it, "If nature fails, the hatchery can always supply some oysters. They are our ace in the hole."

Powered Oyster Dredge Boats
of Over Five Tons

T HIS is a list of the powered oyster dredge boats of five tons and over—steam, naphtha, gasoline, diesel—that worked the waters between New York and Boston from the 1870s to the present. I have made no particular attempt to list the buy boats, freighters, and auxiliaries, although many are given. However, I have included those auxiliaries that I know worked, part of the time at least, on private beds.

Most of the data in the list came from the various editions of *Merchant Vessels of the United States* which has been issued annually by the government since the late 1860s. Other sources, such as master carpenter's certificates, trade magazines, and oystermen themselves, were also consulted.

To keep up with the changing times few vessels remained exactly as they were when launched. Nearly all showed some changes in either name, dimensions, engines, owners, home ports—in fact every item except the official number. This stayed with the vessel throughout its life in spite of all other alterations. Those buying used boats seemed to have made the most changes, not only with the names and home port but often with the length (for more capacity), tonnage, and sometimes even depth. The data generally refers to the vessel's earliest years as a power boat and represents, therefore, only one point in her existence.

The gross tonnage of a vessel is the total capacity of the interior of the hull and the enclosed space on deck, with certain exemptions, measured in units of 100 cubic feet to the ton. The net tonnage is gross tonnage minus deductions for crew's quarters, engine space, and wheelhouse, thereby giving the available cargo space upon which dues and taxes are charged. Tonnages have been rounded off to the nearest ton.

The length and depth given are custom house measurements and do not equal the overall or waterline length and draft. The definition of "length" varied slightly as well as other registered dimensions, but was generally the measurement along the deck taken from "the fore part of the outer planking on the side of the stem to the after part of the main stern post of screw steamers and to the after part of the rudder post of all other vessels." It can be seen then that the overall length is invariably several feet more than the registered length. For example, the *General's* designed overall length is 62'6" whereas the registered or documented length is recorded as 58'3".

Depth is not the same as draft, but vertical distance measured from the underside of the deck beams, amidships, to the ceiling of the hold.

In the remarks column, the phrase "sloop (cat, or schooner) originally" means that the vessel was indeed a sloop initially but had an engine installed later. She may, therefore, be an auxiliary or completely converted; there is no way of distinguishing here or from the *Merchant Vessels of the United States*. In some cases, however, one can sense that the smaller vessels are more likely auxiliaries.

The owner's name and home port—either where the boat was registered or in some cases where she berthed—also represent, of course, items during one moment in the vessel's career. They are not necessarily the most significant ones.

The M. C.—master carpenter—means the boss or head carpenter in a shipyard or if the boat were built mainly by one man—his name. Sometimes the M.C. is given, sometimes the shipyard. For example, Reuben R. Greene is recorded as the M.C. for some vessels; for others, the Greene Brothers. Furthermore, "builder" may mean either the M.C. or the shipyard. My choices here and elsewhere were for the most part arbitrary.

Although the list is fairly complete and certainly representative, there are bound to be some omissions, especially of the early vessels and of those that oystered only a very short time. It is, however, the only extensive compilation of such vessels available. Those marked with an asterisk were steam powered during all or part of their existence. Unless otherwise stated all the other vessels were either gas or diesel powered.

Official Number	Name	Gross Tons	Net Tons	Length	Beam	Depth	Year Built	Where Built	Remarks
106204	A. and W. Manee	11	7	34.0	15.1	3.9	1883	Tottenville, N.Y.	Sloop originally
105929	A. Booth	74	50	82.2	23.4	5.9	1880	Talbot County, Md.	Freighter, schooner originally
107294	*A.C. Brown	22	15	48.0	15.5	5.2	1897	Tottenville, N.Y.	A.C. Brown & Sons, builder
107541	A.C.D.	14	13	39.4	14.0	3.7	1900	South Boston, Mass.	600 bu., M. Dewing, owner, Providence, R.I.
205393	A.C. Frazer	30	19	49.3	17.6	5.4	1908	Port Jefferson, N.Y.	Home port, N.Y.C.
106586	*Active	59	40	50.8	16.8	5.7	1888	Port Jefferson, N.Y.	Mather and Wood, builders
107172	*Active	31	25	40.0	14.5	3.8	1895	East Providence, R.I.	Home port, Providence, R.I.
204202	Ada M. McNeil	9	8	36.2	14.6	3.5	1907	New Haven, Conn.	Sloop originally
106110	Ada Velma	21	15	43.4	15.4	4.6	1882	Northport, N.Y.	Sloop, steam, gas
205624	*Addie L. Lowndes	131	89	88.4	26.5	9.1	1908	Tottenville, N.Y.	A.C. Brown and Sons, builder
106356	*Addie V	21	12	57.7	14.5	5.8	1885	Bayville, N.Y.	30 h.p. steam engine
106856(1)	Adele	6	5	30.2	11.5	3.5	1891	East Providence, R.I.	Sloop yacht
105513	*Adeline	16	8	40.0	12.2	3.8	1875	Cold Spring, N.Y.	Home port, Bridgeport, Conn.
105179	Admiral	28	24	57.6	17.3	5.1	1872	New Brunswick, N.J.	Schooner, sloop, gas, diesel
107816	A.E. Vreeland	21	18	43.0	15.9	4.4	1902	Stratford, Conn.	Home port, N.Y.C.
157374(2)	*A.F. Merrell	31	15	54.6	13.9	5.5	1893	South Norwalk, Conn.	Named after oysterman of N.Y.C.

(1) Renamed *Stranger*
(2) Formerly *Dexter K. Cole*

Official Number	Name	Gross Tons	Net Tons	Length	Beam	Depth	Year Built	Where Built	Remarks
107328	Agile	9	7	34.2	11.5	3.4	1897	Patchogue, N.Y.	John M. Schmeelk, owner, N.Y.C.
203265	Ajax	11	10	38.7	11.3	3.0	1906	South Norwalk, Conn.	Leslie Gamble, M.C.
107829	Alarm	13	12	42.8	13.8	3.6	1903	Patchogue, N.Y.	Westerbeke Bros., owners, West Sayville, N.Y.
107698(1)	Albert	14	9	41.2	15.4	3.6	1901	Tottenville, N.Y.	A.C. Brown & Sons, builders
106193	*Alberta	23	13	50.6	13.4	4.8	1883	South Norwalk, Conn.	Richards & Weed, builders
106578(2)	*Albert J. Hoyt	47	24	63.5	16.5	4.7	1888	Port Jefferson, N.Y.	Mather & Wood, builders
204002(3)	Alert	14	12	48.0	14.5	4.0	1907	Greenport, N.Y.	Waterman E. Field, Jr., owner, Providence, R.I.
105829(4)	Alexine Davison	13	12	42.3	16.3	3.0	1878	Rockaway, N.Y.	Auxiliary sloop
204135	Alice	37	25	56.1	18.5	5.8	1907	Tottenville, N.Y.	J.S. Ellis & Son, builders
106426	Alida V	6	6	29.3	13.3	3.3	1886	Patchogue, N.Y.	First Great South Bay sloop converted
211946	A. Lincoln Ford	19	16	40.7	15.3	4.6	1913	Tottenville, N.Y.	Edgar J. Ellis, M.C.
105355	Alonzo E. Smith	18	18	50.4	17.5	4.4	1873	Port Jefferson, N.Y.	Sloop originally
107235	Alpha	8	7	30.3	11.2	3.3	1896	Freeport, N.Y.	Home port, Patchogue, N.Y.
202065	Alpha	7	7	30.4	11.4	3.7	1905	Stamford, Conn.	W.S. Merritt, owner, Stamford, Conn.

(1)Sistership of Earle   (3)Name changes: P. & B. No. 2, Albert, Whitecap
(2)Renamed Etta May   (4)Renamed Edith

No.	Name						Year	Place	Notes
77043[1]	*Alvina H. Still*	14	13	55.8	17.0	3.0	1892	Bayport, N.Y.	Home port, N.Y.C.
145295[2]	*Amanda*	75	37	69.5	18.0	6.8	1882	Port Jefferson, N.Y.	Home port, New Haven, Conn.
201093	*Amanda Bishop*	29	27	59.4	18.8	5.4	1904	Patchogue, N.Y.	Sloop originally
204837	*Amanda F. Lancraft*	146	99	82.0	24.4	8.6	1907	Greenport, N.Y.	Lengthened by Alberton Const. Co, Greenport, N.Y.
85618[3]	*Americana*	108	73	106.5	22.1	7.3	1880	Mystic Bridge, Conn.	Formerly Block Island ferry
203036	*Americus*	73	60	70.5	22.5	6.4	1906	Tottenville, N.Y.	Sistership of *Columbia*
100202[4]	*Amerique*	19	16	56.0	14.0	4.5	1877	East Haven, Conn.	Converted from steam to 45 h.p. gas
107156[5]	*A.M. Low*	18	12	35.4	12.1	4.0	1892	South Norwalk, Conn.	Wm. Taylor, M.C.
739	*Anna Brown*	48	45	63.6	21.7	5.0	1866	Westfield, N.Y.	Schooner originally
106284	*Anne*	13	6	34.2	14.8	3.7	1884	Smithtown, N.Y.	Capt. L. H. Malloy's converted sloop
418	*Ann Gertrude*	14	13	40.0	15.2	4.3	1851	Patchogue, N.Y.	Auxiliary sloop
1397[6]	*Annie*	72	49	39.9	15.2	5.8	1868	Bristol, R.I.	Sloop, paddle, screw steamer
106875	*Annie*	5	5	26.3	12.2	3.8	1883	Saunderstown, R.I.	Catboat originally
226119	*Anne*	11	9	37.3	13.9	3.4	1926	New Haven, Conn.	John J. Lickteig, owner, New Haven, Conn.
106776	*Annie G*	31	28	61.0	17.7	4.9	1890	Nyack, N.Y.	Sloop originally
203255	*Annie M*	48	33	49.1	16.7	4.5	1898	Warwick, R.I.	Edmund H. Matteson, owner, Warren, R.I.

[1] Formerly *James Morrissey*
[2] Formerly *The Hoyt Bros. Co.*
[3] Formerly *George W. Danielson*
[4] Formerly *Ivernia*
[5] Renamed *Pausch Bros. I*
[6] Renamed *Dreadnaught*

Official Number	Name	Gross Tons	Net Tons	Length	Beam	Depth	Year Built	Where Built	Remarks
77295[1]	*Ardelia	51	34	51.0	15.5	5.6	1898	Essex, Mass.	M. Dewing Co., owner, Providence, R.I.
107394	Argo	10	9	33.0	13.0	3.3	1885	Islip, N.Y.	Sloop originally
106821	*Argus	22	11	42.0	12.2	5.9	1891	Port Jefferson, N.Y.	James M. Bayles and Son, builders
106879	Ariel	6	6	32.0	13.4	5.0	1882	South Norwalk, Conn.	Auxiliary sloop
107493	Arline	14	12	53.2	13.0	4.0	1899	Merrick, N.Y.	Originally an inland freighter
106677	Artemisia	10	9	37.2	13.6	3.0	1889	New Haven, Conn.	Schooner-watch boat
106971	Arthur B	8	8	34.6	13.6	3.3	1892	Bayport, N.Y.	Sloop originally
107811	Arthur J	12	8	40.4	11.4	3.6	1902	Bridgeport, Conn.	Reuben R. Greene, M.C.
107573	Arthur L	13	9	37.7	12.4	4.9	1899	Brooklyn, N.Y.	Naphtha powered originally
107446	Arthur R. Fling	11	10	33.7	13.5	4.5	1898	Atlantic City, N.J.	Sloop originally
106261	Athlon	33	27	52.5	17.0	6.9	1884	Brooklyn, N.Y.	Sloop yacht originally
85831[2]	Audrey	8	7	42.0	13.0	3.0	1884	Patchogue, N.Y.	Home port, Patchogue, N.Y.
107837	Automatic	14	9	44.5	13.0	3.8	1903	Bridgeport, Conn.	Reuben R. Greene, M.C.
106418[3]	Avalon	40	27	58.2	20.7	6.0	1886	Islip, N.Y.	Schooner yacht originally

[1] Formerly J.W. Stubbs, later Woco
[2] Formerly sloop George H. Shaffer
[3] Renamed Sea Coast

Number	Name						Year	Home Port	Remarks
3569	*Baby Ruth	19	10	38.0	12.0	4.0	1892	East Providence, R.I.	Robert Pettis, owner, Providence, R.I.
96647[1]	Beacon	38	26	62.5	17.1	5.2	1902	Huntington, N.Y.	Beacon Oyster Co., owner, Newport, R.I.
2458	Bella Cooper	21	18	47.7	16.3	3.8	1866	Jersey City, N.J.	Once a passenger boat
2768	Belle Breckenridge	14	13	46.5	16.0	4.2	1871	Bellport, N.Y.	Sloop originally
2932	Bellport	12	12	30.0	12.5	3.2		Bellport, N.Y.	Sloop, naphtha, gas
3399	*Bernice	13	6	41.9	9.4	2.8	1888	East Providence, R.I.	10 h.p. steam engine, Home port, Bristol, R.I.
141700[2]	Bertha	15	14	43.5	12.2	4.0	1901	New Haven, Conn.	18 h.p. Standard engine
3344	Bessie	16	15	37.9	14.0	4.3	1866	Noank, Conn.	Sloop originally
3253	B.F. Jane	81	35	74.4	26.6	5.5	1883	Stony Brook, N.Y.	Schooner originally M.T. Smith & Co., builder
3872	Bivalve	14	11	48.2	16.8	4.0	1901	Patchogue, N.Y.	
212814	Bivalve	14	12	32.2	15.6	4.2	1914	Tottenville, N.Y.	36 h.p. gas engine John F. James & Sons, builder
231139[3]	Bluepoints	171	146	92.6	28.5	8.9	1931	Essex, Mass.	
3327	*Bond-Currier	95	67	67.0	17.5	5.7	1885	Stratford, Conn.	Ash. A. Bond, M.C.
3924	Breakwater	14	12	47.9	16.0	3.5	1902	Greenport, N.Y.	Thomas Oyster Co., owner, New Haven, Conn.
3005	*Brookhaven	50	30	61.0	15.0	4.0	1872	Brooklyn, N.Y.	1000—bu. capacity
3116	Bulab Potter	6	5	30.6	13.0	3.0	1879	Patchogue, N.Y.	Cat, sloop, gas boat
5909	*Cambria	90	66	69.8	20.8	6.8	1871	Greenport, N.Y.	Received first gas engine license

[1] Formerly Helen Stanley
[2] Formerly Leah A. Wedmore
[3] Formerly Clara C. Raye

Official Number	Name	Gross Tons	Net Tons	Length	Beam	Depth	Year Built	Where Built	Remarks
5943	Captain	21	17	54.5	17.7	4.6	1871	Bayport, N.Y.	Sloop originally
127473	Captain	14	13	50.0	15.0	3.3	1900	Greenport, N.Y.	Originally 25 h.p. gas engine
240467[1]	Captain	57	26	61.6	23.2	6.3	1940	Amburg, Va.	Long Island Oyster Farms, Inc., owners, N.Y.C.
127412	Capt. Dan	8	8	29.5	13.0	4.4	1900	Stratford, Conn.	James Fyfe, owner, Glenwood Landing, N.Y.
238252	Carol	10	7	34.7	10.8	4.1	1939	Leonardo, N.J.	Home port, Perth Amboy, N.J.
91867[2]	Carolyn Raye	74	50	78.7	24.2	7.1	1886	Stratford, Conn.	Bluepoints Co., Inc., owner, Sayville, N.Y.
205852	Carrie H	11	10	33.0	12.7	4.0	1908	Norwalk, Conn.	Oscar Anderson, M.C.
203720[3]	Carrie H. Still	37	29	56.8	17.6	5.2	1906	Patchogue, N.Y.	Geo. M. Still, owner, N.Y.C.
126832	Carrie H.T.B.	6	5	29.8	13.0	3.3	1892	Patchogue, N.Y.	Sloop originally
127008	*Carrie V	17	8	38.0	14.0	4.0	1893	South Norwalk, Conn.	Wm. Taylor, M.C.
224325	Catherine M. Wedmore	37	25	56.3	18.2	6.0	1924	West Mystic, Conn.	Bloom Bros., owner, South Norwalk, Conn.
126835	*C.B. Lowndes	28	14	64.0	14.2	5.6	1891	Bridgeport, Conn.	W.B. Hunt, M.C.
110802[4]	*C.D. Parmelee	91	65	70.3	21.0	7.7	1888	New Haven, Conn.	144 h.p. engine
126327	*Ceres	16	8	45.0	14.3	3.8	1885	Norwalk, Conn.	400-bu. capacity

[1] Formerly Jane D
[2] Formerly Mikado, City Point
[3] Formerly W.H. Bishop
[4] Formerly Richard W. Law

Official No.	Name			Length	Beam	Depth	Year	Place	Notes
235915	Chamaroy	57	39	63.7	20.0	7.4	1937	Brooklyn, N.Y.	Narragansett Bay Oyster Co., owner, Providence, R.I.
203783[1]	Chas. E. Hopkins	18	12	44.7	14.8	4.2	1906	Bridgeport, Conn.	Greene Bros., builders
126479	Charles F. Dayton	8	8	34.8	13.5	3.9	1888	Patchogue, N.Y.	Catboat originally
127501	Charles W. Lynde	66	40	84.0	20.6	5.4	1901	Patchogue, N.Y.	Schooner originally
126710	C.H. Green	19	17	49.3	16.0	4.6	1891	Bayport, N.Y.	Sloop originally
126208	Christeen	11	10	38.4	15.1	3.9	1883	Glenwood, N.Y.	Sloop originally
126376[2]	*City of Bridgeport	588	340	144.8	28.4	10.0	1886	Port Jefferson, N.Y.	Ferry boat
91867[3]	*City Point	141	96	78.7	24.2	7.1	1886	Stratford, Conn.	Home port, New Haven, Conn.
125050	Clara A. Palmer	15	14	41.5	15.3	4.2	1872	Glenwood, N.Y.	Sloop originally
231139[4]	Clara C. Raye	171	146	92.6	28.5	8.9	1931	Essex, Mass.	4,500–bu. capacity
213548	Clara D	6	5	29.9	10.3	2.9	1909	Woodmere, N.Y.	Emery Dexsey, owner, Lynnbrook, N.Y.
126345[5]	*Cleo	30	15	44.0	13.0	5.4	1886	New Haven, Conn.	Geo. M. Graves, builder
127492	Climax	10	8	38.0	12.1	3.7	1900	Bridgeport, Conn.	Reuben R. Greene, M.C.
127656	Columbia	9	8	42.4	13.0	3.0	1902	Amityville, N.Y.	Originally a side-wheeler passenger boat
203037[6]	Columbia	78	65	70.5	22.5	6.4	1906	Tottenville, N.Y.	A.E. Ellis & Son, builder
243214	Columbus	7	5	30.2	11.7	3.2	1931	Sayville, N.Y.	Long Island Oyster Farms, Inc., owners, N.Y.C.

[1] Renamed T.H.C.
[2] Renamed H.C. Rowe & Co.
[3] Formerly Mikado, renamed Carolyn Raye
[4] Renamed Bluepoints
[5] Renamed Mildred
[6] Sistership of Americus

Official Number	Name	Gross Tons	Net Tons	Length	Beam	Depth	Year Built	Where Built	Remarks
127286	Commander	47	40	68.0	16.4	5.8	1898	Baltimore, Md.	Designed by P. Elsworth
125145	Commodore	25	22	58.0	18.4	5.0	1873	Islip, N.Y.	Sloop originally
252258	Commodore	33	27	60.5	18.9	4.5	1947	West Haven, Conn.	Original owners, J. & J.W. Elsworth Co., N.Y.C.
126038	Contest	12	12	38.1	16.8	4.0	1882	Northport, N.Y.	Auxiliary sloop
209451	Convoy	14	12	37.0	15.3	5.0	1911	Tottenville, N.Y.	Home port, Patchogue, N.Y.
127317[1]	Coulter and McKenzie	14	10	42.0	12.8	4.1	1899	Patchogue, N.Y.	Capt. Chas. B. Crane, Greenport, N.Y.
127543	Crescent	14	12	46.5	13.6	3.9	1901	Rockaway Beach, N.Y.	Chas. K. Wedmore, owner, New Haven, Conn.
127705	Crescite	14	10	46.6	14.0	3.4	1902	Bridgeport, Conn.	Reuben R. Greene, M.C.
125931	*C.S. Conklin	53	34	54.0	15.0	4.0	1881	South Norwalk, Conn.	H.J. Lewis Oyster Co., owner, Bridgeport, Conn.
207302	C.S. Sofield	40	33	55.2	18.8	5.7	1910	Tottenville, N.Y.	Designed by Edward J. Ellis
127608	Cultivator	17	11	44.2	15.5	4.0	1902	Quincy, Mass.	Once owned by Wellfleet Oyster Co, Wellfleet, Mass.
127488	Cupid	14	11	45.6	15.9	4.6	1900	Patchogue, N.Y.	Once owned by Cedar Island Oyster Co., N.Y.

[1] Renamed Maria

Number	Name					Year	Home Port	Remarks
127036	Curiosity	44	74.0	18.4	3.8	1894	Patchogue, N.Y.	Once a stern-wheel passenger boat
126288(1)	*C.W. Hoyt	70	64.1	16.4	4.0	1857	New Haven, Conn.	Rebuilt in 1885
157245	*Daisy	6	34.0	10.3	4.0	1889	Patchogue, N.Y.	Andrew Radel Oyster Co., owner, South Norwalk, Conn.
157050	*Daisy E. Smith	69	65.4	20.0	5.2	1881	New Haven, Conn.	1000–bu. capacity
202805	Daniel and Carrie	14	51.6	13.9	4.4	1906	Bristol, Me.	Home port at one time, Providence, R.I.
6565(2)	Daniel Tomkins	80	80.5	25.5	5.5	1867	Stony Point, N.Y.	Schooner
6669	Dan Sooy	15	43.7	16.7	4.0	1870	Smith Landing, N.J.	Schooner originally
253063	Dauntless	24	37.4	16.9	6.8	1947	East Norwalk, Conn.	Originally designed as V-bottom power yacht
201669	David R. Dodge	14	45.9	13.7	3.2	1905	Bridgeport, Conn.	Reuben R. Greene, M.C.
157640	Decker	10	37.5	11.6	3.4	1890	Freeport, N.Y.	Home port, Patchogue, N.Y.
201077	Decomab	9	34.0	12.2	3.8	1904	Stratford, Conn.	Home port, Patchogue, N.Y.
157374(3)	*Dexter K. Cole	31	54.6	13.9	5.5	1893	South Norwalk, Conn.	Wm. Taylor, M.C.
201824	Dixie	13	37.2	12.2	4.2	1,905	Brooklyn, N.Y.	Home port, N.Y.C.
157249	*Doctor	16	42.0	10.5	4.8	1889	New York, N.Y.	Once a yacht and towboat
1397(4)	*Dreadnaught	81	68.6	17.5	6.4	1868	Bristol, R.I.	Andrew Radel Oyster Co., owner, Bridgeport, Conn.

(1) Renamed Precursor (3) Renamed A.F. Merrell
(2) Renamed Normandic (4) Formerly Annie

Official Number	Name	Gross Tons	Net Tons	Length	Beam	Depth	Year Built	Where Built	Remarks
136588	Eagle	9	8	35.0	10.6	3.3	1896	Patchogue, N.Y.	Warren Oyster Co., Warren, R.I.
136946(1)	Earle	14	9	41.2	15.7	3.6	1901	Tottenville, N.Y.	A.C. Brown & Sons, builder
7930	*Early Bird	9	7	31.4	13.0	3.4		Greenport, N.Y.	First oyster steamer
231607	Eben A. Thacher	47	31	59.8	19.5	6.1	1932	Fairhaven, Mass.	Originally a freighter
137049	Edenia	13	7	42.4	16.0	4.0	1902	Tottenville, N.Y.	Built for A.F. Merrell, N.Y.C.
135126	Edgar Bernard	16	14	41.5	15.7	4.3	1875	Staten Island, N.Y.	Sloop originally
105829(2)	Edith	20	13	55.2	15.6	3.3	1878	Rockaway, N.Y.	Sloop originally, lengthened
136174(3)	*Edith A	31	15	46.1	15.4	6.2	1891	South Norwalk, Conn.	Joseph Vroom & John Ayers, builders
136864	Edith Louise	18	12	46.5	15.7	4.4	1900	Atlantic City, N.J.	Sloop originally
201488	Edna A	8	7	31.2	13.5	3.6	1882	Bay Shore, N.Y.	Catboat originally
136869	*Edna Chase	113	71	76.5	19.4	5.8	1901	Northport, N.Y.	Fore and aft compound engine
200327(4)	Edw. F. Leeds	28	21	55.4	16.8	4.6	1903	Stratford, Conn.	William E. Bedell, M.C.
217969	Eleanor A. Warner	42	22	55.3	20.6	6.1	1919	Patchogue, N. Y.	Empire Shellfish Distributors Inc., owner, N.Y.C.
136902(5)	Elizabeth	69	58	85.2	21.2	5.7	1901	Baltimore, Md.	Home port, Baltimore, Md.
8749	Elizabeth Jones	15	14	43.5	17.0	3.2	1871	Port Richmond, N.Y.	Sloop originally

(1) Sistership of Albert
(2) Formerly Alexine Davison
(3) Renamed Stirling
(4) Renamed Hampton
(5) Renamed Jane

135084	Ella	7	7	36.9	12.0	3.8	1874	Rockaway Beach, N.Y.	Sloop originally
135609	Ella May	12	11	42.0	12.4	3.4	1882	Patchogue, N.Y.	Schooner originally
8963	Ella V. Lillie	9	9	35.3	13.7	3.6	1873	Barnegat, N.J.	Sloop originally
137033	Ellen J	13	7	42.4	16.0	4.0	1902	Tottenville, N.Y.	Fred Lovejoy, owner, East Norwalk, Conn.
200100	Ellen S	15	13	49.5	14.3	3.2	1903	Bridgeport, Conn.	Lengthened 12' in 1911
200401	Elrena	11	8	32.0	12.9	3.8	1903	Glenwood, N.Y.	Lengthened later
136047	Elsie	6	6	27.4	11.0	3.4	1889	Bayville, N.Y.	Sloop originally
136875	Elsie K	12	9	42.0	14.0	4.5	1901	South Norwalk, Conn.	Naphtha engine
136878	Emily	8	6	30.4	12.5	3.6	1901	Rowayton, Conn.	John S. Ayers, M.C.
8369	Emily J	16	15	43.0	15.4	3.3	1868	Merrick, N.Y.	Sloop originally
135682	*Emily Mansfield	51	26	55.0	17.0	5.3	1883	New Haven, Conn.	Geo. M. Graves, builder
225419(1)	Emma & Ruth	64	28	77.9	23.8	5.8	1926	Dorchester, N.J.	Schooner
8599	Emma Frances	18	17	57.0	14.7	3.0	1869	Norwalk, Conn.	Sloop originally
136130	*Emma K	32	16	59.0	16.5	5.8	1890	Glen Cove, N.Y.	Once a towboat
135406	*Empress	9	7	44.5	10.5	3.2	1879	Youngsport, N.Y.	Originally a steam yacht
	Ensign (registration questionable) J. & J.W. Elsworth Co. boat								
135283(2)	*Enterprise	36	28	57.3	14.9	4.5	1877	Norwalk, Conn.	W.H. Lockwood, owner, Norwalk, Conn.
136817	Eric	14	9	42.0	14.1	4.2	1900	New Haven, Conn.	Named after Eric T. Ball, New Haven, Conn.
135837(3)	Estelle Gerber	6	5	34.0	12.0	3.0	1885	Sayville, N.Y.	Sloop

(1)Renamed Norman L. Jeffries, Frank M. Flower   (3)Renamed Sarah L.
(2)Renamed Wm. T. Lancraft

Official Number	Name	Gross Tons	Net Tons	Length	Beam	Depth	Year Built	Where Built	Remarks
80760(1)	Esther B	37	25	59.1	18.3	6.0	1880	Greenport, N.Y.	Ernest E. Ball, owner, New Haven, Conn.
8470	Esther Fraser	23	21	44.8	17.8	4.7	1868	Patchogue, N.Y.	Sloop originally
106578(2)	*Etta May	99	49	75.5	16.5	4.7	1888	Port Jefferson, N.Y.	Home port, Bridgeport, Conn.
136391	Eulalia	11	9	34.0	13.5	4.0	1893	Patchogue, N.Y.	Sloop originally
137048	Eureka	12	10	42.0	14.2	3.8	1902	Patchogue, N.Y.	Later lengthened
136213	Eurybia	14	13	37.4	13.5	6.3	1888	Brooklyn, N.Y.	Sloop yacht originally
200601	Evelyn	24	16	46.7	14.5	4.1	1904	West Haven, Conn.	Once owned by F. Mansfield & Sons, New Haven, Conn.
203768	Excelsior	9	8	38.0	13.3	3.6	1906	Patchogue, N.Y.	Excelsior Blue Point Oyster Co., owner, West Sayville, N.Y.
120244	Falcon	21	13	48.5	16.4	4.6	1876	Mauricetown, N.J.	Schooner originally
120593	*Falcon	46	23	68.0	15.0	6.0	1884	South Norwalk, Conn.	Richards and Weed, builders
120718(3)	*Fannie C. Hart	476	394	142.8	30.0	10.6	1888	Manitowoc, Wis.	Passenger carrier
9731	Fannie Scofield	7	6	30.0	12.2	3.3	1870	Williamsburg, N.Y.	Sloop originally
121027	Fannie W	5	5	33.5	9.9	2.9	1896	Patchogue, N.Y.	First Long Island gas boat
203359	Fannie W	28	19	58.7	18.6	5.2	1906	Greenport, N.Y.	Once owned by Royal Toner, Southold, N.Y.
120734	Favorite	9	8	31.1	12.8	4.4	1888	Seabright, N.J.	Sloop originally

(1) Formerly *Wizard*
(2) Formerly *Albert J. Hoyt*
(3) Renamed *Rowe*

Number	Name						Year	Place	Remarks
120584	*F.C. and A.E. Rowland	97	48	70.0	22.2	5.4	1884	Darien, Conn.	Dexter Cole, M.C. Schooner originally
9923	Fearless	30	20	54.0	16.0	6.4	1870	Bath, Me.	Home port, Greenport, N.Y.
218696	Fern	9	5	29.4	10.6	4.0	1917	West Haven, Conn.	Sloop to steamer
9935	Fleetfoot	47	31	41.4	16.3	4.8	1870	Bridgeport, Conn.	Owned by F. Mansfield & Sons Co., New Haven, Conn.
238258(1)	F.L. Homan	34	23	53.7	18.1	5.3	1939	Warren, R.I.	
120079	*Flora	20	10	41.0	12.4	4.3	1873	Shellyville, Mass.	Home port, Perth Amboy, N.J.
203263	Flora	30	20	51.3	16.7	4.6	1906	Bridgeport, Conn.	Reuben R. Greene, M.C.
200305(2)	Flora Ball	20	13	45.4	16.0	3.0	1903	Greenport, N.Y.	Eric T. Ball, owner, New Haven, Conn.
120350	Florence	8	7	35.0	13.2	3.6	1878	Oyster Bay, N.Y.	Sloop originally
120519	*Florence	102	75	81.0	18.3	5.7	1882	Setauket, N.Y.	Home port, Bridgeport, Conn.
120391	Flying Cloud	8	7	34.4	13.3		1879	Patchogue, N.Y.	Sloop originally, naphtha power
210784	*F. Mansfield & Sons Co.	214	88	100.0	29.0	8.4	1912	Milford, Del.	C.M. McLaury, designer, W. Abbott, builder
248760(3)	40 Fathom No. 39	25	11	44.8	16.0	6.3	1945	Washington, D.C.	Home port, New Orleans, La.
120868	Four Brothers	5	5	25.1	12.0	3.6	1890	Newport, R.I.	Catboat originally
121051(4)	*Four Sisters	28	19	45.8	16.5	5.5	1897	Glenwood, N.Y.	Joshua Bedell, builder
130741(5)	Foxy Grandpa	6	6	30.7	13.2	3.3	1897	Patchogue, N.Y.	Home port, Patchogue, N.Y.

(1) Renamed Suzanne
(2) Formerly Grace Fordham
(3) Renamed Skimmer I
(4) Renamed Vernie S
(5) Formerly Norma

Official Number	Name	Gross Tons	Net Tons	Length	Beam	Depth	Year Built	Where Built	Remarks
204676	Frank A. Koellmer	20	15	47.2	15.0	4.8	1907	Stratford, Conn.	Wm. E. Bedell, M.C.
121242	Frank C. Pettis	17	14	45.7	14.1	3.6	1902	Bridgeport, Conn.	Reuben R. Greene, M.C.
121257	*Frank E. Brown	18	12	52.0	15.6	3.9	1902	Stratford, Conn.	Named after New Haven oysterman
225419(1)	Frank M. Flower	64	28	77.9	23.8	5.8	1926	Dorchester, N.J.	Frank M. Flower & Sons, Inc., owners, Bayville, N.Y.
121058	*Frank T. Lane	99	56	71.7	21.7	5.1	1897	Tottenville, N.Y.	Stern wheeler originally
120463	*Freddie W. Decker	20	14	65.0	13.0	5.0	1881	Norwalk, Conn.	Yacht originally
120471	*Fred F. Brown	42	29	53.2	14.2	4.0	1882	Northport, N.Y.	Henry J. Lewis, owner, Bridgeport, Conn.
121007(2)	*Fulton Market	158	77	132.8	28.0	6.6	1895	Noank, Conn.	Fisherman
120583	F.W. Gordon	13	13	41.5	15.7	4.3	1884	Bay Shore, N.Y.	Sloop originally
85615	*G.C. Dean	16	11	50.9	14.2	4.0	1878	Tottenville, N.Y.	Originally a Philadelphia steamer
237126	General	53	39	58.2	20.2	7.4	1938	Thomaston, Me.	Sistership of Harvester
228281	George C. Bell	84	76	87.2	24.3	6.5	1929	Dorchester, N.J.	Oyster carrier
85133	George D. Allen	15	12	45.8	15.3	3.9	1871	Patchogue, N.Y.	Sloop originally
10918	George F. Carman	40	36	55.5	19.1	6.0	1865	Patchogue, N.Y.	Ernest E. Ball, owner, New Haven, Conn.

(1) Formerly Emma & Ruth, Norman L. Jeffries   (2) Renamed H.C. Rowe & Co., Oyster Bay

202498	*George H. Billo*	14	12	46.8	16.6	3.0	1905	Patchogue, N.Y.	Bluepoints Co, Inc, owner, West Sayville, N.Y.
86591	*Geo. H. Mott*	14	13	45.8	15.0	4.0	1901	Long Island City, N.Y.	Home port, Patchogue, N.Y.
85831[1]	*George H. Shaffer*	8	8	33.0	13.4	3.2	1884	Patchogue, N.Y.	Originally a catboat
85958[2]	*George Kingston*	12	11	35.8	15.0	3.8	1887	Oakdale, N.Y.	Sloop
216411	*Geo. L. Jr.*	13	11	40.2	13.6	4.9	1918	Great Kills, N.Y.	Sharp stern
213745	*George L. Thompson*	20	19	45.0	15.4	5.0	1915	Bristol, R.I.	Rebuilt 1915
86333	**George M. Long*	68	35	51.0	17.0	6.0	1895	Noank, Conn.	Home port, New London, Conn.
86592	*Geo. S. Brush*	14	13	41.0	14.1	4.0	1901	Patchogue, N.Y.	Bluepoints Co, Inc, West Sayville, N.Y., owner
10972	*George S. Page*	53	29	71.5	24.6	5.1	1868	Astoria, N.Y.	Schooner originally
202335	*George T*	25	23	46.5	17.3	4.5	1905	Tottenville, N.Y.	W.H. Ellis, builder
85618[3]	**George W. Danielson*	131	103	106.5	21.6	8.5	1880	Mystic Bridge, Conn.	Block Island ferry
85387	*George W. Moger*	12	8	35.0	12.2	3.0	1875	Patchogue, N.Y.	Sloop originally
85047	*Georgianna*	14	6	41.0	15.6	3.4	1869	Mariner Harbor, N.Y.	Sloop originally
85964	*Georgie M*	7	6	36.7	11.8	3.3	1886	Bay Shore, N.Y.	Auxiliary sloop
208516	*G.H. Church*	36	19	54.5	16.4	4.9	1911	Noank, Conn.	Originally fisherman and freighter
86640	*Gladys*	10	7	33.2	13.4	3.8	1902	Tottenville, N.Y.	Home port, N.YC.
203348	*Gladys Adell*	8	7	33.0	13.0	3.0	1906	Sayville, N.Y.	Home port, Patchogue, N.Y.
205966	*Gladys L*	26	22	45.7	16.7	5.1	1909	Tottenville, N.Y.	80 h.p. Twentieth Century gas engine

(1) Renamed *Audrey*   (3) Renamed *Americana*
(2) Renamed *Progress*

Official Number	Name	Gross Tons	Net Tons	Length	Beam	Depth	Year Built	Where Built	Remarks
208675[1]	Gloria B	41	28	57.4	18.9	6.6	1911	Tottenville, N.Y.	Thomas Oyster Co., owner, New Haven, Conn.
85479	*Golden Gale	18	9	36.0	9.0	4.0	1876	Noank, Conn.	500-bu. capacity
85722	*Gordon Rowe	57	29	62.7	18.0	6.0	1882	New Haven, Conn.	Geo. M. Graves, builder
211737	Gordon K	10	10	33.0	10.0	3.0	1908	New Haven, Conn.	Home port, New Haven, Conn.
209047	Gosome	7	6	34.2	13.0	3.0	1911	Sayville, N.Y.	Fisherman later
203024	Governor	32	22	52.7	17.4	5.2	1906	Stratford, Conn.	Wm. E. Bedell, builder
200305[2]	Grace Fordham	14	12	48.4	16.0	3.0	1903	Greenport, N.Y.	Albertson Shipyard, builder
231045	Grace P. Lowndes	26	18	52.4	18.6	4.2	1931	Stratford, Conn.	Lowndes Oyster Co., owner, South Norwalk, Conn.
86015	Gracie and Emily	9	7	33.5	14.4	3.8	1888	Patchogue, N.Y.	Auxiliary sloop
10889	Gray Eagle	12	11	35.7	15.3	4.2	1868	New Haven, Conn.	Sloop originally
250337	Greenport	50	34	62.5	20.6	7.7	1946	Rockland, Me.	Sistership of Milford
209989	G.S. Terry	15	13	39.9	14.0	4.6	1912	Stratford, Conn.	C.D. Wicks, M.C.
86409	Guess	14	10	37.4	12.6	5.0	1898	Stratford, Conn.	Wm. E. Bedell, builder
86637	G. Vanderburg	13	11	44.2	14.2	4.0	1902	Patchogue, N.Y.	Originally had a 16 h.p. Globe engine
76006[3]	*H.A. Barnes	65	43	69.6	16.4	4.7	1878	Glenwood, N.Y.	Home port, New Haven, Conn.

[1] Formerly Pausch Bros. IV
[2] Renamed Flora Ball
[3] Formerly Joshua Bedell

	Name							Home port	Remarks
200327[1]	Hampton	28	21	55.4	16.8	4.6	1903	Stratford, Conn.	Ernest E. Ball, owner, Greenport, N.Y.
96011	Harriet C	8	7	32.0	12.7	4.3	1889	Keyport, N.J.	Sloop originally
95650	*Harry	77	50	82.0	23.6	6.6	1881	Tottenville, N.Y.	Home port, N.Y.C.
237127	Harvester	53	39	58.2	20.2	7.4	1938	Thomaston, Me.	Sister ship of *General*
11993[2]	*H.A. Stevens	13	7	50.0	12.0	3.0	1869	East Haven, Conn.	Converted from a schooner, c. 1880
96231	*Hattie	9	6	36.9	9.3	4.8	1893	Bridgeport, Conn.	Yacht originally, H.B. Robbins, builder
93353[3]	*Hattie Bell	27	19	60.8	14.7	4.7	1902	Bridgeport, Conn.	Capt. Jacob I. Housman, N.Y.C.
95880	Hattie F. Burcham	6	5	29.3	12.7	3.3	1886	Patchogue, N.Y.	Cat originally
95118	Hattie J	10	9	38.0	13.5	3.6	1871	Smithville, N.Y.	Auxiliary sloop
95758	Hattie M. Bird	15	14	43.0	16.2	4.5	1883	Patchogue, N.Y.	Schooner originally
96672[4]	*H.C. Ellis	13	7	43.2	15.6	4.6	1903	Tottenville, N.Y.	400–bu. capacity
121007[5]	*H.C. Rowe & Co.	387	320	132.8	28.0	6.6	1895	Noank, Conn.	500 h.p. steam engine
126376[6]	*H.C. Rowe & Co.	500	340	144.8	28.4	10.0	1886	Port Jefferson, N.Y.	J.M. Bayles & Son, builder
212624	Helen Marion	10	9	39.3	12.7	3.4	1888	Patchogue, N.Y.	Elmer Murdock, owner, Sayville, N.Y.
96647[7]	Helen Stanley	27	17	60.4	17.1	4.5	1902	Huntington, N.Y.	Jacob Ockers, owner, West Sayville, L.I.
95036	Henry Albin	10	9	30.5	13.0	3.6	1870	New York, N.Y.	Sloop originally
11449	Henry Clay	11	7	41.0	13.3	3.1	1867	Port Richmond, N.Y.	Sloop originally

[1] Formerly Ed. F. Leeds
[2] Renamed Pioneer
[3] Formerly Martha J. Sutter
[4] Renamed Sterling
[5] Formerly Fulton Market, Oyster Bay
[6] Formerly City of Bridgeport, Rosalie
[7] Renamed Beacon

Official Number	Name	Gross Tons	Net Tons	Length	Beam	Depth	Year Built	Where Built	Remarks
130274(1)	*Henry C. Rowe	220	135	120.6	23.4	8.5	1883	Port Jefferson, N.Y.	Hauled four dredges
96285(2)	Henry D. Siminson	20	19	43.5	16.9	4.9	1895	Patchogue, N.Y.	Sloop
95697	*Henry J	42	26	63.0	18.6	6.2	1882	South Norwalk, Conn.	Richards and Weed, M.C.
205207	Henry Warren	11	10	36.0	13.0	3.4	1908	Touisset, Mass.	Freighter originally
201880	Herald	6	6	33.0	11.7	4.6	1905	New Haven, Conn.	Home port, New Haven, Conn.
96007	H.F. Hilderbrant	5	5	28.7	12.9	3.3	1887	Patchogue, N.Y.	Catboat originally
206866	*Hiawatha	13	11	36.4	13.0	5.0	1909	Warren, R.I.	W.E. Field, owner, Warwick, R.I., gas to steam
96653	Highland Light	14	12	48.0	14.5	3.5	1902	Greenport, N.Y.	D. Atwood Co., owner, Boston, Mass.
96666	Hilda	14	10	36.5	14.3	4.0	1903	Oyster Bay, N.Y.	Home port, Cold Spring, N.Y.
95421	Hope	12	11	37.5	14.8	4.4	1875	South Brooklyn, N.Y.	Sloop yacht originally
256559	Hope	17	14	42.2	15.2	4.9	1948	Greenwich, Conn.	Clarence E. Chard, owner, Greenwich Conn.
95645	Hoyden	12	11	32.0	12.6	4.3	1881	Patchogue, N.Y.	Sloop originally
95831	*H.S. Lockwood	70	35	61.3	15.4	6.0	1884	South Norwalk, Conn.	Richards and Weed, M.C.
100138	*Ida Frank	10	10	38.2	14.0	4.2	1874	Oakland, R.I.	Sloop originally E.W. Talmadge, owner, South Norwalk, Conn.
100121	Ida May	10	7	37.2	14.1	3.3	1874	Northport, N.Y.	

(1) Formerly *Nonowantuc*
(2) Renamed *Wm. H. Robbins*

Number	Name			Length	Beam	Depth	Year	Home port	Remarks
225147	Ida May	16	11	45.0	15.5	4.3	1925	Oyster Bay, N.Y.	Frank Flower, builder
100649	Ideal	11	7	36.7	12.1	3.7	1898	Bridgeport, Conn.	Reuben R. Greene, M.C.
202855	*I.E. Brown	133	105	72.3	22.2	8.0	1906	Tottenville, N.Y.	A.C. Brown and Sons, builder
100679	Inner Beach	8	7	30.1	12.1	3.6	1898	East Rockaway, N.Y.	Auxiliary steam engine
100277	*I.P. Mersereau	32	21	48.0	14.0	5.0	1881	Tottenville, N.Y.	Home port, N.Y.C.
155331(1)	Irene and Pearl	26	12	55.2	16.0	4.0	1898	Patchogue, N.Y.	Home port, Norfolk, Va.
257961(2)	Iron Oyster	294	199	151.5	23.2	10.8	1942	Camden, N.J.	J. Waldron Bayles, owner, N.Y.C.
100378	*Isaac E. Brown	69	34	50.0	16.4	6.0	1885	New Haven, Conn.	1400-bu. capacity
202018	Isabella	15	10	47.2	17.0	2.5	1905	Bridgeport, Conn.	Greene Bros., builders
100537	Isa M	14	11	48.2	13.8	3.5	1889	Northport, N.Y.	Sloop originally H.C. Monsell, owner, Greenport, N.Y.
91106(3)	*Island Belle	60	26	74.0	18.0	4.4	1878	Espy, Pa.	Was a Norwalk ferry
100455	*Itbiel	31	15	49.6	15.8	5.0	1889	Port Jefferson, N.Y.	Mather & Wood, M.C.
100531	Ivah Ray	11	7	37.9	14.5	3.8	1892	Seabright, N.J.	Auxiliary sloop
100202(4)	*Ivernia	13	7	56.0	14.0	4.5	1877	East Haven, Conn.	900-bu. capacity
100599	Ivy	8	5	35.9	10.3	4.5	1895	Port Washington, N.Y.	Naphtha engine
77289	Jacob Ockers	13	12	39.8	12.8	3.2	1898	Patchogue, N.Y.	Sloop originally George Bishop, builder
200638	Jacob Ockers	29	27	56.0	18.6	5.4	1904	Patchogue, N.Y.	

(1) Formerly Oysterman
(2) Formerly LCI-47 (U.S.N.)
(3) Formerly Modjeska, Storm Signal
(4) Renamed Amerique

Official Number	Name	Gross Tons	Net Tons	Length	Beam	Depth	Year Built	Where Built	Remarks
235024	James B	80	69	69.4	21.6	7.2	1936	Stratford, Conn.	Andrew Radel Oyster Co., owner, Bridgeport, Conn.
25949(1)	*James Everard	93	53	123.0	18.0	9.5	1878	Newburgh, N.Y.	Steam yacht originally
13937(2)	*James Morgan	69	41	45.0	17.2	5.8	1822	Poughkeepsie, N.Y.	Schooner originally
77043(3)	James Morrissey	17	16	43.0	17.0	4.4	1892	Bayport, N.Y.	Sloop
77016	James Mulvey	18	7	42.0	16.4	4.5	1892	Greenwich, N.J.	Sloop originally
76584	*James W. Boyle	41	24	68.3	18.0	5.5	1885	Athens, N.Y.	1000-bu. capacity
76157	*J. and G.H. Smith	42	21	67.0	17.5	5.5	1880	East Haven, Conn.	1000-bu. capacity
136902(4)	Jane	71	62	85.3	21.2	5.2	1901	Baltimore, Md.	Freighter
240467(5)	Jane D	57	26	61.6	23.2	6.3	1940	Amburg, Va.	C. DeGraff, owner, Riverhead, N.Y.
201670	Janice D. Pettis	13	8	40.5	13.8	3.2	1905	Bridgeport, Conn.	Robert Pettis, owner, Providence, R.I.
77175	Jap	16	15	47.3	16.6	2.9	1895	Bellport, N.Y.	Originally schooner
76708(6)	*Jennie	18	14	39.0	12.5	4.2	1867		300 bu.
209493	Jennie	10	9	33.0	13.7	3.3	1911	Innwood, N.Y.	Home port, N.Y.C.
77074	Jennie Ockers	7	6	30.0	13.0	3.3	1892	Patchogue, N.Y.	Sloop originally
76558	Jennie Treadwell	8	7	33.8	14.0	3.5	1885	Patchogue, N.Y.	Cat and sloop originally
76997	Jennie Tucker	6	5	29.5	13.0	3.2	1891	Patchogue, N.Y.	Sloop originally
76671	Jennie Wicks	6	5	28.1	12.5	3.2	1887	Patchogue, N.Y.	Cat originally
76608	*Jeremiah Smith	179	111	86.2	22.8	7.2	1885	West Haven, Conn.	Once a passenger boat, diesel later
76637	Jerry Brown	24	13	45.0	16.4	4.5	1885	Bayport, N.Y.	Sloop originally
76828	Jesse Johnson	8	7	35.0	13.1	3.1	1889	Patchogue, N.Y.	Auxiliary sloop

(1) Formerly Vedette
(2) Renamed Saltesea
(3) Renamed Alwina H. Still
(4) Formerly Elizabeth
(5) Renamed Captain
(6) Formerly Wave

No.	Name						Year	Home port	Notes
77424	*Jessie	26	18	47.4	11.8	4.7	1894	Providence, R.I.	3-cylinder Automatic engine
76599	*Jessie Clayton	56	28	72.0	18.0	6.2	1885	South Norwalk, Conn.	Richards and Weed, M.C.
77048	Jessie G	6	5	29.5	12.9	3.0	1892	Sayville, N.Y.	Auxiliary sloop
77219	Jessie R	17	15	49.5	15.5	4.9	1896	Patchogue, N.Y.	W.H. Rowland & Co., owner, New Haven, Conn.
77516	J.H.B.	15	12	45.0	16.0	4.0	1902	Brookhaven, N.Y.	Home port, Patchogue, N.Y.
76651	*J. Howard Lowndes	72	36	75.0	18.9	6.5	1886	South Norwalk, Conn.	Richards and Weed, M.C.
76817	J.H. Still	32	29	58.2	17.8	5.0	1889	Bayport, N.Y.	Sloop originally
110508(1)	*J. J. Hagerty	53	26	75.3	17.7	6.4	1882	Tottenville, N.Y.	At one time a towboat
77503	John Keeley, Jr.	11	10	40.0	12.7	3.7	1901	Patchogue, N.Y.	DeWitt Conklin, M.C.
77020	John Lundy	27	25	59.0	16.5	5.1	1892	Tottenville, N.Y.	Schooner originally
111116(2)	*John L. Wade	35	24	54.6	15.3	7.1	1896	Athens, N.Y.	At one time a towboat
259609	Johnnie	6	6	37.9	9.0	3.0	1949	Crocheron, Md.	Robert Henning, owner, N.Y.C.
206274	John Stuart	27	18	51.0	17.5	3.7	1909	West Haven, Conn.	Beacon Oyster Co., owner, Wickford, R.I.
77475	John S. Waples	14	9	52.4	16.6	4.0	1901	Pocomoke City, Md.	Sloop originally
76672	*John W. Dodge	59	25	50.4	17.6	4.4	1887	Pawtuxet, R.I.	Sloop originally Ran to W. Washington Market, N.Y.C.
81751(3)	Joseph B. Glancy	19	15	47.8	16.3	4.8	1901	Bridgeport, Conn.	Sloop originally
76711	Joseph C. Knapp	38	36	51.5	21.0	5.0	1887	Greenport, N.Y.	

(1) Formerly Rambler
(2) Formerly Robert White
(3) Formerly W.H. Hoy

Official Number	Name	Gross Tons	Net Tons	Length	Beam	Depth	Year Built	Where Built	Remarks
76609	*Josephine	126	85	69.0	21.0	6.2	1885	Stratford, Conn.	Moses B. Hart, M.C.
77137	Joseph Murray	79	62	73.0	24.6	4.9	1894	Milford, Del.	Schooner originally 1000 bu.
76006[1]	*Joshua Bedell	61	31	56.4	16.4	4.6	1878	Glenwood, N.Y.	
75906	*Joshua Leviness	91	65	77.2	22.0	4.7	1876	City Island, N.Y.	Home port, N.Y.C.
76498	*J.P. Thomas	79	48	62.0	18.0	5.6	1884	New Haven, Conn.	Geo. M. Graves, builder
91760[2]	Judge Moore	27	13	62.3	13.7	5.4	1885	Tarrytown, N.Y.	Home port, Eastport, Me.
76314	*Jupiter	54	40	68.0	20.0	6.0	1882	Darien, Conn.	Dexter Cole, M.C.
204853	J. Van Wyen	14	12	44.4	15.3	3.4	1908	Patchogue, N.Y.	Bluepoints Co. Inc, owner, West Sayville, N.Y.
77295[3]	*J.W. Stubbs	51	34	51.0	15.5	5.6	1898	Essex, Mass.	Home port, Wellfleet, Mass.
14391	Kansas City	18	14	48.0	16.1	4.5	1881	Greenport, N.Y.	Sloop originally
14461	*Kate C. Stevens	104	52	85.0	25.5	6.8	1887	Stratford, Conn.	Moses B. Hart, M.C.
200010	Katherine	26	20	47.8	13.0	5.5	1903	Jersey City, N.J.	Yacht originally
14425	Katie G	14	11	36.2	14.5	3.9	1884	City Island, N.Y.	Sloop originally Bill Ciaurro, owner, Bridgeport, Conn.
161171	Katy Did	14	11	51.0	14.5	3.8	1901	Bridgeport, Conn.	Greene Brothers, builders
14478	*Kickemuit	60	30	52.5	17.4	4.7	1888	Noank, Conn.	Once a fisherman
208758	Kickemuit	10	8	28.0	11.6	3.6	1880	Warren, R.I.	Benjamin D. Brooks, owner, Warwick, R.I.
205262[4]	King Fisher	55	49	77.5	18.4	5.4	1908	Darien, Conn.	Yacht originally

(1) Renamed H.A. Barnes
(2) Formerly Marion
(3) Renamed Ardelia, Woco
(4) Formerly Mañana

Official No.	Name			Length	Breadth	Depth	Year	Where built	Remarks
161198	*Kingston	65	39	67.0	21.3	6.3	1902	Kennebunkport, Me.	Home port, New Haven, Conn.
231325	Klondike	33	22	55.2	17.5	5.8	1931	Brooklyn, N.Y.	Beacon Oyster Co., owners, Wickford, R.I.
248599[1]	K38	25	11	44.8	16.0	6.3	1945	Washington, D.C.	Cedar Island Oyster Co., Inc., owners, Greenport, N.Y.
140532	Laura B	10	9	34.8	14.0	4.0	1882	Patchogue, N.Y.	Sloop originally
207379	Laura R	30	20	49.3	17.6	5.4	1910	Port Jefferson, N.Y.	Wm. E. Hunt, M.C.
141134	*Laurel	41	20	57.0	13.5	5.0	1891	Tottenville, N.Y.	A.C. Brown and Sons, builders
141700[2]	Leah A. Wedmore	10	10	46.3	11.8	3.0	1901	New Haven, Conn.	Home port, New Haven, Conn.
141530	*Lena S	18	14	47.5	15.0	4.6	1898	Northport, N.Y.	Named after Capt. Henry Scudder's daughter
141771	L.F. Terry	14	13	41.5	15.5	3.7	1902	Patchogue, N.Y.	Shelter Island Oyster Co., owner, N.Y.
140651	Libbie D	12	10	41.5	14.0	4.0	1883	Patchogue, N.Y.	Sloop originally
140482	Libbie M	12	12	39.0	15.0	4.0	1881	Greenwich, Conn.	Sloop originally
140488	Lida May	7	7	34.8	12.4	3.7	1881	Stamford, Conn.	Sloop originally
140730	Lieutenant	14	12	40.0	16.0	4.5	1884	Islip, N.Y.	Auxiliary sloop
203666	Lieutenant	21	17	44.4	14.9	4.9	1906	Tottenville, N.Y.	J. & J.W. Elsworth, Co., owner, N.Y.C.
232023	Lill	6	5	34.1	11.1	2.8	1907	New Haven, Conn.	Elwood Keister, owner, New Haven, Conn.
140475	Lillie B. Dayton	9	8	38.4	12.5	3.0	1881	Patchogue, N.Y.	Cat originally
204676[3]	Linwood	20	15	47.2	15.0	4.8	1907	Stratford, Conn.	Home port, Providence, R.I.

[1] Formerly *40 Fathom No. 38* [3] Formerly *Frank A. Koellmer*
[2] Renamed *Bertha*

Official Number	Name	Gross Tons	Net Tons	Length	Beam	Depth	Year Built	Where Built	Remarks
202314	Lister	13	12	35.0	13.3	4.8	1905	Bridgeport, Conn.	Schooner originally
271326	Little Tom	32	16	41.6	15.3	7.2	1956	Tarpon Springs, Fla.	Long Island Oyster Farms, Inc, owner, Greenport, L.I. Home port, N.Y.C.
235181(1)	Live Carp	6	5	32.0	11.5	2.8	1856	Sayville, N.Y.	Sloop originally
140307	Lizzie	5	5	28.5	11.6	2.8	1873	Babylon, N.Y.	Sloop originally
140356	*Lizzie	14	13	38.8	15.0	5.7	1879	Oyster Bay, N.Y.	Sloop originally
140687	Lizzie D. Bell	16	13	38.3	16.0	4.3	1883	City Island, N.Y.	1000-bu. capacity
140677(2)	*Lizzie E. Woodend	67	42	61.6	15.9	4.5	1883	Northport, N.Y.	Jacob Houseman, owner, N.Y.C.
140548	*Lizzie H.	34	24	63.0	18.8	4.7	1882	Tottenville, N.Y.	Originally a "water boat"
141788	Lizzie Pettigrove	12	5	35.3	13.6	4.7	1902	Boothbay, Me.	Sloop originally
140372	L.J. Dayton	12	8	36.4	14.4	4.2	1879	Port Jefferson, N.Y.	Cape Ann Oyster Co., owner, Providence, R.I.
208635	Lola	18	15	30.0	12.9	6.0	1894	Providence, R.I.	Sloop originally
141089	Lola L	13	12	31.0	14.5	4.0	1890	Northport, N.Y.	Tallmadge Bros., owners, Norwalk, Conn.
141171	*Lola M	35	17	58.2	15.9	5.0	1891	Tottenville, N.Y.	
141303	Lorena B	8	6	36.6	12.5	3.6	1893	South Norwalk, Conn.	Auxiliary sloop
140921	Loretta	6	5	30.5	12.4	3.0	1888	Patchogue, N.Y.	Cat originally
140845	*Loretto	19	9	54.5	11.2	5.5	1886	Brooklyn, N.Y.	Steam yacht originally
140729	Lottie B	13	9	35.5	15.5	4.4	1884	Mount Sinai, N.Y.	Sloop originally
141747	*Lottie B	21	14	57.6	17.6	6.5	1901	Tottenville, N.Y.	1000-bu. capacity

(1) Formerly S.V. Rogers
(2) Renamed Pioneer

Number	Name						Year	Home port	Notes
140400	*Lonisa H*	11	11	35.2	14.3	4.0	1880	Northport, N.Y.	Sloop originally
201558	*Lonisa O*	13	11	45.0	14.9	3.4	1904	Patchogue, N.Y.	Named after Jacob Ockers' daughter
226334	*Louise Ockers*	19	13	45.2	15.2	4.0	1927	Stratford, Conn.	Fred Ockers, owner, West Sayville, N.Y.
206476	**Lonis R*	64	51	69.9	20.8	5.8	1909	Stratford, Conn.	Wm. E. Bedell, M.C.
141493	*Loyalty*	9	9	34.3	12.6	4.0	1894	Portland, Me.	Cat, sloop, gas
141413	*L. R. Hand*	17	12	42.0	15.0	4.7	1896	Patchogue, N.Y.	Sloop originally
141774	*L. R. Hand*	14	12	48.6	16.0	4.0	1901	Bridgeport, Conn.	Built for Capt. Ferdinand Downs, Greenport, N.Y.
140770	**Luzerne Ludington*	74	37	54.0	17.0	6.0	1885	New Haven, Conn.	Geo. M. Graves, builder
210949	*Lydia*	41	31	54.8	20.4	5.0	1913	New Haven Conn.	Home port, Providence, R.I.
93220	**Mabel & Ray*	26	18	44.4	15.9	5.7	1899	Stratford, Conn.	Home port, N.Y.C.
93181	*Mabel Holland*	13	12	43.5	14.3	4.0	1901	Rockaway, N.Y.	Home port, Patchogue, N.Y.
91262	**Mabel L. Stevens*	31	21	60.6	16.3	4.8	1880	South Norwalk, Conn.	Moses Hart, builder
210210	*Mabel V*	8	6	30.0	11.6	3.6	1912	Stratford, Conn.	Home port, N.Y.C.
91997	*Madaline Brandt*	6	5	29.2	12.6	3.0	1887	Patchogue, N.Y.	Cat originally
92522	*Maggie S. Myers*	24	21	50.0	18.1	5.2	1893	Bridgeton, N.J.	Schooner originally
91022(1)	*Maggie T. Young*	8	8	36.0	12.5	3.5	1877	Greenport, N.Y.	Sloop
202974	*Magician*	57	52	78.4	19.4	6.2	1906	Greenport, N.Y.	Bluepoints Co., Inc., owner, N.Y.C.
205262(2)	*Mañana*	63	52	77.5	18.4	5.4	1908	Darien, Conn.	Yacht

(1) Renamed *Nadine*
(2) Renamed *King Fisher*

Official Number	Name	Gross Tons	Net Tons	Length	Beam	Depth	Year Built	Where Built	Remarks
213106	Margaret Raye	65	55	63.5	20.5	4.7	1915	Greenport, N.Y.	Long Island Oyster Farms, Inc., Northport, N.Y.
200988	Marguerite	16	12	42.4	15.6	6.8	1904	Eastport, Me.	Schooner originally
127317[(1)]	Maria	32	29	51.5	13.0	4.6	1899	Patchogue, N.Y.	G.F. Greene, Jr., owner, Warren, R.I.
93173	Marie	6	6	30.0	11.9	3.0	1901	Amityville, N.Y.	Sloop originally
91760[(2)]	*Marion	27	13	62.3	13.7	5.4	1885	Tarrytown, N.Y.	Home port, N.Y.C.
93150	Marjorie	6	5	31.7	11.7	3.2	1897	Sayville, N.Y.	Sloop originally
93013	*Martha	16	11	42.7	16.3	4.8	1900	Tottenville, N.Y.	Geo. C. Brown, M.C.
93353[(3)]	*Martha J. Sutter	17	12	43.8	14.4	4.7	1902	Bridgeport, Conn.	Home port, N.Y.C.
92246	Mary A	11	10	30.0	13.8	4.0	1886	City Island, N.Y.	Sloop originally
91576	Mary A. Marshall	9	9	33.6	13.6	3.7	1883	Tottenville, N.Y.	Sloop originally
90432	Mary Ella	13	11	39.0	15.8	3.0	1872	Rye, N.Y.	Sloop originally
91565	Mary Jane	9	7	31.5	13.3	3.5	1883	N.Y.C.	Sloop originally
93203	Mary Lou	15	14	38.8	13.9	4.5	1901	South Boston, Mass.	M. Dewing Co., owner, Providence, R.I.
93227	*Mary S. Lewis	138	99	88.0	22.0	8.5	1901	Port Jefferson, N.Y.	Mather and Wood, M.C.
202407	Mascot	59	42	71.0	20.2	6.6	1905	Greenport, N.Y.	Andrew Radel Oyster Co., owner, Norwalk, Conn.
92793	Maud	7	7	32.5	13.5	3.6	1897	Patchogue, N.Y.	Sloop originally
214647	Mayflower	13	11	34.1	10.8	4.1	1916	Oyster Bay, N.Y.	Frank M. Flower, owner, Oyster Bay, N.Y.

[(1)] Formerly Coulter and McKenzie
[(2)] Renamed Judge Moore
[(3)] Renamed Hattie Bell

92551	*M. Dewing	71	51	50.0	19.7	5.4	1893	Boston, Mass.	1000-bu. capacity
91766	*Medea	54	27	67.0	18.2	6.2	1885	South Norwalk, Conn.	Richards and Weed, M.C.
91867[1]	*Mikado	77	51	55.6	18.6	5.7	1886	Stratford, Conn.	Moses B. Hart, M.C.
92764	*Mildred	123	66	96.7	20.6	6.8	1897	Tottenville, N.Y.	A.C. Brown, builder
126345[2]	Mildred	27	18	53.6	17.6	5.2	1886	New Haven, Conn.	F. Mansfield & Sons, Co, owner, New Haven, Conn.
92511	Mildred Hall	14	13	42.0	16.0	4.0	1893	Bayport, N.Y.	Sloop originally
250336[3]	Milford	50	34	62.5	20.6	7.7	1946	Rockland, Me.	Long Island Oyster Farms, Inc, owner, Northport, N.Y.
16973	Millard F. Houseman	15	5	42.9	15.3	3.5	1858	Greenville, N.J.	Sloop originally
91232	*Minnie B	27	14	56.0	15.6	3.5	1880	Port Jefferson, N.Y.	800-bu. capacity
92971	Minnie C	42	25	68.2	19.4	5.6	1899	Greenport, N.Y.	Sloop originally
91979	Minnie T. Rackett	8	7	30.8	13.2	5.2	1888	Greenport, N.Y.	Sloop originally
203955	*Miranda	95	36	78.0	20.5	6.6	1907	Kennebunk, Me.	Home port, New Haven, Conn.
91217	Mist	6	5	31.3	11.1	3.3	1880	Canarsie, N.Y.	Sloop originally
91655	Mizpah	12	11	33.0	14.0	3.0	1884	New Bedford, Mass.	Schooner yacht originally
92573	M. J. Fitzsimmons	39	39	58.6	21.3	4.8	1894	Tottenville, N.Y.	Schooner originally
92215	Moccasin	15	15	45.0	13.6	5.6	1890	City Island, N.Y.	Sloop yacht originally
91106[4]	Modjeska	46	36	74.0	13.0	4.0	1878	Espy, Pa.	Home port, Norfolk, Va.
201725	Mollie M	15	13	48.2	16.3	3.0	1905	Patchogue, N.Y.	George Bishop, builder

[1] Renamed *City Point, Carolyn Raye*
[2] Formerly *Cleo*
[3] Sistership of *Greenport*
[4] Renamed *Storm Signal, Island Belle*

Official Number	Name	Gross Tons	Net Tons	Length	Beam	Depth	Year Built	Where Built	Remarks
90801	*Molly	29	19	34.5	13.8	3.6	1875	Poughkeepsie, N.Y.	Charles W. Bell, owner, Rowayton, Conn.
204826	M.P. McDonagh	50	43	73.8	20.6	6.2	1907	Greenport, N.Y.	Greenport Basin and Construction Co., builder
93199	Myra Inman	11	8	37.0	14.8	4.0	1901	Gloucester, Mass.	R.R. Higgins Co., owners, Boston, Mass.
93006	Myrtle	14	13	54.0	16.5	3.4	1900	Patchogue, N.Y.	Lengthened to 69.7' at Andrew Radel's yard, Port Jefferson, L.I.
91823	*Mystery	97	72	72.4	20.5	6.1	1886	Tottenville, N.Y.	Northport Oyster Co., owner, Northport, N.Y.
91022[1]	Nadine	8	8	36.0	12.5	3.5	1877	Greenport, N.Y.	Home port, Greenport, N.Y.
211045	Napeague	50	40	50.6	20.5	6.5	1913	Tottenville, N.Y.	Cedar Island Oyster Co., owner, Greenport, N.Y.
130628	Narika	7	7	34.4	11.6	4.6	1893	Fall River, Mass.	Sloop yacht originally
130872[2]	Narragansett	15	11	35.1	13.9	4.8	1900	New Haven, Conn.	Narragansett Bay Oyster Co., owners, Providence, R.I.
130952	Nassau	9	7	38.0	11.7	3.8	1901	Freeport, N.Y.	Home port, Patchogue, N.Y.

[1] Formerly *Maggie T. Young*
[2] Renamed *Star*

216

Official No.	Name	Gross tons	Net tons	Length	Breadth	Depth	Year	Home port / place	Remarks
130474	*Nellie	16	8	37.6	12.7	4.5	1890	East Providence, R.I.	Stern–wheeler originally
130578	Nellie	8	8	25.6	12.7	3.4	1891	Smithtown, N.Y.	Sloop originally
130734	Nellie Bly	7	7	29.3	12.1	3.4	1897	East Rockaway, N.Y.	Home port, Patchogue, N.Y.
130258	Nena A. Rowland	38	36	54.0	20.4	6.3	1883	South Norwalk, Conn.	Richards and Weed, M.C.
130683	Nettie	5	5	30.8	11.5	2.8	1876	Bellport, N.Y.	Sloop originally
130730	Nettie Bell	9	9	36.0	12.2	3.4	1896	Freeport, N.Y.	Home port, Patchogue, N.Y.
130869	Nianta	7	6	29.4	12.3	4.0	1900	Patchogue, N.Y.	Home port, Patchogue, N.Y.
130936	Night Hawk	14	11	36.8	12.2	4.3	1901	Fall River, Mass.	Home port, N.Y.C.
130274[1]	*Nonowantuc	220	135	120.6	23.4	8.5	1883	Port Jefferson, N.Y.	Passenger boat
130726[2]	Nora E. Lawson	8	6	50.0	11.8	3.3	1896	Monie, Md.	Schooner, oyster freighter
6565[3]	Normandic	79	65	80.5	25.5	5.5	1867	Stony Point, N.Y.	J. Richards Nelson, owner, Providence, R.I.
225419[4]	Norman L. Jeffries	64	28	77.9	23.8	5.8	1926	Dorchester, N.J.	Elsie M. Jeffries, owner, Port Norris, N.J.
130741	Norna	6	6	30.7	13.2	3.3	1897	Patchogue, N.Y.	Sloop
155424	*Old Colony	207	121	86.0	25.4	7.9	1901	Bridgeport, Conn.	Reuben R. Greene, M.C.
204854	Olive B. Van Dusen	50	44	66.3	22.0	5.2	1908	Patchogue, N.Y.	Auxiliary schooner
1440[5]	Orient	13	11	38.5	14.2	4.3	1867	Brooklyn, N.Y.	Home port, N.Y.C.
155076	Oscar	7	6	32.0	11.4	4.0	1883	Freeport, N.Y.	Sloop originally
155143	*Ostrea	69	47	68.0	19.6	6.4	1887	Port Jefferson, N.Y.	Home port, Bridgeport, Conn.

[1] Renamed *Henry C. Rowe*
[2] Renamed *Water Gypsy*
[3] Formerly *Daniel Tomkins*
[4] Formerly *Emma & Ruth*, renamed *Frank M. Flower*
[5] Formerly sloop *Annie Marshall*

Official Number	Name	Gross Tons	Net Tons	Length	Beam	Depth	Year Built	Where Built	Remarks
216547	Overseer	11	7	37.6	9.6	3.4	1918	Chincoteague, Va.	Wimbrough Brothers, builders
155378	Owl	9	6	35.7	12.2	4.0	1900	Bridgeport, Conn.	Reuben R. Greene, M.C.
121007[1]	*Oyster Bay	158	77	132.8	28.0	6.6	1895	Noank, Conn.	Freighter
213475	Oysterette	12	10	42.0	12.0	2.5	1910	Inwood, N.Y.	Freeman Sprague, owner, Inwood, N.Y.
255533	Oysterette	10	7	29.0	12.3	4.6	1948	East Norwalk, Conn.	Wallace Bell, builder
155331[2]	Oysterman	14	13	42.0	14.8	4.2	1898	Patchogue, N.Y.	H.J. Lewis, owner, Bridgeport, Conn.
204049	Oyster Transport	29	24	70.2	17.2	4.0	1907	Greenport, N.Y.	Freighter, Greenport, N.Y.
204002[3]	P. & B. No. 2	14	12	48.0	14.5	4.0	1907	Greenport, N.Y.	John C.F. Shepard, owner, Providence, R.I.
248265	Pastime	8	8	31.2	13.2	3.6			Charles Weeks, owner, Bridgeport, Conn.
150503	*Pansy	11	10	40.4	11.6	4.0	1890	Patchogue, N.Y.	400-bu. capacity 10 h.p. Globe
209243	Patrol	14	12	41.3	14.9	3.7	1911	New Haven, Conn.	Andrew Radel Oyster Co., South Norwalk, Conn.
150801	Paul Raymond	8	7	35.8	13.0	3.6	1898	Freeport, N.Y.	Home port, Patchogue, N.Y.

(1) Formerly *Fulton Market*, renamed *H.C. Rowe & Co.*   (3) Renamed *Alert, Whitecap*
(2) Renamed *Irene and Pearl*

No.	Name						Year	Place	Notes
150877	*Pausch Bros.*	14	11	45.5	13.7	4.6	1900	Stratford, Conn.	Wm. E. Bedell, M.C.
107156[1]	*Pausch Bros. I*	18	12	35.4	12.1	4.0	1892	South Norwalk, Conn.	Pausch Bros. Oyster Co., owner, Port Chester, N.Y.
204842	*Pausch Bros. No. 2*	11	8	46.0	13.5	2.5	1907	Bay Shore, N.Y.	Bluepoints Co., Inc., owner, West Sayville, N.Y.
208675[2]	*Pausch Bros. IV*	41	28	57.4	18.9	6.6	1911	Tottenville, N.Y.	Pausch Bros. Oyster Co., owner, Port Chester, N.Y.
201954	*Pearl*	13	9	40.0	13.0	3.5	1905	Cos Cob, Conn.	F.T. Palmer, M.C.
205615	*Pearl D. Evans*	23	9	56.1	16.0	4.5	1908	Weems, Va.	B.D. Rooks, owner, Providence, R.I.
210002	*Peconic*	58	50	64.7	20.5	6.5	1912	Tottenville, N.Y.	Peconic Bay Oyster Co., owner, Greenport, N.Y.
20006	*Pelican*	11	9	34.8	14.0	3.4			Home port, N.Y.C.
19704	**Peri*	22	21	42.9	16.8	5.5	1848	Huntington, N.Y.	First with steam hoisters
150851	*Petrel*	13	8	43.5	13.5	4.2	1900	Bridgeport, Conn.	Reuben R. Greene, M.C.
150606	*Phebe Cochran*	10	9	33.8	14.0	3.4	1892	Patchogue, N.Y.	Auxiliary sloop
150596	*Pigeon*	12	10	46.4	14.0	4.7	1890	Greenport, N.Y.	Home port, Barnstable, Mass.
233979	*Pine Island*	23	20	47.7	20.0	3.1	1935	Bayville, N.Y.	Scow type. H. Butler Flower, owner, Bayville, N.Y.

[1] Formerly *A.M. Low*
[2] Renamed *Gloria B*

Official Number	Name	Gross Tons	Net Tons	Length	Beam	Depth	Year Built	Where Built	Remarks
11993(1)	*Pioneer	44	22	48.0	13.5	3.6	1869	East Haven, Conn.	Home port, New Haven, Conn.
140677(2)	*Pioneer	36	25	61.6	15.9	4.5	1883	Northport, N.Y.	Home port, Camden, N.J.
150676	Pioneer	7	5	30.0	12.8	2.9	1888	Patchogue, N.Y.	Home port, Patchogue, N.Y.
126288(3)	*Precursor	41	20	64.0	16.0	4.4	1885	New Haven, Conn.	Home port, Port Jefferson, N.Y.
208304	Priscilla	31	18	44.0	18.6	5.0	1910	Warren, R.I.	Eddie B. Blount, owner, Warren, R.I.
85958(4)	Progress	14	12	38.0	15.2	4.2	1887	Oakdale, N.Y.	Home port, Patchogue, N.Y., Davis Brothers, builders
150569	Psyche	10	9	32.0	14.9	3.2	1892	Cold Spring, N.Y.	Sloop originally H.W. Porter, owner, Stratford, Conn.
150895	Push	10	7	39.0	13.7	3.3	1901	Stratford, Conn.	
253016(5)	Quinnipiac	194	176	95.5	29.9	7.0	1943	Kingston, N.Y.	Long Island Oyster Farms, Inc., owner, Greenport, N.Y.
110508(6)	*Rambler	53	26	75.3	17.7	6.4	1882	Tottenville, N.Y.	Once a towboat
111326	Ramsden	13	11	39.5	14.0	4.0	1901	Ocean Side, N.Y.	Home port, Patchogue, N.Y.
262317	Raymond M	17	8	39.0	12.2	6.6	1925	New Bedford, Mass.	Thomas J. Higgins, owner, Newport, R.I.

(1) Formerly H.A. Stevens
(2) Formerly Lizzie E. Woodend
(3) Formerly C.W. Hoyt
(4) Formerly George Kingston
(5) Formerly YCK-5 (U.S.N.)
(6) Renamed J.J. Hagerty

No.	Name						Year	Home Port	Remarks
110827	*Red Cedar*	8	7	32.6	13.3	3.3	1889	Bellport, N.Y.	Sloop originally
207186	*Resolute*	47	33	71.3	18.0	4.8	1910	Tottenville, N.Y.	Sea Coast Oyster Co., owner, New Haven, Conn.
111143	*Rhoda E. Crane*	14	10	47.1	13.6	4.4	1897	Stratford, Conn.	Wm. E. Bedell, builder
110802[1]	**Richard W. Law*	114	57	70.3	20.2	6.0	1888	New Haven, Conn.	Weekend excursion boat, New Haven, Conn.
202336	*Richmond*	18	17	40.3	16.3	4.4	1905	Tottenville, N.Y.	Lester & Tener, owners, N.Y.C.
110758	**Ripple*	36	18	48.0	16.2	5.2	1887	South Norwalk, Conn.	Richards and Weed, M.C.
204825	*Rival*	18	14	48.0	15.3	5.0	1907	Greenport, N.Y.	H.C. Rowe, owner, New Haven, Conn.
215576	*Robert M. Utz*	37	30	52.8	18.1	5.3	1917	Tottenville, N.Y.	Home port, Greenport, N.Y.
111050	**Robert Pettis*	31	20	45.9	16.8	5.1	1893	New Haven, Conn.	Home port, Providence, R.I.
111116[2]	**Robert White*	36	24	54.6	15.3	7.1	1896	Athens, N.Y.	100 h.p. steam engine
21815	*Rosabell*	23	21	54.0	15.9	4.4	1865	Patchogue, N.Y.	Sloop originally Ferry, N.Y.C.
126376[3]	**Rosalie*	500	340	144.8	28.4	10.0	1886	Port Jefferson, N.Y.	Wm. Rudolph, owner, West Sayville, N.Y.
209276	*Rose*	10	8	50.2	10.0	2.5	1911	Sayville, N.Y.	Sloop originally, Jacob Ockers, owner, West Sayville, N.Y.
111011	*Rosella*	8	7	34.0	14.0	3.4	1892	Patchogue, N.Y.	

[1] Renamed C.D. Parmelee
[2] Renamed John L. Wade
[3] Formerly City of Bridgeport, renamed H.C. Rowe & Co.

Official Number	Name	Gross Tons	Net Tons	Length	Beam	Depth	Year Built	Where Built	Remarks
210442	Rover	9	7	37.0	9.8	2.6	1896	Merrick, N.Y.	David Bush, owner, Mariners Harbor, N.Y.
120718(1)	*Rowe	476	394	142.8	30.0	10.6	1888	Manitowoc, Wis.	360 h.p., crew of 13
251498(2)	Rowe	281	191	107.2	27.0	12.3	1943	Solomons, Md.	M.M. Davis & Son, Inc., builder
111401	Roy	18	12	42.2	13.4	5.3	1902	Warren, R.I.	Originally naphtha powered
110759	*Ruel Rowe	147	73	81.5	20.0	7.4	1887	Stratford, Conn.	2400-bu. capacity
111275	*Russell T	22	16	50.0	14.2	4.6	1900	Greenport, N.Y.	Lengthened 10' in 1902
115548	Sabrina	14	8	43.4	16.2	3.5	1877	Riverside, N.J.	Sloop originally
201876	Sachuest	14	13	35.8	12.0	4.8	1903	Neponset, R.I.	H.W. Milliken, owner, Warwick, R.I.
115606	*Sadie	11	8	39.5	9.3	4.0	1878	Brooklyn, N.Y.	250-bu. capacity Home port, Stamford, Conn.
116618	Sadie M	15	12	44.2	15.2	4.2	1894	Patchogue, N.Y.	Geo. H. Mott, owner, Inwood, N.Y.
116581	Sagitta	8	7	34.5	14.3	3.6	1893	Patchogue, N.Y.	Geo. Chase, owner, Devon, Conn.
13937(3)	Saltesea	34	27	54.6	17.4	5.1	1822	Poughkeepsie, N.Y.	American Oyster Co., owner, New Haven, Conn.

(1)Formerly Fannie C. Hart (3)Formerly James Morgan
(2)Formerly FS-42, FP-42

No.	Name						Year	Home port	Notes
117081	Samuel Chard	22	22	43.6	16.6	5.6	1901	Greenwich, Conn.	Auxiliary sloop
117236	Samuel Fleet	10	9	33.2	14.0	4.0	1903	Patchogue, N.Y.	Auxiliary sloop
115962	Sarah Ann Carpenter	65	45	75.0	25.8	5.7	1883	Tottenville, N.Y.	Auxiliary schooner; freighter
117245	Sarah B	14	9	39.0	13.4	4.1	1903	Stratford, Conn.	Andrew Radel Oyster Co., owner, South Norwalk, Conn.
115084	Sarah Eldert	17	15	40.7	16.5	4.0	1872	Keyport, N.J.	Sloop originally
115360	Sarah E. Miller	9	9	37.0	14.4	3.7	1875	Islip, N.Y.	Sloop originally
135837[1]	Sara L	6	5	34.0	12.0	3.0	1885	Sayville, N.Y.	Fred Lovejoy, owner, East Norwalk, Conn.
174138	Scow No. 2	21	21	57.6	14.2	3.0			Bluepoints Co., Inc., owner, West Sayville, N.Y.
77219[2]	Sea Coast	44	33	69.3	19.6	6.2	1896	Patchogue, N.Y.	Home port, New Haven, Conn.
106418[3]	Sea Coast	75	40	83.6	22.2	7.9	1886	Islip, N.Y.	Sea Coast Oyster Co., owner, New Haven, Conn.
261392	Sea Foam	10	9	34.0	11.3	4.1	1941	Ipswich, Mass.	Sea Coast Oyster Co., owner, New Haven, Conn.
204207[4]	*Sea Gate	244	165	122.2	27.2	8.5	1907	Newburg, N.Y.	Ferry
116796	Sea Gull	14	12	48.2	13.0	4.0	1897	Stratford, Conn.	Wm. E. Bedell, builder
201905[5]	Sea Gull	14	13	46.0	14.6	3.6	1905	Stratford, Conn.	H.C. Rowe, owner, New Haven, Conn.

(1) Formerly *Estelle Gerber* (3) Formerly *Avalon* (5) Formerly *Wayward*
(2) Formerly *Jessie R* (4) Renamed *Seawanhaka*

223

Official Number	Name	Gross Tons	Net Tons	Length	Beam	Depth	Year Built	Where Built	Remarks
204853[1]	Sea Horse	14	12	44.4	15.3	3.4	1908	Patchogue, N.Y.	K.F. Stein owner, Home port, N.Y.C.
203434[2]	Sealshipt	243	165	97.4	25.0	7.4	1906	Northport, N.Y.	Bluepoints Co., Inc., owner, West Sayville N.Y.
209210[3]	Sealshipt No. 38	17	12	39.0	18.0	4.4	1911	Northport, N.Y.	Home port, Greenport, N.Y.
117161	Sea Pigeon	9	7	31.1	12.6	3.1	1902	Oceanus, N.Y.	Naphtha powered
204207[4]	Seawanhaka	181	123	122.2	27.2	8.5	1907	Newburg, N.Y.	J. Waldron Bayles, owner, Oyster Bay, N.Y.
117252	S.E. Johnson	14	8	60.0	15.6	3.6	1903	Seabright, N.J.	Home port, Perth Amboy, N.J.
222846	Sergeant	35	24	55.2	20.0	3.7	1923	Milford, Del.	J. & J.W. Elsworth Co., owner, N.Y.C.
115195	S.E. Smith	7	7	45.0	10.3	2.8	1870	Milford, Conn.	Schooner originally
229413	Sheppard Campbell	57	52	73.2	21.8	6.3	1930	Dorchester, N.J.	L.A. Campbell, owner, New Brunswick, N.J.
116993	Siesta	8	6	34.0	11.3	3.6	1900	Patchogue, N.Y.	Burned in Patchogue, N.Y., 1908
225432	Signal II	20	14	46.0	12.0	5.8	1926	New York, N.Y.	Yacht and watch boat, J. Waldron Bayles, owner, N.Y.C.
203784	Siguan	18	14	44.5	14.8	4.2	1906	Bridgeport, Conn.	Reuben R. Greene, M.C.

[1] Formerly *J. Van Wyen*
[2] Formerly *Supervisor*, renamed *Wind*
[3] Renamed *Thimble Islands*
[4] Formerly *Sea Gate*

No.	Name	Gross	Net	Length	Breadth	Depth	Year	Home Port	Owner/Builder
218550	*Sir Thomas*	11	7	38.4	13.4	4.0	1902	Bridgeport, Conn.	H.I. Brown, owner, New Haven, Conn.
117037	*Siva*	33	30	55.0	16.6	5.0	1901	Stratford, Conn.	Wm. E. Bedell, builder
248760[1]	*Skimmer 1*	25	11	44.8	16.0	6.3	1945	Washington, N.C.	General Foods Corp., owner, N.Y.C.
248554[2]	*Skimmer 2*	25	11	44.8	16.0	6.3	1945	Washington, N.C.	General Foods Corp., owner, N.Y.C.
248598[3]	*Skimmer 3*	25	11	44.8	16.0	6.3	1945	Washington, N.C.	Helen Hesto, owner, Philadelphia, Pa.
248761[4]	*Skimmer 4*	25	11	44.8	16.0	6.3	1945	Washington, N.C.	Vernon Tuttle, owner, N.Y.C.
115826	*Smith Bros.*	64	48	63.5	20.0	5.0	1882	New Haven, Conn.	Geo. M. Graves, builder
211119	*Smith Bros.*	166	128	82.0	23.5	6.1	1913	Bridgeport, Conn.	Lake Torpedo Boat Co., builder
23587	*Smith V. Rogers*	12	11	44.4	16.0	3.3	1867	Patchogue, N.Y.	Sloop originally Home port, Bridgeport, Conn.
202535	*Sneckner*	6	6	27.6	9.9		1905	Stamford, Conn.	Home port, Bridgeport, Conn.
117043	*Sophie Harms*	14	13	42.0	13.6	3.8	1901	Bridgeport, Conn.	Home port, N.Y.C.
115391	*Spark*	36	21	45.7	14.4	4.5	1875	Brooklyn, N.Y.	Narragansett Oyster Co., R.I.
116113	*Sparkle*	11	10	36.7	13.6	4.0	1886	Pleasant Plains, N.Y.	Eric T. Ball, owner, New Haven, Conn.
203724	*Standard*	299	203	102.0	31.0	9.7	1906	Tottenville, N.Y.	A.C. Brown and Sons, builder

(1) Formerly 40 Fathom No. 39
(2) Formerly 40 Fathom No. 36
(3) Formerly 40 Fathom No. 37
(4) Formerly 40 Fathom No. 40

Official Number	Name	Gross Tons	Net Tons	Length	Beam	Depth	Year Built	Where Built	Remarks
22429	Stanley Howard	14	13	44.5	17.7	3.6	1865	Northport, N.Y.	Auxiliary sloop, named after Stanley Howard Lowndes
130872(1)	*Star	37	25	51.9	14.6	5.8	1900	New Haven, Conn.	Andrew Radel Oyster Co, owner, Bridgeport, Conn.
116569	*Star Fish	12	6	39.9	9.3	4.3	1893	Port Jefferson, N.Y.	James E. Bayles, builder
96672(2)	Sterling	13	7	43.2	15.6	4.6	1903	Tottenville, N.Y.	F.F. Brown, owner, New Haven, Conn.
136174(3)	Stirling	21	18	46.1	15.4	6.2	1891	South Norwalk, Conn.	Home port, Bridgeport, Conn.
91106(4)	*Storm Signal	46	36	74.0	13.0	4.0	1878	Espy, Pa.	Home port, Norfolk, Va.
106856(5)	Stranger	6	5	30.2	11.5	3.5	1891	East Providence, R.I.	Home port, Providence, R.I.
201349	Stranger	40	33	62.4	20.0	5.5	1904	Tottenville, N.Y.	J. S. Ellis & Son, builder
81337(6)	*Stratford	98	67	100.6	22.1	7.0	1891	Bridgeport, Conn.	Designed by A. J. Hoyt
206463(7)	*Success	30	20	59.0	16.0	5.2	1909	Baltimore, Md.	M. Dewing Co, owner, Warren, R.I.
203434(8)	*Supervisor	214	136	91.4	25.0	7.4	1906	Northport, N.Y.	Dexter Cole, designer
116122	Susie B	9	8	36.7	12.8	3.4	1883	Patchogue, N.Y.	Sloop formerly

(1) Formerly Narragansett
(2) Formerly H.C. Ellis
(3) Formerly Edith A
(4) Formerly Modjeska, renamed Island Belle
(5) Formerly sloop yacht Adele
(6) Formerly William H. Hoyt
(7) Formerly Success, U.S.S. No. 2912
(8) Renamed Sealshipt, Wave

116647	*Susie C*	9	8	34.7	13.3	4.4	1894	Greenwich, Conn.	Auxiliary sloop, Samuel Chard, M.C.
116157	*Susie R*	9	8	40.8	13.2	3.2	1886	Brooklyn, N.Y.	Sloop originally F. Mansfield & Sons, owner, New Haven, Conn.
238258(1)	*Suzanne*	34	23	53.7	18.1	5.3	1939	Warren, R.I.	
23581(2)	*S.V. Rogers*	6	5	32.0	11.5	2.8	1856	Sayville, N.Y.	Sloop
116608	*Sword Fish*	9	9	41.2	9.6	2.6	1887	South Norwalk, Conn.	Sharpie; J.L. Richards, M.C.
23790	*S.W. Truslow*	23	15	50.5	17.9	5.1	1869	Moriches, N.Y.	Sloop originally
23051	*Sylph*	12	12	40.0	15.7	3.5		Greenport, N.Y.	Rebuilt in 1912
117249	*Sylvester Decker*	26	21	49.4	14.8	4.6	1903	Bridgeport, Conn.	Peter & Fred Decker, owners, East Norwalk, Conn.
145765	*Tartar*	14	9	45.7	14.2	4.0	1898	Peekskill, N.Y.	Home port, N.Y.C.
145544	*Teal*	5	5	28.0	12.5	3.8	1886	South Norwalk, Conn.	Richards and Weed, M.C.
206688	*Thalassa*	11	11	37.1	11.0	3.4	1909	Warren, R.I.	Once a passenger boat
203783(3)	*T.H.C.*	18	15	44.7	14.8	4.2	1906	Bridgeport, Conn.	Named for Thomas H. Connelly, R.I.
145295(4)	*The Hoyt Bros. Co.	75	37	69.5	18.0	6.8	1882	Port Jefferson, N.Y.	Home port,
203462	*The Limit*	13	7	42.4	16.0	4.0	1906	Tottenville, N.Y.	Home port, New Haven, Conn.
145903	*Theodore Roosevelt*	14	13	40.6	13.5	4.0	1901	Patchogue, N.Y.	Home port, Cold Spring, N.Y. Weeks & Co., builders

(1) Formerly *F.L. Homan* (3) Formerly *Chas. E. Hopkins*
(2) Renamed *Live Carp* (4) Renamed *Amanda*

227

Official Number	Name	Gross Tons	Net Tons	Length	Beam	Depth	Year Built	Where Built	Remarks
209210(1)	Thimble Islands	17	12	39.0	18.0	4.4	1911	Northport, N.Y.	Elijah S. Ball, owner, New Haven, Conn.
145881	Town Harbor	14	12	47.2	13.0	4.3	1901	Greenport, N.Y.	Home port, Greenport, N.Y.
202006	20th Century	13	11	44.2	14.2	4.0	1905	Patchogue, N.Y.	Home port, Patchogue, N.Y.
145739	Two Sisters	13	12	43.2	13.3	4.0	1897	Oakdale, N.Y.	Geo. M. Still, owner, N.Y.C.
25318	Ulrica	11	10	40.1	13.9	3.6	1899	Sayville, N.Y.	Home port, Patchogue, N.Y.
25949(2)	*Vedette	93	53	102.8	18.8	9.5	1878	Newburg, N.Y.	Phillips Phoenix of Ward, Stanton & Co, designer
25975	Vendean Chief	10	9	36.5	13.6	3.4	1877	South Norwalk, Conn.	Home port, Patchogue, N.Y.
211510(3)	*Vera Gordon Rowe	357	297	100.0	29.0	8.4	1913	Milford, Del.	C.M. McLaury, builder
161748	Verena	9	8	37.7	12.5	4.6	1895	Harwich, Mass.	Sloop originally
121051(4)	Vernie S	28	22	45.6	16.2	5.7	1897	Glenwood, N.Y.	Sea Coast Oyster Co., owner, New Haven, Conn.
161844	Victor	14	12	42.7	13.0	4.0	1899	Patchogue, N.Y.	Westerbeke Bros., owner, West Sayville, N.Y.
225005	Victoria	10	7	29.0	12.1	4.8			Frederic Goodsell, owner, Stratford, Conn.

(1) Formerly Sealship No. 38   (3) Formerly Edith B, Catherine Johnson, Lighter 161 (U.S.N.), Catherine Johnson, Sorensen Bros.
(2) Renamed James Everard   (4) Formerly Four Sisters

Number	Name						Year	Home Port	Notes
25652	Victorine	15	13	43.0	16.4	3.7	1852	Hempstead, N.Y.	Sloop originally
161726	Vigil	12	11	44.0	13.3	4.2	1893	Port Jefferson, N.Y.	Auxiliary schooner
161831	Vindex	11	7	41.2	12.2	3.6	1898	Bridgeport, Conn.	Reuben R. Greene, M.C.
161525	*Virginia	54	27	64.5	18.6	5.5	1884	New Haven, Conn.	1000–bu. capacity H.J. Lewis, owner, Bridgeport, Conn.
204060	*Waldron B	54	36	66.5	18.6	6.4	1907	Stratford, Conn.	Wm. E. Bedell, M.C.
80570	Walter R. Smith	13	13	39.5	14.9	5.0	1876	Freeport, N.Y.	Sloop originally
81206	*Waneta	19	9	38.2	14.4	4.3	1888	City Island, N.Y.	Archibald Robertson, M.C.
81781	*Warwick	49	29	51.2	16.5	4.8	1901	East Providence, R.I.	Home port, Newport, R.I.
130726[1]	Water Gypsy	10	9	50.0	11.8	3.3	1896	Monie, Md.	Schooner, freighter
81148	Watson	12	12	40.0	13.8	3.8	1887	Bayonne, N.J.	Home port, N.Y.C.
76708[2]	*Wave	18	14	39.0	12.5	4.2	1867		U.S. steamer
201905	Wayward	14	13	46.0	14.0	3.6	1905	Stratford, Conn.	Wm. E. Bedell, M.C.
208058	W. D. Anderson	10	8	40.0	11.6	3.4	1910	Darien, Conn.	John H. Oberlander, M.C.
81863	We Three	14	12	48.0	14.5	3.5	1903	Greenport, N.Y.	Tuthill & Higbee, builders
203720[3]	W. H. Bishop	33	24	56.8	17.6	5.2	1906	Patchogue, N.Y.	Fishing boat originally
81751[4]	W.H. Hoy	19	15	47.8	16.3	4.8	1901	Bridgeport, Conn.	Reuben R. Greene, M.C.
204002[5]	Whitecap	14	12	48.0	14.5	4.0	1907	Greenport, N.Y.	Blount Seafood Corp., owner, Warren, R.I.

[1] Formerly *Nora E. Lawson*
[2] Renamed *Jennie*
[3] Renamed *Carrie H. Still*
[4] Renamed *Joseph B. Glancy*
[5] Formerly *P. & B. No. 2, Alert*

Official Number	Name	Gross Tons	Net Tons	Length	Beam	Depth	Year Built	Where Built	Remarks
81195	Wilbur D	12	10	44.0	15.2	4.0	1888	Patchogue, N.Y.	Sloop originally
81105	*Wm. A. Cumming	76	41	65.0	16.3	5.1	1885	South Norwalk, Conn.	Richards and Weed, M.C.
80673	*William Alexander	38	32	59.9	15.0	6.8	1878	Rockaway, N.Y.	Reed and Franklin, owners; Bridgeport, Conn.
81337(1)	*William H. Hoyt	91	46	77.6	17.8	7.7	1891	Bridgeport, Conn.	Wm. E. Hunt, M.C.
80670	*William H. Lockwood	49	30	55.6	16.0	5.9	1878	South Norwalk, Conn.	1000-bu. capacity
96285(2)	Wm. H. Robbins	20	18	39.0	16.6	4.9	1895	Patchogue, N.Y.	Home port, Patchogue, N.Y.
81134	William H. Rowe	17	16	43.3	16.5	4.6	1886	Bay Shore, N.Y.	Home port, Patchogue, N.Y.
81786	William McKinley	14	13	45.8	14.9	4.0	1901	Patchogue, N.Y.	Jacob Ockers, owner, West Sayville, L.I.
81092	*William M. Merwin	64	35	56.3	16.5	4.9	1885	Milford, Conn.	1000-bu. capacity,
81870	Wm. Penn	8	8	38.9	14.6	3.6	1903	Forked River, N.J.	Sloop originally
80722	William Scott	9	9	34.1	13.3	3.5	1878	Rockaway, N.Y.	Sloop originally
135283(3)	*Wm. T. Lancraft	65	45	66.0	20.4	6.6	1877	Norwalk, Conn.	Ernest E. Ball, owner, New Haven, Conn.
202874	Willie K	13	11	42.2	15.3	3.6	1906	Patchogue, N.Y.	Jacob Ockers, owner, West Sayville, L.I.
81731	Willie M	14	12	56.0	14.3	3.6	1900	Greenport, N.Y.	Jacob Ockers, owner, West Sayville, L.I.

(1) Renamed Stratford
(2) Formerly Henry D. Siminson
(3) Formerly Enterprise

No.	Name						Year	Built at	Remarks
81457	Will-o-the-Wisp	8	7	31.9	11.9	4.6	1893	Bridgeport, Conn.	H.J. Lewis Oyster Co., owner, Stratford, Conn.
203434(1)	Wind	115	78	97.4	25.0	7.4	1906	Northport, N.Y.	Dragger, Joshua W. Murphy, owner, New Bedford, Mass.
214057	Winifred	25	23	45.1	15.2	5.5	1916	Nyack, N.Y.	Home port, Bridgeport, Conn.
81522	Winnie Kane	11	10	32.5	12.1	6.0	1895	Friendship, Me.	Sloop, H.J. Lewis Oyster Co., owner, Stratford, Conn.
81872	*W.I. Stevens	75	48	73.4	23.0	6.8	1903	Bridgeport, Conn.	Reuben R. Greene, M.C.
80760(2)	Wizard	40	35	64.0	18.3	6.0	1880	Greenpoint, N.Y.	Sloop yacht originally
77295(3)	Woco	51	34	51.1	15.5	5.6	1898	Essex, Mass.	Home port, Providence, R.I. George Bishop, builder
205380	Wolverine	14	12	48.5	16.5	3.2	1908	Patchogue, N.Y.	Power scow
204151	W.W.	21	14	58.8	13.9	3.0	1907	Patchogue, N.Y.	Home port, Newport, R.I.
81033	*Wyona	26	13	58.6	12.0	3.0	1884	North Kingston, R.I.	Home port, Patchogue, N.Y.
27026	X.L.	14	13	43.5	14.6	3.8	1903	Bay Shore, N.Y.	Home port, Patchogue, N.Y.
27022	X-Ray	32	22	55.7	16.4	5.6	1898	Bridgeport, Conn.	Reuben R. Greene, M.C.
226122	Zlobdnera	11	8	36.6	10.1	5.9	1926	Naugatuck, Conn.	Setauket Oyster Co., owner, New Haven, Conn.
28139	Zola	7	7	32.2	11.2	3.8	1899	Riverhead, N.Y.	Cat originally

(1) Formerly Supervisor, Sealshipt
(2) Renamed Esther B
(3) Formerly J.W. Stubbs, Ardelia

Notes

CHAPTER 1. *The Oyster and Its Cultivation*

1. Ernest Ingersoll, *The Oyster Industry* (Washington: Goverment Printing Office, 1881), p. 19.

2. *Ibid.*

3. Zara Jones Powers, ed., *Ancient Town Records,* Vol. III, [of] New Haven Town Records, 1684–1769, p. 769.

4. Rollin G. Osterweis, ed., *Three Centuries of New Haven, 1638–1938,* p. 104.

5. John Fanning Watson, *Annals of New York,* p. 284. *Annals and Occurrences of New York City and State in the Olden Time* (Philadelphia: Henry F. Anners, 1846).

6. Ingersoll, p. 112.

7. *The Writings of Henry David Thoreau,* Cape Cod and Miscellanies (Boston and New York: Houghton Mifflin Co., 1906), Vol. 4, p. 82.

8. Ingersoll, p. 95.

CHAPTER 2. *The History of Oystering in the North*

1. Ernest Ingersoll, *The Oyster Industry* (Washington: Government Printing Office, 1881), p. 61.

2. *Ibid.,* p. 61.

3. *Ibid.,* p. 63.

4. *Ibid.,* p. 95.

5. Joseph William Collins, *Notes on the Oyster Fishery of Connecticut* (Washington: Government Printing Office, 1891), p. 469.

6. Ingersoll, p. 64.

7. State of Connecticut, *Sixteenth Annual Report of the Fish Commissioners, and First Annual Report of the Shell-Fish Commission* to the General Assembly, January Session, 1882, p. 125.

8. G. Agassiz, "The Romance of the Oyster" from *National Magazine*, January, 1909, p. 452.

9. Marinus Van Popering and Joseph B. Glancy, "History of the Shellfish Industry in Great South Bay, New York" (unpublished, 1947), p. 7.

10. Ernest Ingersoll, *The Oyster Industry* (Washington: Government Printing Office, 1881), p. 98.

11. Agassiz, p. 459.

12. State of New York. Bureau of Marine Fisheries, *Statutes of*, 1908, Article XII, Chapter 130, Sec. 201-a.

13. *Fishing Gazette*, October 10, 1896, p. 643.

14. Ingersoll, p. 99.

15. Agassiz, p. 459.

16. *Fishing Gazette*, December 11, 1909, p. 1596.

17. Van Poppering and Glancy, p. 1.

18. State of New York, Forest, Fish and Game Commission, *Eleventh Annual Report*, 1906, p. 56.

19. Jenny L. Hopkins, *An Oyster Village, Cosmopolitan*, October, 1891, p. 720.

20. Burton A. Kollmer, "The Yesterday of the Oysterman" from *The Staten Island Historian*, vol. 3, number 3, (July, 1910).

21. *Ibid.*, p. 19.

22. *Ibid.*, p. 19.

23. Ingersoll, p. 112.

24. Charles Frederick Stansbury, "An Oyster of the Great Kills" from *Outing, April,* 1903, p. 29.

25. Ingersoll, p. 91.

26. New York Historical Society Quarterly, vol. 36, no. 4, (October, 1952), p. 400.

27. Abrams C. Dayton, *Last Days of Knickerbocker Life in New York* (New York: G. P. Putnam's Sons, 1897), pp. 128, 134.

28. Meryle R. Evans, "Knickerbocker Hotels and Restaurants," *New York Historical Society Quarterly*, vol. 36, no. 4 (October, 1952), p. 400.

29. Edward G. Porter, *Rambles in Old Boston, New England* (Boston: Cupples, Upham and Company, 1887), p. 275.

30. *The Oysterman and Fisherman*, February 4, 1916, p. 7.

31. Ernest Ingersoll, *The Oyster Industry* (Washington: Government Printing Office, 1881), p. 30.

32. Levi Whitman, *Massachusetts Historical Collections III*, as quoted by Ingersoll, p. 18.

33. Ingersoll, p. 24.

34. David L. Belding, "The Shell Fisheries of Massachusetts" in *The Oysterman and Fisherman*, November, 1912, p. 28.

CHAPTER 3. *The Oyster Ashore*

1. Ernest Ingersoll, *The Oyster Industry* (Washington: Government Printing Office, 1881), p. 122.

2. *Ibid.*, p. 128.

3. *Ibid.*, p. 126.

4. *Ibid.*, p. 81.

5. *Fishing Gazette*, November 12, 1910, p. 1428.

CHAPTER 4.   *Shucking, Measuring, and Shipping*

1. Ernest Ingersoll, *The Oyster Industry* (Washington: Government Printing Office, 1881), p. 84.

2. *Fishing Gazette*, August 2, 1913, p. 990.

3. *The Oysterman and Fisherman*, December 26, 1913, p. 16.

4. *Ibid.*, January 16, 1914, p. 13.

5. *U.S. Commission of Fish and Fisheries, Report of the Commissioner for 1873–74 and 1874–75*, Part III, p. 308.

6. *Suffolk County News*, "Progressive Sayville Edition," 1915.

7. Joseph William Collins, *Notes on the Oyster Fishery of Connecticut* (Washington: Government Printing Office, 1891), p. 479.

8. *Ibid.*

CHAPTER 5.   *Hand Implements*

1. Marion Brewington, *Chesapeake Bay Log Canoes and Bugeyes* (Cambridge: Cornell Maritime Press, Inc., 1963), p. 92.

2. Ernest Ingersoll, *The Oyster Industry* (Washington: Government Printing Office, 1881), p. 247.

3. *Ibid.*, p. 249.

4. P. deBroca, *op. cit.*, p. 292.

5. Brewington, p. 93.

6. T. D. Lethbridge, *Boats and Boatmen* (New York: Book Collectors Society) p. 40.

CHAPTER 6.   *Oyster Tonging Boats*

1. Ernest Ingersoll, *The Oyster Industry* (Washington: Government Printing Office, 1881), p. 80.

2. From a scrapbook entitled *New Haven Old and New: Oyster Industry*, vol. 13, no. 2, the Arnold Buyot Dana Collection at the New Haven Colony Historical Society.

3. *Ibid.*

4. Henry Hall, *Report of the Ship-building Industry of the United States*, 1892, (Washington: Government Printing Office, 1884), Tenth Census of the United States, p. 29.

5. *Ibid.*, p. 30.

6. *Ibid.*, p. 32.

CHAPTER 7. *The Sailing Oyster Dredgers*

1. Howard I. Chapelle, *American Small Sailing Craft* (New York: W. W. Norton & Company, Inc., 1951), p. 245.

2. *Bi-Centennial History of Suffolk County*, 1885, p. 107.

3. *Bridgeport Sunday Post*, May 26, 1963.

CHAPTER 8. *The Sailing Freighters*

1. Samuel Eliot Morison, *History of Maritime Massachusetts* (Boston: Houghton Mifflin Company, 1961), p. 306.

2. Howard I. Chapelle, *The National Watercraft Collection* (Washington: Government Printing Office, 1960), p. 196.

3. Ernest Ingersoll, *The Oyster Industry* (Washington: Government Printing Office, 1881), p. 25.

CHAPTER 9. *Powered Oyster Boats*

1. *Baltimore Sun*, August 6, 1886.

2. *Frank Leslie's Illustrated Newspaper*, October 15, 1859.

3. Connecticut. Fifth Annual Report of the Bureau of Labor Statistics for the year ending November 30, 1889. (Hartford: The Case, Lockwood & Brainard Company, 1890).

4. Joseph William Collins, *Notes on the Oyster Fishery of Connecticut* (Washington: Government Printing Office, 1891), p. 467.

5. *Sea World*, August 4, 1879.

6. *Fishing Gazette*, March 26, 1898, p. 208.

7. *Ibid.*, January 5, 1907, p. 22.

8. *Ibid.*, June 21, 1913, p. 795.

9. *New Haven Register*, January 3, 1932.

CHAPTER 10. *Oystering on the Natural Beds*

1. Shell-Fish Commissioners. *First Annual Report* (1882), pp. 45, 46; (1894), pp. 35-45.

2. Ernest Ingersoll, *The Oyster Industry* (Washington: Government Printing Office, 1881), p. 82.

3. State of Connecticut Laws Relating to Shell-Fisheries January 1969. Conn. State Shell-Fish Commission, Milford, Conn.

4. *Fishing Gazette*, September 17, 1904, p. 760.

CHAPTER 12. *Oystering in the 1970s*

1. David L. Belding, "The Shell Fisheries of Massachusetts" in *The Oysterman and Fisherman*, November 1912, p. 29.

2. William Firth Wells, *Early Oyster Culture Investigations by the New York State Conservation Commission* (1920–1926). State of New York Conservation Department, Division of Marine and Coastal Resources, p. 45.

Glossary

Adductor muscle   The large muscle that opens and closes the shells of a bivalve.

Ark   *See* Barge, oyster.

Bank   The southern term for oyster bed; same as bar.

Bar   The southern term for oyster bed; same as bank.

Bar, oyster   An eating place where oysters and other seafood are served at a counter or bar.

Bay, oyster   A section of a restaurant set off or apart from the main section where oysters and other seafood are served.

Barge, oyster   The floating New York City oyster market vessel which was a flat bottom barge or scow with a house built on it. Sometimes called scow or ark.

Bed   The term used in the northern states to denote a place where oysters grow naturally or where they are cultivated. Cultivated beds are frequently classed as seed, growing, fattening and holding beds. *See also* Bank, Bar, Reef, Rock.

Bed, natural   An oyster bed where oysters grow naturally without cultivation.

Bedding   The act or practice of transplanting oysters to be left down a short time, and usually taken up before winter sets in. *See also* Laying down.

Bench   The platform in an opening house upon which oysters are opened.

Block   The conical or square block of wood having an iron chisel or chisellike metal fixed in its top upon which bills of oysters are broken with a hammer in the cracking method of oyster opening.

Blue Points, Bluepoints   Oysters originally found off Blue Point, a town on Great South Bay, Long Island, New York. The name referred to any oyster native or transplanted to Great South Bay. Now it may mean any small, well-shaped oyster from Long Island or, in fact, anywhere.

Box oyster   A market oyster from four to ten years old generally sent in the shell. The name came from the old practice in New York of sending these large oysters in boxes rather than in the ordinary barrel.

Brands   Oyster brands such as Blue Points, East Rivers, Cotuits, White Rocks (Norwalk) refer to the nearest place—town, river, harbor, or reef—where they are harvested. More recently it may refer to the size or shape of the oysters rather than their place of origin.

Brood oysters   Oysters used for spawning.

Bull rake   *See* Rake.

Can, Oyster   The variously shaped metal receptacle for shipping raw, shucked oysters.

Cellar, oyster   A nineteenth-century New York restaurant located below street level that specialized in serving oysters.

Count   The method of selling and buying oysters by enumeration instead of by bulk or volume, especially used at the New York City floating oyster markets.

Cracking   A method of opening oysters by breaking or cracking the bill of the oyster with a special hammer before severing the adductor muscle with an oyster knife.

Cullentines   The smallest grade of oysters, (they are about two years old), are used for stews and are sent shucked in cans and kegs.

Culling   The act of separating oysters from extraneous shells and debris and or sorting them according to size.

Culls   Next to the poorest grade oysters. Culled out oysters. Also, three-year-old shucked oysters for stews.

Cultch   In oyster culture, the shells, gravel, or other material placed in the water upon which the oyster, at the end of the free-swimming stage, attaches or sets.

Cultivate   To raise oysters artificially by catching the larvae, usually on planted oyster shells, at the end of the free-swimming stage, and then caring for them until they reach market size. It also refers to the growing of oysters from transplanted seed oysters.

Designation   The right of cultivating or planting oysters on a specific piece of ground designated for it by oyster commissioners or other authorities; also, the stretch of ground so designated.

Drag   A dredge or the act of dredging. Term for dredge used by Prince Edward Island, Cape Cod oystermen and others.

Dredge   An instrument for bringing up oysters from under water consisting of a metal frame with a scraping edge, with or without teeth, and a metal basket or a two-part bag of heavy twine and iron links to hold the catch. It is dragged over (or along) the oyster bed and lifted to the boat by a cable, rope, or chain.

Drink   To drink, soak, or float oysters was the practice of placing them on special floats or on the bottom over one or more tides in water of less salinity than that in which they grew. It was thought that this cleaned, freshened, and improved the meat, but it actually added fresh water—an adulteration, and did not improve its quality; in fact it removed ingredients and was a source of infection if they were "drunk" in polluted water.

East Rivers   The old term for oysters grown anywhere from the East River in New York City to New Haven, Connecticut.

Ecology   The study of the relationship of living things with their environment.

Extra   Large oysters five–years–old or older which were sent in the shell but are now shucked and used mostly for stews.

Farm   A tract of sea bottom where oysters are cultivated.

Fatten   To drink or float oysters. Also to bed down or plant for growth.

Float   The platform or raft of planks upon which oysters are placed and subjected to brackish or fresh water to be "drunk" before being taken to market. *See also* Drink.

Franchise   The right or privilege to oyster given by a government to an individual or group of individuals.

Grounds   The beds or area where oysters are found or grown.

Hamper   An oyster basket holding two bushels used in New York.

House, oyster   The building where oysters are prepared in or out of the shell, for shipment to market. Variously called opening, shucking, or packing house, shop, or plant. Also, an eating place where oysters are served as a specialty.

House, packing   An oyster house where oysters are canned, barreled, or processed in some way.

House, watch   A shanty built on the shore or on piles at the oyster beds from which the beds may be guarded.

Jag   A lot, parcel, or quantity of oysters of indefinite size, such as a jag or load of oysters aboard a boat.

Jingle Shell   A mollusk having a flat, thin, translucent shell. It frequently competes for space with the oyster. Also used as oyster cultch.

Keg, oyster   A small wooden keg once used in Connecticut and elsewhere for shipping raw shucked oysters.

Knife, oyster   A special knife with various shapes for opening oysters.

Larva   The early form of an animal that passes through a metamorphosis to reach the fundamentally different adult state.

Laying down   The act or practice of transplanting oysters usually in waters close to shore for a few months (spring and summer) to increase in size and flavor. *See* bedding.

Market oysters   Oysters offered for sale or sold for human consumption, usually four- or five-year-olds.

Meat, oyster   The part of the oyster without the shells that is eaten.

Metamorphosis   The radical change in the physical form of the setting oyster larvae at the end of the free-swimming period.

Mop or star mop   A contrivance, consisting of an iron framework from which hang lines strung with coarse cotton, that is dragged along the bottom to entangle and catch starfish. Also called star tangle.

Natives   Oysters that are native to or grown in the general area where they are sold.

New Haven oyster hammer   A square, blunt-headed hammer with a wooden handle used to break the oyster shell before opening with a knife.

Opener   Usually refers to one who opens or shucks oysters in an oyster opening shop.

Oystering   The act or business of taking oysters for any reason, such as for seed, market, transplanting or eating.

Oyster, raw   An unprocessed oyster removed from its shells.

Oyster, wild   An uncultivated naturally grown oyster.

Pail, oyster   A wooden, typically tapered and returnable shipping container holding from four to six gallons of raw oysters with various patented devices for locking the cover down.

Phytoplankton   Microscopic marine plant cells which are food for the oyster.

Planting   Usually refers to removing and planting seed oysters from one place to another for better growth and flavor.

Rake   A long–handled rake, usually with long tines (teeth) curved into a semicircle, for gathering oysters or clams in water of moderate depth. Also called a bull rake.

Reef   The term used in the Gulf of Mexico and Florida for oyster bed. *See also* Bank, Bar, Rock.

Rock   The term used in the Chesapeake Bay and southward for a natural oyster bed. It refers to the accumulations of old compacted, broken shells on the bottom. *See also* Bank, Bar, Reef.

Runner   Vessels that carry bought or dredged oysters from the beds to market.

Saddle Rocks   The trade name or brand in New York and vicinity of the finest oysters, originally found off Great Neck, Long Island or Norwalk, Connecticut.

Salinity   The degree of being salty expressed in parts per thousand of total salt.

Saloon, oyster   Special eating place for oysters.

Sandbagger   A popular nineteenth-century plumb-stemed, square sterned, sloop-rigged centerboard racing boat. Sand bags shifted by the crew plus their own weight acted as the only ballast on these boats with large sail areas.

Scow   A beamy, flat-bottom, square-ended boat or vessel with or without sails or motive power used in sheltered waters for commercial work. Also refers to the hulls and house structures of the old floating New York oyster markets. *See also* Barge, oyster.

Seed   Oysters used for transplanting purposes. Any oysters not ready for market.

Set   The newly settled or metamorphosed oysters. Also called spat.

Shellermen   Men who gathered oyster shells to be used as cultch from the bottom
   of the Housatonic River in Stratford, Connecticut.

Shelling   The spreading or planting of shells upon the bottom to act as cultch.
   Also the work done by the shellermen of the Housatonic River.

Shuck, shock (New England)   To open oysters or clams.

Shucker   One who opens oysters or clams. *See* Opener.

Side knifing   A method of opening oysters by grasping the oyster in one hand,
   forcing the oyster knife's blade between the shells (valves) on the side, and
   severing the adductor muscle.

Skimmer   The flat, shallow pan or tray with a perforated bottom in which the
   freshly opened oysters in oyster shops are placed to allow the liquor or other
   extraneous material to drain away before canning or packaging.

Sounds   The trade name or brand for oysters grown in Staten Island Sound, New
   York.

Spat   *See* Set.

Spawn   The free-swimming oyster larvae.

Spawning   The releasing of the male oyster's sperm and the female's ova.

Stabbing   A method of opening oysters by holding or wedging the oyster on the
   bench, inserting the slightly flexible knife between the valves and severing the
   adductor muscle.

Tangles   *See* Mop.

Tongs   A hand-operated implement for gathering oysters (in depths of up to roughly
   30′) consisting of two long wooden handles or stales pivoting like scissors
   and bearing opposing baskets with teeth on the bottom.

Transplant   To remove and plant oysters from one place to another. The act of
   spreading or planting such oysters.

Tub, oyster   A wooden, shipping oyster container much used in New York City
   before 1910. It was shaped like a butter tub, generally held about six gallons
   of oyster meats, and was kept cool by a chunk of ice placed in the center.
   Sometimes referred to as a large oyster pail.

Valve   One of the two shells of a bivalve.

Bibliography

Agassiz, G. "The Romance of the Oyster," in *National Magazine*, January, 1909, p. 452.

Bi-Centennial History of Suffolk County, 1885, p. 107.

Bolitho, Hector. *The Glorious Oyster*. New York: Horizon Press, 1961.

Brewington, Marion. *Chesapeake Bay Log Canoes and Bugeyes*. Cambridge: Cornell Maritime Press, Inc., 1963.

Bridgeport Sunday Post, May 26, 1963.

Brooks, William. *The Oyster: A Popular Summary of a Scientific Study*. Baltimore: The Johns Hopkins Press, 1891.

Carpenter, O.G. *Robbins Island Oyster, New Suffolk, Long Island*. South Norwalk: The Andrew Radel Oyster Co., 1935.

Chapelle, Howard I. *American Small Sailing Craft*. New York: W.W. Norton Company, Inc., 1951, p. 245.

——. *The National Watercraft Collection*. Washington: Government Printing Office, 1960, p. 196.

Churchill, Edward Perry. *The Oyster and the Oyster Industry of the Atlantic and Gulf Coasts*. Bureau of Fisheries Doc. No. 890, Washington: Government Printing Office, 1920.

Collard, Allan Ovenden. *The Oyster and Dredgers of Whitstable*. London: Joseph Collard, 1902.

Collins, Joseph William. *Notes on the Oyster Fishery of Connecticut*. Doc. No. 169, Washington: Government Printing Office, 1891.

Commercial Fisheries Review. Vol. 10, No. 9, Washington, 1948.

Connecticut. Shell-Fish Commissioners. *Annual Report*, 1882–1969.

Connecticut. *Fifth Annual Report of the Bureau of Labor Statistics for the year end-*

ing November 30, 1889. Hartford: The Case, Lockwood & Brainard Company, 1890.

Danenberg, Elsie Nicholas. *The Romance of Norwalk.* New York: States History Company, 1929.

DeBroca, Lieut. P. *On the Oyster Industries of the United States.* Vol. XVI, Part III. Report of the Commissioner for 1873–74 and 1874–75. Washington: Government Printing Office, 1876, pp. 271–320.

Eyton, T.C. *A History of the Oyster and the Oyster Fisheries.* London: Jan Van Voorst, 1858.

Fishing Gazette (The). New York, 1884–present.

Galtsoff, Paul S. *The American Oyster: Crassostrea Virginica Gmelin.* Washington: Government Printing Office, 1964.

Gutsell, James S. *Oyster-cultural Problems of Connecticut.* Washington: Government Printing Office, 1924.

Hopkins, Jenny L. "An Oyster Village," *Cosmopolitan,* October, 1891.

Hopson, W.B. *An Essay on the Oyster Industry of the United States.* New York: Sea World Publishing Company, 1885.

Ingersoll, Ernest. *The Oyster Industry: Tenth Census of the United States.* Washington: Government Printing Office, 1881.

Kollmer, Burton A. "The Year of the Oysterman," *The Staten Island Historian,* 111:3, July, 1910.

Lethbridge, T.D. *Boats and Boatmen.* New York: Book Collectors Society, p. 40.

Loosanoff, Victor. *The American or Eeastern Oyster.* Circular No. 205, Bureau of Commercial Fisheries, U.S. Fish and Wildlife Service, Department of the Interior. Washington: Government Printing Office, March, 1965.

Lyle, Charles H. *Fishery Statistics of the United States 1965.* Bureau of Commercial Fisheries, U.S. Fish and Wildlife Service, Department of the Interior. Washington: Government Printing Office, 1967.

Massachusetts. *A Report upon the Mollusk Fisheries.* Boston: Wright and Potter Printing Co., 1909.

Massachusetts. *A Report upon the Quahaug and Oyster Fisheries.* Boston: Wright and Potter Printing Co., 1912.

Matthiessen, George C. *A Review of Oyster Culture and the Oyster Industry in North America.* Woods Hole: Oceanographic Institution, 1970.

Morison, Samuel Eliot. *History of Maritime Massachusetts.* Boston: Houghton Mifflin Company, 1961, p. 306.

Nelson, J. Richards. *Some Principles of Oyster Dredging.* New Brunswick: New Jersey Agricultural Experiment Station, Bulletin No. 443, 1927.

New Haven Old and New: Oyster Industry. Vol. 13, No. 2, in a scrapbook in the Arnold Buyot Dana Collection at the New Haven Colony Historical Society.

New York. Forest, Fish and Game Commission. *Eleventh Annual Report,* 1906, p. 56.

New York. State Commissioners of Fisheries. *Second Report of the Oyster Investigation and of Survey of Oyster Territory, for the years 1885 and 1886.* Albany: The Argus Company Printers, 1887.

New York. Statutes of Bureau of Marine Fisheries. Article XII, Chapter 130, Sec. 201-a, 1908.

Osterweis, Rollin G., ed. *Three Centuries of New Haven, 1638–1938.* New Haven: Yale University Press, 1953.

Oyster Epicure (The): A collation of Authorities on the Gastronomy and Dietetics of the Oyster. New York: White, Stokes and Allen, 1883.

Oysterman (The) and *Oysterman and Fisherman (The)*, 1905–1916.

Pease, H.D. "The Oyster—Modern Science Comes to the Support of an Ancient Food," in *Journal of Chemical Education.* October, 1932.

Philpots, John R. *Oysters, And All About Them.* 2 vols. London: John Richardson & Co., 1891.

Powers, Zara Jones, ed. *Ancient Town Records*, Vol III, New Haven Town Records, 1684–1769.

Prytherch, Herbert Francis. *Investigation of the Physical Conditions Controlling Spawning of Oysters and the Occurrence, Distribution, and Setting of Oyster Larvae in Milford Harbor, Connecticut.* Washington: Government Printing Office, 1929.

——. *Improved Methods for the Collection of Seed Oysters.* Washington: Government Printing Office, 1930.

Rhode Island. Commissioners of Shell Fisheries. *Annual Report*, 1904, 1909, 1911, 1913.

Rowe, Henry C. "The Oyster Industry of Connecticut." In *History of Connecticut*, edited by Norris Osborn. New York: The State's History Company, 1925.

Smith, Hugh. "Oysters: The World's Most Valuable Water Crop," *The National Geographic Magazine*, vol. 24, No. 3, 1913.

Stetson, Judy. *Wellfleet: A Pictorial History.* South Yarmouth: The Wellfleet Historical Society, 1963.

Stevenson, Charles. *A Bibliography of Publications in the English Language Relative to Oysters and the Oyster Industry.* Washington: Government Printing Office, 1894.

Suffolk County News. "Progressive Sayville Edition," 1915.

Sweet, Gordon. "The Northern Oyster Industry 1600 to 1950: A Study in Conservation," *The New England Social Studies. Bulletin*, vol. 8, 1951.

——. "Oyster Conservation in Connecticut: Past and Present," *The Geographical Review*, October, 1941.

The Writings of Henry David Thoreau, Cape Cod and Miscellanies. Boston and New York: Houghton Mifflin Co., 1906, vol. 4, p. 82.

Tressler, Donald K. *Marine Products of Commerce.* New York: The Chemical Catalog Company, 1923.

U.S. Commission of Fish and Fisheries. *Report of the Commissioner for 1873-74 and 1874–75.* Part III, p. 308.

Van Popering, Marinus, and Glancy, Joseph B. "History of the Shellfish Industry in Great South Bay, New York." Unpublished, 1947.

Watson, John Fanning. *Annals and Occurrences of New York City and State in the Olden Time.* Philadelphia: Henry F. Anners, 1846.

Wells, William Firth. *Early Oyster Culture Investigation by the New York Conservation Commission, 1920–1926.* New York: State of New York Conservation Department, 1969.

Wright, John K., ed. *New England's Prospect: 1933.* New York: American Geographical Society, 1933.

Yonge, C.M. *Oysters.* London: Collins Clear-Type Press, 1960.

Index

The seventh volume in the American Maritime Library
OYSTERING FROM NEW YORK TO BOSTON
has been composed in Linotype Garamond by
P & M Typesetting, Inc., printed by Halliday
Lithograph Corporation, and bound by The Chas.
H. Bohn Co., Inc.

Published for Mystic Seaport, Inc., by
Wesleyan University Press

The great oyster excitement – scene at the oyster bed with two hundred fifteen vessels